*exploring*

# ILLUSTRATION

*Michael Fleishman*

**THOMSON**

**DELMAR LEARNING** ™

Australia Canada Mexico Singapore Spain United Kingdom United States

**THOMSON**

—★—

**DELMAR LEARNING**

**Exploring Illustration**
Michael Fleishman

**Vice President, Technology and Trades SBU:**
Alar Elken

**Editorial Director:**
Sandy Clark

**Acquisitions Editor:**
James Gish

**Development Editor:**
Jaimie Wetzel

**Marketing Director:**
Cindy Eichelman

**Channel Manager:**
Fair Huntoon

**Marketing Coordinator:**
Mark Pierro

**Production Director:**
Mary Ellen Black

**Production Manager:**
Larry Main

**Production Editor:**
Thomas Stover

**Art/Design Coordinator:**
Rachel Baker

**Technology Project Manager:**
Kevin Smith

**Editorial Assistant:**
Marissa Maiella

Library of Congress Cataloging-in-Publication Data:

Fleishman, Michael, 1951-
    Exploring illustration /
    Michael Fleishman.—1st ed.
      p.  cm.
Includes index.
      ISBN 1–4018–2621–0
    1. Illustration of books—
    Technique.   I. Title.
NC960.F57 2003
741.6'4—dc22
                                    2003020026

## NOTICE TO THE READER

# *dedication*

To my wife, Joanne, and my sons, Cooper and Max—my source of strength and joy: Thanks for that little nudge in the morning.

# table of contents

TABLE OF CONTENTS

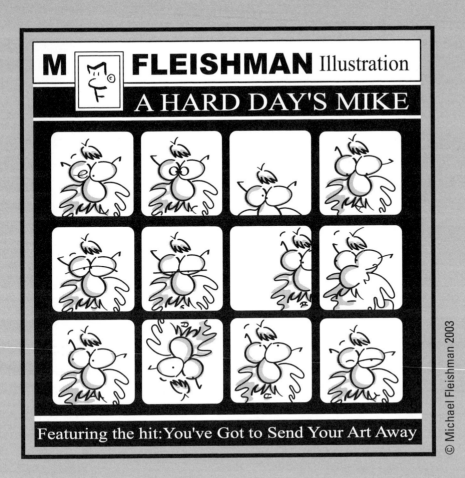

exploring illustration

# *preface*

## INTENDED AUDIENCE

If you were stuck on a desert island (with your client just on the other side of the sand dune, waiting for that job), what are the brushes you hope made it off the wreck of the good ship Winslow Homer?

Of course, we're simply trying to make a point. But reading this book just might throw you a lifeline to the answer. *Exploring Illustration* is designed to immerse the reader in both the theory and practice of illustration—a heady mix of promise and challenge.

That mix involves process and product, metaphor and mechanics, not to mention analog directions and digital trends. Intended for a college illustration program, *Exploring Illustration* was actually written for all *students* of illustration, regardless of where they are on the learning curve or professional ladder.

## BACKGROUND OF THIS TEXT

*Exploring Illustration* was written to address a variety of concerns. If you survey the field, it becomes apparent that illustration teachers are looking for a "good illustration book." Students often ask for a resource text to supplement their illustration endeavors. But many teachers—myself included—have yet to find a book that works for *them,* in *their* classroom. There are books we suggest, but without a full endorsement.

If you are devoted to education, and you teach illustration, you are—more than likely— an active and proactive teacher. If you love to paint and draw, and are a freelance illustrator, it's a safe bet you are passionate about the art and occupation of illustration.

After years of juggling the classroom and the field, you probably have some things to say about illustration, and much to articulate about being (or becoming) an illustrator.

This is your kind of book!

*Exploring Illustration* responds to student needs, present market concerns, and emerging visual objectives. This is accomplished by examining influences and connections, current thinking and modern method, as well as historical and available tools. We do this by exploring a cornucopia of techniques with a broad range of viewpoints (and a variety of personalities).

How does one write a book like this? There's stuff you know, of course. Obviously, one takes the usual academic route of referencing classic and current resources. And then you enjoy the privilege of working with some 75 gifted individuals who graciously (and generously) share their wisdom and experience, expertise and talents.

What do you need to utilize a book like this? Well, definitely a basic core of artistic knowledge, creative ability, and mechanical dexterity. You shouldn't presume that *Exploring Illustration* is the holy grail of illustration instruction. And it's not the magic key to fame, fortune, or booming business opportunities— all this you must make for yourself.

Primarily, *Exploring Illustration* asks the reader to possess the desire to learn, and the open mind to make learning happen. Sure, every textbook might assume this or state it outright. But as it is also said: when the student is ready, the teacher will come.

## TEXTBOOK ORGANIZATION

The book is logically laid out. Chapter 1 covers the first steps: the beginnings of the illustration process— how to generate ideas, then turn those ideas into illustration. We look at concepts and discuss sketching, thumbnails, roughs, comprehensives, and the finish.

Chapter 2 deals with the fundamental building blocks: concept and composition, value, color, line, pattern, and texture.

In Chapter 3 we look at subject matter: portraiture and figure drawing, various editorial and advertising venues; conceptual and narrative illustration. Topics include: collage/montage; cartoon, caricature and fantasy; exteriors and interiors; organic and mechanical; alternative/new wave/cutting-edge; gallery, as well as non-objective arts.

© Daryll Collins

Chapter 4 considers connections and directions: history; culture and taste; cross-cultural and ethnic references. We discuss schools, genres, and styles; inspirations, peers, and heroes.

Chapter 5 is concerned with dry media; Chapter 6 with the wet stuff—painting and drawing. Chapter 7 elaborates on this and targets pen, brush, and ink. Chapter 8 introduces you to extended techniques like stencil and airbrush; scratchboard and woodcut; graffiti and calligraphy; as well as 3-D process.

Chapter 9 explores collage, cut paper, and fabric, while Chapter 10 is our digital overview and analysis.

## FEATURES

- Opening objectives clearly state learning goals of each chapter.

- Illustrations are used generously to enhance the concepts learned.

- Profiles of successful illustrators offer practical advice and words of wisdom.

- Step-by-step procedures break down the mechanics behind the creative inspiration.

- Review questions and exercises reinforce material presented in each chapter.

- Exercises challenge students to apply techniques and employ the concepts that are presented.

- A full color insert showcases beautiful artwork, creative encouragement, and technical expertise from the illustrators.

© Michael Fleishman 2003

# HOW TO USE THIS TEXT

## ▶ Objectives

Learning Objectives start off each chapter. They describe the competencies readers should achieve upon understanding the chapter material.

## ▶ Notes and Tips

Notes and Tips provide special hints, practical techniques, and information to the reader.

## ▶ Step by Step

Created by accomplished illustrators, the Step-by-Step diagrams are interspersed throughout the text and allow readers to learn the illustration process right from the professionals.

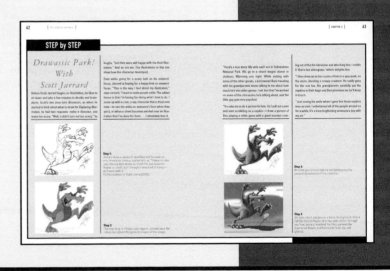

## Profiles

These career profiles are located at the end of each chapter. Each features a successful illustrator in the field.

## Sidebars

Sidebars appear throughout the text, offering additional valuable information on specific topics.

## Review Questions and Exercises

Review Questions and Exercises are located at the end of each chapter and allow the reader to assess their understanding of the chapter. Exercises are intended to reinforce chapter material through practical application.

# INSTRUCTOR'S GUIDE ON CD

Our instructor's guide on CD-ROM supplements the written text and continues the curriculum. This electronic manual offers even more illustration galleries, chapter assignments, related projects, and discussion questions. It was developed to assist teachers in planning and implementing their instructional programs, not to replace the text.

# ACKNOWLEDGMENTS

The author is indebted to the many artists who contributed to *Exploring Illustration.* It would not have been the same book without their commitment and enthusiasm, priceless content assistance and, of course, *superb* illustration! Thanks must also be extended to those educators and professionals who consulted on the manuscript—your time and energy, wit and wisdom were invaluable. Thank you to family and friends for your care and support in general.

Certain chapters and sections really reflect the wonderful interaction that embellished this project. Tom Garrett, Greg Nemec, Lori Osiecki, Robert Saunders, Akiko Stehrenberger, Ilene Winn-Lederer, and Robert Zimmerman collaborated on Chapter 1.

Chapter 2 was also dialogued with Ilene, Robert Saunders, and Greg. Other key correspondents here were Melina Elum, Beth Holyoke, Margaret Parker, Paul Melia (also for Chapter 3), Stan Shaw, and Carla Steiger-Meister. Thanks to Ben Mahan, David Milgrim, and Tad Suzuki (also for Chapter 6), too.

Greg, Akiko, and Robert Zimmerman contributed to Chapter 4, where a reference note is in order: Two books were particularly invaluable (and used extensively) to prepare this chapter. The first volume is *The Illustrator in America* (Watson-Guptill © 2001). Written by educator, writer, and illustrator Walt Reed, the third edition of this fine and important work was edited by Roger Reed, Walt's son.

The second is *200 Years of American Illustration,* with text by Henry C. Pitz (Random House © 1977). Pitz was a reknowned illustrator, teacher, and historian. I bought this book when it was new. You might find some factual errors in this book, but it has been, and remains, a fine resource.

Great thanks to Terry Brown and The Society of Illustrators, who came through with timely and crucial visuals for Chapter 4.

Chapters 8 and 9 could not have been written without all the featured illustrators. Kudos to Margaret Cusack, Tom Garrett, John Jinks, Peter Kuper, Greg Nemec, Lori Osiecki, Margaret Parker, Robert Zimmerman, and Robin Zimmerman.

Thanks to Ilene Winn-Lederer and Robert Zimmerman, along with Chris Spollen and David Julian for their input on Chapter 10, plus a note of thanks to Norton Gusky and Brad Reed here, as well.

Woody Coleman put the word out to the PortSort illustrators, as did Ashley Lorenz at the Lilla Rogers Studio. Special mention to illustrators Greg Manchess and Overton Loyd at this juncture, too—thanks to all of you for helping network the book.

Thanks must go to Janet Kiefer and those folks at Carlisle Publishers Services who put the book together.

A tip of the hat to all the people at Delmar, but especially Jaimie Wetzel, Tom Stover, and a guitar buddy who started it all: Jim Gish. Your editorial eye, technical expertise, and market savvy were always right up front, and I only gained from your counsel and perspective. You know your job, but you never let me doubt that this was *my* book, every step of the way.

Finally: If anyone was left out, my sincere apologies; I'll bring the doughnuts next time around.

*Michael Fleishman*
*2003*

Delmar Learning and the author would also like to thank the following reviewers for their valuable suggestions and technical expertise:

**VICKEY BOLLING,** Graphic Design Department, Art Institute of Atlanta, Atlanta, Georgia.

**LARRY BYERS,** Art Department, St. Louis Community College at Florissant Valley, St. Louis, Missouri.

**KATHLEEN FARRELL,** Visual and Performing Arts Department, Monroe Community College, Rochester, New York.

**TOM GARRETT,** Design Department, Minneapolis College of Art and Design, Minneapolis, Minnesota.

**CHUCK GROTH,** Art Department, St. Louis Community College at Meramec, St. Louis, Missouri.

**STAN SHAW,** Art Department, Pacific Lutheran University, Tacoma, Washington.

**PAUL YOUNG,** Fine and Applied Arts Department, Parkland College, Champaign, Illinois.

## About the Illustrators

*Margaret Adams Parker* is an artist who works primarily as a printmaker and sculptor. She is also an adjunct instructor at Virginia Theological Seminary. She recently completed 20 woodcuts to accompany a new translation of the biblical book of Ruth. More information on the artist and her work may be found on her website www.margaretadamsparker.com.

*Tom Bachtell* is a Chicago-based cartoonist and illustrator. His drawings and caricatures appear each week in "The Talk of the Town" section of *The New Yorker,* and have appeared for many years in "The Hot Sheet" column in *Entertainment Weekly.* He works for numerous not-for-profit and arts organizations in Chicago, as well as for *Newsweek* and *The Wall Street Journal.* Bachtell's cows for Marshall Field's department stores were among the most celebrated in Chicago's popular "Cows on Parade" public art festival in the Summer of 2000.

*Carla Bauer* has had her own design firm for over 23 years. She has been doing woodcuts even longer, both as fine art and illustration. A great adjunct to her business, Bauer speaks of the woodcut process as a wonderful escape and a fine companion. In the most frustrating of times, Bauer seeks solace with her tools and a piece of wood. Contact Carla Bauer at Carla Bauer Design, Inc., 156 Fifth Ave., Suite 1100, New York, NY 10010 by phone: 212-807-8305 or by fax: 212-727-8094.

*James Bennett* attended Bucks County Community College in Pennsylvania and The School of Visual Arts in New York City. Freelancing since 1985 for clients like *Playboy, National Lampoon,* and *The New York Times,* Bennett has also completed children's books with Jerry Seinfeld and Carl Reiner, and received recognition from *Communication Arts, Step by Step Graphics,* and The Society of Publication Designers. He's won a Gold Medal, the Steven Dohanos Award, and the 2001 Hamilton King Award from The Society of Illustrators. Bennett has taught at the School of Visual Arts and lectured at numerous schools and institutions. He resides in Bucks County, Pennsylvania, with his wife Susan and their two young sons.

*Mark Braught* was born in Des Moines, Iowa, attended the Minneapolis College of Art & Design, and received a B.F.A. from Indiana State University. His work has appeared in *CA, Print, Graphis, Step-by-Step,* the New York Art Directors Club, Society of Illustrators, and SILA. Clients include Churchill Downs, Warner Brothers, *Newsweek,* Citibank, Herman Miller, Richards Group, BBDO, Scholastic, The Cincinnati Zoo, and ATP Tennis. He is the illustrator of *P is for Peach* and *Cosmo's Moon,* and is the past president of the Art Director's Club of Indiana. Currently, he resides in Commerce, Georgia, with his wife Laura, five cats, and Charlie the dog.

Assisted by her family of feline muses, *Wendy Christensen* works at Bobcat Mountain Studios in rural New Hampshire. Her award-winning paintings have appeared in books, magazines, and on numerous products, and she's the author of many articles and books on feline topics. A member of the Cat Writers' Association (CWA); The Dog Writers Association of America (DWAA); the Society of Children's Book Writers and Illustrators (SCBWI), as well as the Guild of Natural Science Illustrators, Wendy is represented by Art Licensing International, Inc. (http://www.artlicensinginc.com) and PortSort (http://www.PortSort.com). Contact her at http://www.wendychristensen.com or christensen@wendychristensen.com

*Tom Nick Cocotos* abandoned an engineering career for art (he received an M.F.A. in Illustration from the School of Visual Arts in 1995 and a B.S. in Electrical Engineering from Columbia University in 1988). Heavily influenced by his Greek heritage, Tom enjoys reinterpreting from this timeless style, through the contemporary feel of collage. Clients include *Business Week,* Disney, Doubleday, MTV / VH1, *Newsweek, The New York Times, Playboy, Time,* and *The Washington Post.* Cocotos has won numerous awards, including those from *American Illustration* and the Society of Illustrators. Contact Tom Nick Cocotos at: 360 W 53rd St, #2FE, New York, NY 10019 by phone: 212-620-7556 or online: http://www.cocotos.com or tom@cocotos.com

*Daryll Collins* felt lucky to have parents and teachers who supported his goal of becoming a cartoonist. Graduating from Youngstown State University, he also attended Columbus College of Art and Design. Starting out doing TV news graphics, Collins eventually cartooned for Gibson Greeting Cards (now defunct). Clients include Hallmark, *Sports Illustrated for Kids, Disney Adventures,* McDonald's, and *Time* magazine (Asia). Daryll works out of his home studio, where he lives with wife Marilyn and a variety of pets. Contact Daryll Collins at: daryll@daryllcollins.com, 2969 Ensley Ct. Maineville, OH 45039, by phone: 513-683-9335 or online: http://www. daryllcollins.com

*John Coulter* is a Los Angeles-based illustrator. His clients include *UTNE Reader, Wall Street Journal, Christian Science Monitor, Entertainment Weekly, The Boston Globe,* Great Arrow Cards, Rodale Books, and *OUT* magazine. John grew up on a hog farm in Joy, Illinois. After receiving his B.F.A in Visual Communications from Truman State University, he spent two and a half years in the Dominican Republic as a Peace Corps volunteer. John now lives in Monrovia, California, with his wife Anne and daughter Ava. He is represented by Lilla Rogers Studio and can be reached at 781-641-2787 or lilla@lillarogers.com, http://www.johncoulter.net, and http://www.theispot.com/artist/jcoulter/

*Linda Crockett* has been doing illustration for many years and has been published thousands of times. Her work has received two Gold Medals from the Society of Illustrators and has been shown in the Cleveland Museum of Art and many other galleries and museums. Several pieces are in the permanent collection of the Society of Illustrators in New York City. She creates children's books, greeting cards, and magazine illustrations in her home studio in Euclid, Ohio. Contact Linda Crockett at: 216-731-2675 for phone or fax, 23336 Williams Ave., Euclid, OH 44123 by mail, or online at: twelvetrees@earthlink.net, http://www.sundayparlor. com, http://www.portsort.com, http://www.images.com and http://www.coroflot.com

*Margaret Cusack* creates artwork using fabric as her medium. Born in Chicago, she has lived in New York since 1959. She studied at Pratt Institute, has worked as a graphic designer, art director, and set designer (earning an Emmy award for set design along the way). Her samplers, fabric collage, soft sculpture, and large architectural-scale hangings are commissioned by many clients, from *Time* magazine to the First Unitarian Church of Brooklyn. Contact Margaret Cusack at: 124 Hoyt St. Brooklyn, NY 11217-2215, by phone: 718-237-0145 or online: cusackart@aol.com

*Jeanne de la Houssaye* says, "I planned on being a cowboy, or maybe a doctor. I still think about being a cowboy." She went to art school in the French Quarter of New Orleans, and her client/job list includes:

DDB Needham, HBO, Ketchum Communications, SaraLee, Red Lobster, Disney, and Microsoft. But if you were to ask what makes her the proudest, it would be the smiles she brings to patients at Children's Hospital with her pro bono caricature work. Her name is spelled in 3 parts, with a capital H, and pronounced (in French): *Zhan della HOO say*. She can be contacted online: mardidraw@cox.net, and by phone: 504-957-8981.

*Steve Dininno* graduated with honors from the School of Visual Arts in 1982, and found assignments throughout the newspaper and magazine markets. He soon broke into advertising, book publishing, CDs and licensing, as well as working on annual reports, brochures, posters and direct mail pieces. A partial list of clients includes: Coca-Cola, EMI, Bayer Pharmaceuticals, Jaguar, Blue Cross/Blue Shield, and Panasonic. Lauded by those clients as one of the nicest, funniest and most reliable illustrators out there, Dininno is a widely exhibited painter and printmaker to boot. He lives and works in Woodstock, New York, with his wife, Astrid, and their three cats. Presently on the Woodstock Artists Association Board of Directors and the Board of Advisors of The Woodstock School of Art, Steve has been exclusively represented by the David Goldman Agency since 1992.

*Ali Douglass* began her college education at the School of the Museum of Fine Arts in Boston, and finished at the Kansas City Art Institute with a B.F.A in Illustration. She moved to New York City in 1999 to develop her career as an illustrator, and currently lives in San Francisco, California. Her paintings have been recognized by *American Illustration* and Step-by-Step Graphics, and have been exhibited at the Society of Illustrators in New York. Ali's favorite naptime spot, however, is high up in her treehouse in her hometown of Muncie, Indiana. Ali Douglass can be reached online at ali@alidouglass.com or http://www.alidouglass.com or by phone: 415-695-1202.

*Jim Dryden* lives in the Minneapolis/St. Paul area, and studied art and music at the University of Minnesota. He has a B.F.A in painting and printmaking from the Minneapolis College of Art and Design. A love of travel and exotic places has been a primary influence in Jim's work. He has traveled in Central America and South America, Europe, Asia, and Africa, drawing inspiration and painting in a color palette that speaks of latitudes far south of Minnesota. Jim works for many major corporate clients including General Mills, Honda, and Coca-Cola, to name just a few. He also provides artwork to fine arts groups like the Minnesota Arts Council, and for non-profit causes and organizations such as the American Red Cross. Published in several trade and educational texts (including *Creative JOLT* and *Visual Workout*), Dryden's work has been recognized by the American Society of Illustrators.

*John Dykes* was born in Port Washington, New York, in July, 1960. He attended Syracuse University from 1978–1982, earning a B.F.A in Illustration. He has done many magazine and newspaper illustrations: *Time, Newsweek, U.S. News, The Atlantic Monthly, The New York Times, The Wall Street Journal,* and lots of corporate stuff; Gold and Silver awards, Society of Illustrators of L.A., *Communication Arts, Print,* and Step By Step Graphics. He is a member of the Society of Illustrators and Illustrators' Partnership of America. Contact John S. Dykes Illustration by phone: 203-254-7180, by fax: 203-254-7436, or online at http://www.jsdykes.com and http://theispot.com/artist/dykes

With a degree in art from Iowa State University firmly in hand, *Bill Ersland* knocked on the door of the established design firm Hellman Associates in Waterloo, Iowa. There, for ten years, he honed his skills working with a talented group of illustrators and designers whose clients included some of the country's largest corporations, magazines, and publishers. In 1983 Ersland moved to Stillwater, Minnesota, and embarked on a prolific freelance career. His clients include Scholastic, Deere & Company, Philadelphia's *Inquirer* magazine, Perfection Learning Publishing, and a variety of advertising agencies throughout the Midwest. A member of the Society of Illustrators, Ersland also exhibits through a local gallery featuring historical and Western art.

*Lisa Ferlic* graduated from the University of Wisconsin–Eau Claire with a B.F.A. (emphasis in graphic design). She works and lives in Seattle as a freelance illustrator and graphic designer.

*Sarajo Frieden* is an artist, illustrator, and designer living in Los Angeles where she cross-pollinates happily between traditional paint media and digital software programs. Her work has been featured in numerous award books, such as *American Illustration 21 & 22, 100 Best Album Covers,* and *Illustration West.* Recently featured in *Adobe Master Class: Illustrator Illuminated,* published by Adobe Press, Frieden's prolific illustrations appear nationally and internationally. She's currently illustrating a book for Klutz Press.

Born in Japan, *Tuko Fujisaki* grew up in southern California. At first a sun worshipper, she discovered she loved New York and cafés and started wearing a lot of black—not a good look at the beach. After living in New York, then New Mexico, she finally came to her senses and found a home in Hawaii—the green, the ocean, the sun, and gentle lifestyle. Tuko started her art career as a designer, but quickly moved to illustration because she found it more rewarding. She also found lots of jobs, from corporations to magazine work, educational stuff, even TV. The best reward has been doing what she loves! Tuko Fujisaki can be contacted by phone: 800-208-2456 or by mail: RR2 Box 4797, Pahoa, HI 96778.

*Tom Garrett* has been an Associate Professor at the Minneapolis College of Art and Design since 1985. His illustrations have appeared in *The Atlantic Monthly, Sports Illustrated, Fortune,* and *The Wall Street Journal,* and he has done work for clients like Time Warner, Timex, Mattel, and American Express. Tom has received awards from *Communication Arts* Illustration Annual, *American Illustration,* the Los Angeles Society of Illustrators, the Society of Publication Design, *Print, How,* the New York Art Director's Club, and *Dimensional Illustration.* Contact Tom Garrett at: 612-827-2897 (phone), 612-827-2896 (fax), and online: tomgarrett@visi.com or http://www.tomgarrettillustrator.com

*Jacki Gelb's* unique pen and ink and watercolor style—warm, spirited and loose—has been requested by clients such as American Express, HBO, DuPont, *Bon Appetit,* Perrier-Jouet Champagne, Bank of

Boston, Bloomingdales, the *Wall Street Journal,* UNICEF, and Liz Claiborne. Jacki was honored to illustrate a humanitarian campaign for President Bush's fund for Afghan children sponsored by the White House and Red Cross after 9/11. Both a writer and illustrator, Jacki sees the purpose of her work as bringing a sense of warmth, connectedness, and personality to her clients. She can be reached at: Jacki Gelb Communications, 847-475-1949. Her art website is http://www.gelbillustration.com.

*Jud Guitteau* lives in Portland, Oregon, with his wife Lynn, two children, Annie and Will, and various household pets. Jud has been illustrating for a large variety of corporate and editorial clients since 1988. His style has steadily transformed from pastel and scratchboard to primarily digital, and back again to a combination of acrylic painting and digital work.

*Scott Jarrard* graduated with a B.F.A in Illustration from Brigham Young University. His professional career began at a video-game developer where he designed, created, and animated characters and backgrounds for Nintendo of America, EA, Accolade, MGM Interactive, and Marvel. He is currently working at a design firm as an illustrator. There he has done character design and licensed character work for Sony Entertainment of America, 989 Studios, and THQ. In his spare time he freelances, creating characters, illustrations, and logos for his clients. All of his work is completely digital and is created in Adobe Photoshop and Adobe Illustrator. Scott Jarrard can be contacted at: http://www.scottjarrard.com or scott@scottjarrard.com

*Bill Jaynes* is an artist and educator. He illustrates in a free pen and ink with watercolor style which ranges from whimsical fun to work that dances on the edge of the existential abyss (without falling in). His commercial clients include: *The Wall Street Journal, Forbes* magazine, and the *Los Angeles Times,* as well as many others. Bill has taught illustration at California State University–Long Beach, and the Art Institute of California–Orange County. He enjoys family life, which includes drawing and brainstorming sessions with his young daughters, Julia and Hanna. Bill Jaynes can be contacted at: 2924 Ostrom Ave., Long Beach CA 90815, by phone: 562-420-7209, or online: willieworks@billjaynes.com

*John Jinks* moved to New York City in the mid-80s, started out working for clients in the publishing field, then branched out to advertising as well. Along the way, clients of all genres were included, as were many awards from publications and his peers. His work has appeared in many national ad campaigns with a diverse client base from Broadway musicals to the medical fields. His work can be seen on the Web at *www.jjinks.com.*

Originally from the Boston area, *David Julian* worked and studied at Harvard's Biological labs, attended Massachusetts College of Art, and then relocated to New York City for 17 years. He earned a B.F.A from Pratt Institute. David worked as a designer, art director, and photographer until 1994. A need for a change led him to Seattle for a more relaxed lifestyle, western light, and space. Working in several disciplines, Julian now creates illustration and photography for clients and collectors worldwide. When not working, he enjoys traveling, sea kayaking, exploring, teaching, and assemblages. Julian shares home and studio with wife Cheryl, and Psycho, an agile and amiable three-legged cat. Contact David Julian at http://www.davidjulian.com or by phone: 206-364-9077 or 11516 Sixth Ave NW, Seattle, WA 98177.

Award winning painter and illustrator *Douglas Klauba* was born and raised in Chicago with pencil and paintbrush always in hand. His work is recognized for his dramatic use of lighting in a heroic-deco style (with art nouveau design influences from antique early 20th-century advertising posters). Doug's work has been exhibited at the Society of Illustrators in New York and Los Angeles, the Auditorium Theatre, Lincoln Park Zoo, Chicago Historical Society, and in many private collections in the United States. Contact Douglas Klauba at: http://www.douglasklauba.com

*Milton Knight* was born in 1962 in Mineola, New York. He started drawing, painting, and creating his own attempts at comic books and animation at age two. "I've never formed a barrier between fine art and cartooning," he says. "Growing up, I treasured Chinese watercolors, Breugel, Charlie Brown, and Terrytoons equally." His work has appeared in *Heavy Metal, High Times, National Lampoon, Nickelodeon Magazine* and other publications, plus he has illustrated, designed record covers, posters, candy, and T-shirts. All this, and Knight continues to exhibit his acrylic paintings. His comics titles include *Hugo, Midnite the Rebel Skunk, Slug 'N' Ginger,* and *Hinkley.* He is completing a ten-minute animated film (done solo), and is now in the ink and paint stage.

*Peter Kuper's* illustrations and comics appear regularly in *Time, The New York Times* and *Mad,* where he illustrates "Spy vs. Spy" every month. He has written and illustrated many books, including *Comics Trips,* a journal of his travels through Africa and Southeast Asia, adaptations of Upton Sinclair's *The Jungle,* and numerous short stories by Franz Kafka (all of which can be seen in *Speechless,* a coffee table art book covering his career to date). Peter recently adapted Kafka's *The Metamorphosis,* published by Crown. More of his work can be seen at *www.peterkuper.com*

*Loren Long* grew up in Lexington, Kentucky. He was an illustrator for the Gibson Greeting Card Company in Cincinnati, Ohio, before beginning his freelance career. Since then, he has received numerous accolades for his fluid WPA painting style, including two Gold Medals from the Society of Illustrators in New York. Long's clients include *Time* magazine, *Reader's Digest, Sports Illustrated,* and Lands' End, among many others. Contact Loren at golonggo@yahoo.com or by phone: 513-942-5051.

*PJ Loughran* began his career doing illustrations for the Op-Ed pages of the *New York Times* while attending Parsons School of Design. PJ has since contributed to over 300 publications and campaigns for *Sports Illustrated, Esquire, Time,* Simon and Schuster, *Forbes,* Nike, Scholastic, Burton Snowboards, and many others. He has been recognized by *American Illustration, Print Magazine,* and the Society of Illustrators of New York and Los Angeles, and more. A former design and creative director for Agency.com, PJ helped this interactive/multimedia firm win over 30 awards on projects for Coca-Cola, Nike, and others.

Most recently, PJ is back at Parsons, teaching both illustration and Web design. He's also returned to an earlier passion for music; he's recording and also performing for East Coast audiences.

As a teenager, Detroit-born *Overton Loyd* drew caricatures at state fairs. In 1977, he signed up with musician George Clinton, a turn that has distinguished him as a pop culture illustrator. Loyd helped produce Clinton's Parliament/Funkadelic multimedia stage shows, designed costumes, created album covers, and animated videos. He won Billboard's Best Use of Computer Graphics award in 1983 for his work on the music video *Atomic Dog.* He is well known as the featured caricaturist on the television program *Win, Lose, or Draw.* Contact Overton Loyd at: 530 Molino #218, Los Angeles, CA 90013, by phone: 213-687-7233 or online: http://www.overvision.com

*Ben Mahan* lives on a farm in Morrow County, Ohio, close to the area where he grew up. He is married and has two daughters. Mahan attended the Columbus College of Art and Design (where he teaches part-time) and has worked for Hallmark Cards. He eventually moved to New York City, and began a professional relationship with Jim Henson, the Muppets, and the Sesame Street TV shows. Mahan draws extensively for magazines, greeting cards, and children's books. His art has been chosen for several UNICEF cards. The award-winning illustrator has been recognized by the New York One Show, CA, *Print,* American Institute of Graphic Arts, the Society of Illustrators in New York, the Society of Korean Illustration Art, and the Gallery of Contemporary Art in Rome, Italy.

A native of Kentucky, *Gregory Manchess* earned a B.A. from the Minneapolis College of Art and Design in 1977, but is largely self-taught in drawing and painting. After two years as a studio illustrator, he struck out on his own in 1979. Greg's client work includes covers for *Time, Atlantic Monthly;* a portrait of Sean Connery for the film *Finding Forrester;* three portraits for the History Channel on the tsars of Russia; spreads for *Playboy, Omni, Newsweek, Smithsonian, National Geographic* and numerous book covers. In the fall of 2003, his third children's book, *Giving Thanks* by Jonathan London, was scheduled to be released. He has won numerous awards from the New York Society of Illustrators, including its highest achievement, the Hamilton King Award.

*Greg Maxson* earned his Associates Degree in technical graphics from Purdue University in 1988, and has practiced technical illustration ever since. Greg has provided technical illustrations to large and small corporate and publishing clients such as Ryobi, Los Alamos National Laboratory, *Popular Science, Consumer Reports,* and *Corvette Quarterly.* His work can also be seen in the Illustrator WOW! books, the Artist's & Graphic Designer's Market, and in regular issues of *SBS Digital Design.* Greg also currently works as an illustrator at Precision Graphics and lives in Urbana, Illinois, with his wife Wendy and their son Drake. Contact Greg at: gmaxti@shout.net

*Marti McGinnis,* along with her husband, three dogs, two birds, a Fijian cat from her Peace Corps days, and a lizard she rescued from her local Home Depot check-out line, lives in Evanston, Illinois, and makes her Happy Art when she's not out tending her madcap garden.

*David McGlynn* lives and works in New York City. Born and raised in the Bronx, he received a Bachelor of Fine Arts degree from SUNY Purchase, New York, in 1979, and moved to New York to begin his career. During this period he first began to explore the possibilities of panoramic collages as color contact prints. A veteran of many solo and group exhibitions, David has produced mural-size pieces for installation and touring shows, corporate commissions, and permanent installations at locations such as the AT&T building in New York City. His art is included in various private as well as public collections. Portfolio spreads of his work have been published in *Life* magazine, *Popular Photography,* and more. A successful commercial photo-illustrator, David's work has appeared in numerous publications such as *WIRED, New York, Forbes,* the *New York Times,* and for corporate and advertising clients that include Miller Brewing Company, Absolut Vodka, and Minolta Copiers.

A professional illustrator and painter since 1952, *Paul Melia* has served clients in the health care field, as well as the Fortune 500, the publishing industry, and the government. He is a graduate of the School of the Dayton Art Institute with a Bachelor of Fine Arts degree. Melia's design, illustration, portraits, and water media work have appeared in nearly 300 exhibitions. This includes the prestigious Federation of Canadian Artists—AIM for the Arts International Exhibit 2000 (where he won the top award of $25,000), the American Watercolor Society, and the Communications Arts Annual Exhibit, the New York Society of Illustrators Annual Exhibit's, Ohio Watercolor Society in which he was a five-time gold award winner), and Watercolor USA. His paintings and portraits are represented in numerous corporate and private collections throughout the world. He and his wife, Carole, reside in Dayton, Ohio.

*Ken Meyer Jr.* has been employed in many industries as an artist, using many disciplines. He has produced training materials for educational media companies and the military (where he worked close to Area 51), designed for the Web, and created art for online games (the popular Everquest). Throughout, he has done freelance illustration for the gaming market, comics, mainstream media, and more. He resides in Fairfax, Virginia, with his lovely wife Mona and adorable girls Riley and Avery. Contact Ken Meyer Jr. at: 10108 Spring Lake Terrace, Fairfax, VA 22030 or online: kenmeyerjr@cox.net

*David Milgrim* is a full-time children's book author/illustrator with twelve books to his credit. He has also been a commercial illustrator and graphic designer. He lives in Rhode Island with his wife and child. Some titles include *Cows Can't Fly,* Viking; *Here in Space,* Bridgewater; *My Friend Lucky,* Atheneum; *Thank You Thanksgiving,* Clarion; *The Adventures of Otto* series, Atheneum.

*Mark Monlux* is an award-winning Pacific Northwest illustrator whose freelance career spans over two decades. His involvement in various professional organizations—the Society of Professional Graphic Artists, the Graphic Artists Guild, the Tacoma Ad Club, the NorthWest Designers Association, and Cartoonists Northwest—has contributed to efforts on both the state and national level to improve and protect artists' rights. He currently lives in Tacoma, Washington.

Though *Phillip Mowery* has been a graphic designer in the San Francisco Bay area since 1993, he is a newcomer to the professional illustration field. He began to market his design style in 2002, and quickly landed several jobs. Currently, Phillip is an art director at an advertising agency in San Jose, California, and is happily taking on illustration projects as they come. Contact him at <u>mowerydesign @yahoo.com.</u>

*Joe Murray's* goal since age 5 was to be an artist. He was, at one time, a political cartoonist and an ad agency designer. Opening up his own successful illustration and animation studio, the early 1990s found Joe as head producer and creator of the popular *Rocko's Modern Life,* which aired on Nickelodeon. Joe loves going to work and coming home to his beautiful illustrator/art director wife, Carol Wyatt, and two beautiful daughters, Daisy and Casey. Contact Joe at <u>joemstudio@earthlink.net</u> or by phone: 626-281-8924.

*Gregory Nemec* is one of five siblings, and has more than 150 cousins. He grew up in Des Moines, Iowa, inspired by everything from giant concrete Happy Chef sculptures to Francis Bacon's work at the Des Moines Art Center. Greg attended the University of the Arts in Philadelphia, and was shaped as much by literature classes and seeing transsexuals in the supermarket as he was by his illustration classes. He married a nice girl from Queens, moved to New York City, and currently resides in Pleasantville, New York with his wife, two kids, and one cat. He says his kids inspire him, but he also enjoys movies, telling stories, eating homemade pie, and singing loudly and off key. Contact Gregory Nemec at: 37 Martling Avenue, Pleasantville, NY 10570, by phone: 914-747-6125 or online: <u>me@gregorynemec.com</u>

*Lori Osiecki* likes her job. Born in Shillington, Pennsylvania, Osiecki graduated from the York Academy of Art (now Pennsylvania College of Art and Design) in 1979. She worked for Hallmark Cards for eight years, and began her freelance career in 1987. Lori lives in Mesa, Arizona, with husband Jarek; her two favorite little people, daughter Alex and son Max; and the best dog an illustrator (or anybody else for that matter) could have, George. Contact Lori Osiecki at: 123 W. 2nd St., Mesa, AZ, 85201 or by phone: 480-962-5233, or online at <u>lorio@fastq.com</u>

*Randy Palmer* once worked as a graphic artist for the Air Force and received "secret" clearance to work on documents that would make your blood run cold (not really). He lives in Dayton, Ohio, with his wife Jenny and their daughters, Adrienne and Madeline.

*Led Pants'* Attention-Deficit-Disorder-inducing entertainments combine Heironymous Bosch with the Atari 2600 in a post-modern mixture that's colorful, enthusiastic, wacky, and uninhibited. His clients include Nickelodeon, Disney, Amazon.com, Noggin, and a broad assortment of publications including *Inc., Fast Company, The New York Times,* and *The Atlantic Monthly.* He's been profiled in the best European design magazines, including *Etapes* and Czech *Vogue,* and has won awards from *Print* magazine and *American Illustration.* His website, having been selected for Webmonkey's and Yahoo's Picks of the Week, has generated a broad international fan base. Led Pants lives in San Francisco with his wife, Petunia Pants.

*C.F. Payne* is a 1976 BFA graduate of Miami University, in Oxford, Ohio. After brief studio stints, he began his freelance career in Dallas, Texas, in 1980, and has worked for *Time Magazine, Esquire, Reader's Digest, The New York Times, The Atlantic Monthly, Boys Life, Forbes* and *Mad* magazine, to name just a few. The illustrator has received national acclaim, has won Gold and Silver awards from the Society of Illustrators of both New York and Los Angeles, and received the Hamilton King Award from the Society of Illustrators of New York. C.F. Payne currently works and resides in Cincinnati, Ohio, with his wife, Paula, and children.

*Mike Quon* arrived in New York City over 20 years ago and has been making eye-catching graphic design and illustration ever since. He was raised in Los Angeles, attended UCLA, and furthered his studies at Art Center College. Mike is an author and lecturer as well as a designer, creative director, and illustrator. He also works as a consultant on corporate identity development projects for AOL Time Warner, Estee Lauder/Aveda, JPMorgan Chase, *Fortune* magazine, KPMG Consulting, and UBS PaineWebber. Quon recently mounted a fine arts exhibition at the Society of Illustrators in New York City, and his work is represented in the permanent collections of the Library of Congress and the Wakita Design Museum in Japan. Contact Mike Quon Designation Inc. at 212-226-6024 (phone), 212-219-0331 (fax), or http://www.mikequondesign.com

*Lauren Redniss* lives in New York City. She is a regular contributor to the *New York Times* Op-Ed page, and other publications. Contact Lauren at: lauren.redniss@verizon.net

From his college days in the heart of Oklahoma to his current staff position with the Pittsburgh Post-Gazette, *Rob Rogers* has been creating editorial cartoons with impact. Rogers is nationally syndicated four times weekly by United Feature Syndicate. His cartoons appear in *The New York Times, The Washington Post,* the *Chicago Tribune,* and *The Philadelphia Inquirer.* You'll also find his work in *Newsweek, Business Week, U.S. News & World Report,* and *USA Today.* Rogers and his cartoons have also appeared on NBC's "Today," CBS's "Face the Nation," and ABC's "Good Morning America Sunday." Rogers was a finalist for the Pulitzer Prize in 1999 and received the 2000 Overseas Press Club Award, the 1995 National Headliner Award, and has won eight Golden Quill Awards.

*John Rutherford* spent two years in the United States Infantry, four years at the Art Center School, and has been a San Francisco-based illustrator for some 30 years. Presently, he is pursuing figurative fine art and teaching. His teaching credits include the San Francisco Academy of Art, College of the Redwoods, and Humboldt State University (in Eureka, CA), and the Mendocino Art Center (Mendocino, CA). Contact John Rutherford at: 707-937-2114 or jnjr@mcn.org

*Robert Saunders* is a native of Seattle and graduate of the Rhode Island School of Design in its European Honors Program to Rome. Robert lived for seven years in Italy, where he earned a Master's Degree from Rosary College in Florence, while supporting himself as a musician. Upon returning to the United States he entered the field of full-time illustration for editorial/book publishers, design studios, and advertising agencies. He has worked with hundreds of clients including *The Atlantic, The New York Times, Entertainment Weekly, The Wall Street Journal,* and many Fortune 500 firms. His work has appeared in *Communication Arts, Print,* the *Art Directors Club,* and the annuals of the Society of Illustrators of New York and Los Angeles.

*Bob Selby* was staff illustrator at the *Providence Journal* for 20 years. Covering the U.S. Supreme Court or grinding poverty in Guatemala were all in a day's work for this award-winning illustrator. He has taught Illustration at the Rhode Island School of Design and the University of Massachusetts. A 1993 Fulbright research grant took him to Madrid where he studied the history of caricature in Spain. He currently lives and works as a freelance illustrator in Johnson, Vermont. Recent kudos include a commission for the U.S. Coast Guard and a runner-up award in the first Society of Illustrators Three Dimensional Illustration Biennial in New York.

*Stan Shaw* illustrates for such clients as *The Village Voice, Esquire,* Starbucks, the Seattle Mariners, Nintendo, Rhino Records, Microsoft, DC Comics, ABCNEWS.com, *Vibe,* and The Flying Karamazov Brothers. His work has appeared in *Print, Communication Arts,* and *How* magazines. Shaw also teaches at Pacific Lutheran University, and has taught at the Cornish School of the Arts, and the School of Visual Concepts (both in Seattle, WA). Stan can be reached at drawstanley@harbornet.com or by phone: 253-756-7303.

*Brian Shellito* graduated from the University of Nebraska in 1993 with a bachelor's degree in fine arts, emphasizing painting and drawing. He has worked in the art departments of three daily newspapers as an illustrator and graphic artist. At home in Akron, Ohio, Brian and his wife Susan have two young children, dogs, cats and a couple of lizards.

*Elwood H. Smith* studied at the Chicago Academy of Fine Arts and the Institute of Design at IIT in Chicago. After eight years as an art director, Elwood moved to New York City in 1976, establishing himself as one of the premier professionals in the field of illustration. His clients include *Time, Newsweek,* SONY, Pizza Hut, *Sports Illustrated,* Bell Atlantic, *The New York Times,* Cornell University, Carlsburg Beer, McDonalds, Saturn/GM, Nabisco, Klutz Press, and many more. He has written and illustrated books (as well as two musicals with his wife and representative, Maggie Pickard) for children. In 1983, Elwood and Maggie moved to Rhinebeck, New York, where they live with Sophie, a Scottish Terrier; Girlie, an ancient feline nut-case; and Luigi, the best cat in the world.

*Ken Smith* still lives on the south side of Chicago, where he was born and raised. Ever since he can remember, he has known how to draw—a skill he says has miraculously survived his artistic training. His most enjoyable college class was Engineering Drafting, but it was during Ken's first full-time job drawing heating and air-conditioning components that he learned the finer points of using the french curve, ellipse template, technical pen, and airbrush. He sat down in front of a Macintosh computer at the age of 32, and it only *partially* changed his life—he has not forgotten how to draw! Reach him by phone at 773-373-3015, or by e-mail at smithster@earthlink.net.

*Chris Spollen* has been interviewed by *Byte, HOW, MacWorld, Print,* and *Step-By-Step.* He has lectured at the Art Director's Club of Long Island, the Graphic Artist Guild, the Society of Illustrators, Syracuse University, the Rochester Art Director's Club, and Sacred Heart University, and is listed in the Contemporary Graphic Artists' Who's Who. Spollen received his art training at Parsons School of Design. He participates in a wide variety of markets especially in advertising, publishing, and editorial illustrations. Recent clients have included AT&T, Bell Labs, *Boy's Life, Byte* magazine, Citibank, *Consumer Reports, MacWorld,* Novell, *PC Magazine, Reader's Digest,* Tandem, *Var Business,* and General Motors. "Mediocrity," he says, "is not long hidden from one's fellow artists. I am constantly searching for innovations in both style and technique."

*Akiko Stehrenberger* graduated as the youngest of her class from the Art Center College of Design in Pasadena, CA, where she received her Bachelor's Degree of Fine Art with honors in Illustration. She currently resides in New York pursuing freelance illustration and specializing in the editorial field. Her clients include *SPIN* magazine, the *New York Press,* Lego toys, Disney toys and clothing, Mattel toys, FUBU clothing, TNT, and Canon Camera. Contact Akiko Stehrenberger by phone: 212-330-9073 or online: http://www.akikomatic.com or akiko1024@hotmail.com

Born in Tokyo, *Tadanobu (Tad) Suzuki* now lives in Victoria, British Columbia. Self-taught, Suzuki is represented by Winchester Galleries in Victoria, and Kensington Fine Art Gallery in Calgary, Alberta. He has exhibited in extensive group and solo shows and won the 1998 Myfanwy Spencer Pavelic Award at the Sooke Art Show, the largest juried show on Vancouver Island. Contact Tad at debtad@ islandnet.com

*Sam Viviano* was born sometime in the last century to an anonymous couple in Detroit. Moving to New York City, he was saved from a life of crime by the editors of *Mad* magazine, who assigned him his first cover—#223—in 1980. He quickly became one of the Usual Gang of Idiots, producing movie and television satires, phony ads and, of course, more covers. To stem his seemingly endless output of bad illustration, Sam was asked to become the Art Director of *Mad* in 1999, a position he still sleeps through today. Sam lives in New York with his wife and daughter, who (like his parents) would prefer to remain anonymous. Viviano can be reached (when awake) at: sam.viviano@madmagazine.com.

The Wertzateria has been mixing savvy and professionalism with a wildly expressive style of illustration since 1995. Originally a dance club that *Michael Wertz* hosted in his apartment, the Wertzateria—like its namesake club—produces lively and engaging art that is bright and fun. Michael Wertz can be reached at: http://www.wertzateria.com

A native of Chicago, *Ilene Winn-Lederer* attended the Museum School of the Art Institute of Chicago, followed by training in illustration and graphic design at the Chicago Academy of Fine

Arts. Living in Pittsburgh, Pennsylvania, Ilene has taught illustration and design, and her work is represented in many public and private collections. Her clients include *The Wall Street Journal,* Children's Television Workshop, Simon & Schuster, and Scholastic, Inc. Contact Ilene Winn-Lederer at http://www.winnlederer.com

*Brian Zick* is an old commercial hack who has for eons serviced a whole bunch of *really* really *big* big-time clients (it would be gauche to drop names). His post avant-garde neo-derivative stylings display an amalgam of diverse creative influences (he rips off the best). Brian has yet to write an opera, but he always puts the toilet seat back down, and he never goes to bed without first brushing his teeth.

*Robert Zimmerman* has spent the last 20 years developing a perpetual drawing machine, which is fabricated from nothing but recycled milk jugs, rubber bands, and plastic coat hangers. Once completed, the machine (called the Zimminator, and currently occupying a 40,000-square-foot airplane hangar) is planned to replace him completely. He intends to use his free time to fulfill his lifelong dream of sorting, identifying, and cataloging his collection of petrified ants and writing catchy burlesque show tunes on his guitar. A college dropout and father of two, Robert lives in the mountains of North Carolina. He is known to spend long hours talking to his pet parakeet, Buzz, who understands everything that Robert says and agrees completely with all of his lousy opinions.

*Robin Zimmerman* lives and works in Xenia, Ohio. She learned to Batik in high school and continued to explore the medium at Ohio University. Robin has a place in the north woods of Michigan's Upper Peninsula. There she spends about a month in the summer. "Not long enough," she reflects. Many of her images come from the north woods: the birch and balsam trees, the native birds and flowers there. She travels as often as she can, and is creatively inspired by those journeys.

For as long as she can remember, *Robin Zingone* has had design running through her veins. A compulsive designer, Robin's many trips abroad have inspired every aspect and application of her work. After completing her education (at Parsons both in New York and Paris), Robin traveled extensively overseas. She continues to do so when she is not hard at work here in America for a broad range of clients, including product illustration for Barbie (Mattel), shampoo bottles for Conair, cookbooks for Workman Publishing, and beer glasses for Anheuser Busch. Robin has applied her love of beauty and design to other projects as well. She designed (and built) her own exquisitely lush home, and developed a line of pottery, decorated in her own unique style. Robin lives in Connecticut with her husband, Peter, and an extended family that includes three dogs and two cats.

## QUESTIONS AND FEEDBACK

Delmar Learning and the author welcome your questions and feedback. If you have suggestions that you think others would benefit from, please let us know and we will try to include them in the next edition.

To send us your questions and/or feedback, you can contact the publisher at:

Delmar Learning
Executive Woods
5 Maxwell Drive
Clifton Park, NY 12065
Attn: Graphic Arts Team
800-998-7498

Or the author at:

Edison Community College
1973 Edison Drive
Piqua, OH 45356
937-778-8600
*fleishman@edisonohio.edu* or
*jojobean@infinet.com*

# about the author

▶ Michael Fleishman has been active for the past 30 years as an illustrator, educator, and writer. He was a staff illustrator at Abbey Press, and his freelance client list includes the Children's Television Workshop, Scholastic Press, Pictura AB Sweden, Price Stern Sloan, and Recycled Paper Products.

Mike was a contributing editor at *The Artist's Magazine,* penning many feature articles and two continuing columns on illustration and design. He has written for *How Magazine* and other publications, and was a featured speaker at Design World, the How Design conference of 2002.

© Max Fleishman 2003

Mike is the author of three previous books on the business of illustration and design. His latest book prior to this—*Starting Your Career as a Freelance Illustrator or Designer*—was published by Allworth Press in 2001.

He was formerly a national representative, then president, of the At-Large chapter of the Graphic Artists Guild. Mike has a BS in Art Education, and an MA in Painting and Drawing, from Indiana University of Pennsylvania. He has been teaching art since 1973, and is currently a Commercial Art Instructor at Edison Community College in Piqua, Ohio.

© Cooper Fleishman 2003

Mike lives in Yellow Springs, Ohio, the tiny town that time forgot. He shares home and studio with his beautiful wife, JoJo Beanyhead, and sons Cooper and Max—two inspirational artists who explore illustration with the best of 'em.

My bio illustrations were done by Cooper Fleishman (age 15) and Max Fleishman (age 13). Right up front, I'll admit to being a proud (and biased) father, but I can be objective *Mr. Teacher-head,* too. The art instructor in me also recognizes that both guys are sharp illustrators in this stage of their game.

Professionals? Of course not. Max (whose illustration is above right) and Cooper (whose illustration is lower right) are amateurs in the true, *original* sense of the word: they draw because they *love* to draw. They draw without compensation. They create because they are compelled by an inner drive, a profound interest—and the sheer *fun* of it!

Yes, I love my sons, but I show their drawings to make a point: foster an all-access creative environment, throw in cool tools, and full-throttle inspiration gears up—exactly what *Exploring Illustration* is all about.

## MURPHY'S LAW

In thinking about what to say in the introduction to this book, I realized that (at the risk of being cute) I wanted to discuss a guy I share my studio with—a cat named Murphy. Murphy lives his art, and fulfills his job contract every minute; he is learning in the field, and strives diligently to be exactly who he is.

And who exactly is Murphy? Murphy is a ball of energy, but he understands the vital importance of rest—the "Murph" makes sleep look absolutely *wonderful*. He makes mistakes, but bounces back instantaneously. Murphy jumps at opportunity; when a door is open to him, he goes for it.

Murphy takes his recreation quite seriously. The boy spends long hours in the studio, but gets away from the drawing board (going outside the house, as well) at every opportunity. Murph instinctively *knows* how to play hard and well. A very sweet guy with great people skills, Murphy never hides his appreciation or affection. But he also speaks up when he has to; he lets you know when it's just not working for him.

Murphy seldom skips a meal, and he doesn't short change his personal hygiene. His concentration is intense. When he's really on, he doesn't know the meaning of the word *no;* yet with the proper motivation, he's a fine team player. Murphy's work ethic, spirit of play, and sense of self offer much to think about and emulate. For this illustrator, he's the very definition of a good role model.

Figure | I-01 |

Murphy! (© Michael Fleishman 2003)

# FUNDAMENTALS

Seasoned illustrators—like pro athletes—will tell you that "illustration" is a mental procedure—one must have confidence in what he is doing. It may seem a funny starting point for an illustration *techniques* text, but I want to make a statement.

Your cause *is* a bit righteous (as in good, upright, honorable, and honest). And you have a noble charge—nothing more than an unshakable faith in, and a distinct appreciation of, your own unique abilities. Realize, too, that the act of illustration can satisfy on a gut level (some might say a *soul* level). But also keep it humble; understand that the process can be pure pleasure, and know in your heart that *that's okay, too.*

# THE "BIZ"

As you read these words, the illustration "biz" will be going only one of two ways—up or down, it's that simple. But frankly, *Exploring Illustration* is not really a book about the state of the illustration business or marketing strategies.

As a freelance illustrator trying to keep his business afloat, I hardly make light of all this (or the real-world ramifications of my little off-hand opener in the previous paragraph). I deal with the state of the illustration business every day, and so will you. Hey, I'll talk marketing strategies with you *anytime*.

## Both Sides of the Coin

When I set about approaching contributors for this book, some illustrators were, shall we say, *reluctant* to participate. They did not have "a lot of spare time to give away free advice," and felt that due to the extreme nature of the current marketplace, they weren't "interested in sharing what has taken a career to develop."

Concerned that a book about illustration techniques would encourage "would-be illustrators toward a career that may be close to impossible to get started, given that market," a few questioned the wisdom and motivation behind such a project. Why "benefit people who might end up being my competition, at a time when the market is already saturated with illustrators?" I had one illustrator, with tongue, I hope, planted firmly in cheek, tell me that he didn't want to give up the recipe for the "secret sauce."

Paranoia? Hardly. A bad case of the grumps? No. These folks—good, upright, honest, honorable (and incredibly talented) illustrators, one and all—must be heard and respected. If this book nurtures your technique in any way, I still cannot promise you a boom market, nor will I paint a false picture of the possibilities.

But, as illustrator Elwood Smith will tell you, "If there is one thing I've learned from my nearly 40 years as an illustrator, it is this: remain as open and flexible as you can.

"Everything is changing more quickly than ever before," observes Smith. "Trust me, I was there back then. Keep a tight grip on your optimism—muck about in the artistic soup of your pure creative self as much as possible. Remain vigilant, keep those creative fires tended."

So feel the burn; make that burn (and maybe discover the formula for your own secret sauce).

# DECISIONS

Artist and educator Carla Steiger-Meister shared this with me: "Seeing is one of the basic ways we know the world, and creating an image makes order out of chaos. Illustration helps the viewer to focus on a selected number of elements to form the image."

The focus is on decision making. It's about the many forks in the road—on *your* path—to making an illustration. Those little junctures where you decide what you're going to do are the very core of your process—of what you are going to make, what the image is going to be.

You'll make more than a few stops along the way. Decision after decision . . . and it all adds up to your process and your particular manner of expression.

That expression is highly individual. Okay, so perhaps, after that job from hell, you'll moan and groan, "I'll never be a great illustrator. I'll never be as good as ___ (you can fill in the blank)." And maybe you won't be. But you *could* learn to be a *better* illustrator, and you *can* improve. Just as you can practice kicking a soccer ball, so can you practice the art of illustration.

# MAKE THE JUMP

Somebody, somewhere said, "Risk inescapably precedes growth." Wise advice. You should always *go for it.* Keep your feet firmly on the ground, but don't plant them there.

Sure, baby steps usually come first, but babies don't stay slow for long, as anyone who has attempted to keep up with a toddler at full speed will attest. Have just enough adult in you to appreciate possible consequences, but keep taking risks. Illustrator Paul Melia puts it nicely: "Taking chances keeps the illustrator improving and growing—it's the evolution of your spirit. Your talent comes out progressively as you work hard and follow your intuition."

Have fun, because this *is* fun. Work hard, because frankly, you will have little choice. My career has been built on long, passionate hours doing something I love. And that's what exploring illustration—that's what *Exploring Illustration*—is really about!

© John S. Dykes

PART

# WHAT IS ILLUSTRATION?

Let's preface our section on illustration theory by briefly addressing what "illustration" is. According to a rather long dictionary definition, illustration is "the art or process of producing or providing a drawing, photograph, or diagram that accompanies and complements a printed, spoken, or electronic text." An "illustration" can also clarify or explain: "Let me give you an illustration."

An illustration can describe. The nature of this description can be photographic (or realistic, if you prefer)—an accurate visual report. In other words, the eyes have it.

Or the illustration may hit a little higher or lower—it can make a stylistic or metaphorical point or describe an emotional sense or physical state. By that extension, then, an illustration can also impact, intrigue, or provoke.

Bottom line, both illustrative art and gallery art ask the viewer to do one thing: *Look at me.* One basic difference, however, is that an illustration must usually answer the core questions of *who, what, when, where,* and *why* for the viewer. Gallery art—the so-called "fine art"—doesn't necessarily have to do this at all.

Maybe the *fine* in the label "fine art" means it's just fine the way it is. Of course, this "fine art" can also accurately report details, and provoke deep thought or powerful emotion. Gallery art can make profound political, social, and cultural statements, as well as lightly entertain.

So, illustration and gallery art both tell tales or send messages (see Figure I-1). The trouble is, our ready-made definitions and tags don't quite stick all the time. The gallery artist (with enough backbone) is free to create without commercial restraint. As long as you don't care about labels, sales, or critics, you can paint or draw what you please. The commissioned illustrator doesn't enjoy this artistic perk (sure, an illustrator can also reject labels, sales, and critique, but I doubt this artist will stay in *business* very long).

We can, then, define *illustration* as art with a definite purpose. This is *not* to say that gallery arts have *no* purpose, but illustration must *do* and do it *on demand*. Illustrators, remember: *your art is being prepared for reproduction*. You face the multilevel challenge of insuring artistic merit and maintaining quality control—your little masterpiece must be fit for page or display.

Figure | I-1a |

*Guy Cubed* is a portfolio piece, an illustration pushing my cubist approach (and selling *me*). It addresses what I do with a grid, my line style (and media work), color direction, and value sense. (© Michael Fleishman 2003)

Figure | I-1b |

*Confab* was a portfolio illustration, but in another vein; for an older, entirely separate portfolio. Here, I am selling pen and ink work. The illustrations in this portfolio demonstrate a kinetic line that plays with figure/ground—something decidedly distinct from my cubist stuff. I would not hesitate to exhibit the *Guy Cubed* or *Confab* originals (and in fact, I have). (© Michael Fleishman 2003)

Figure | I-1c |

Drawn with a brush, the spot drawings are also done in ink, but are obviously different from b; they would not be in the same portfolio. I wouldn't pair this humorous style with the line (or conceptual) approach of *Confab*. I would certainly choose to exhibit these spots in an *illustration show*, but these drawings weren't done for exhibition purposes. (© Michael Fleishman 2003)

Figure | **I-1d and I-1e** |

*Pig Map* (above) and *Right to the Left* (right), are gallery art—not done for print—and somewhat dissimilar paint explorations. The figure is an energetic exercise in bold color and intense brushwork; the big ham is a study in subtle gradated color harmony. Both pieces could be viable illustrations; these painterly techniques are very page-worthy. (© Michael Fleishman 2003)

Figure | **I-1f** |

*Milhouse* is an experimental caricature that actually made it into my portfolio. Depending on just how tiny, small line drawings are enlarged some 200-600 percent (via photocopier or scan. On *Milhouse* I even crumpled the paper surface before I started drawing, and purposely worked with a clunky broad-tip marker).

The result: instant, effortless (and fabulous) line character! I bring this art into Photoshop, where I continue to manipulate line quality. I then add color in Photoshop or Illustrator, depending on the look I'm after. (© Michael Fleishman 2003)

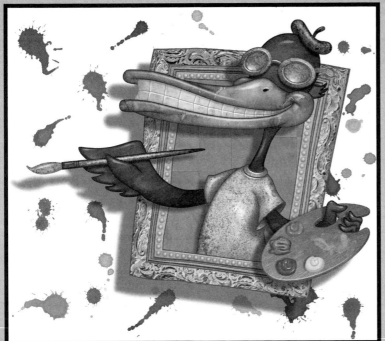

© Brian Zick 1998

Getting It Down

*"What I've come to realize is that it's definitely a thought process. There are a lot of different answers to one problem, and spitting out the one you think is going to work best is the key. That's part of why an art director should be hiring you; not just for your drawing skills, but for your sensibilities too."*

**PJ Loughran, illustrator and educator**

*"So many illustrators—entry-level and pro—occasionally 'hit the wall' when looking at a blank canvas or screen. This is actually a very healthy experience towards the creative process—to 'hit the wall' and go past it. It's like the restart button for your brain to flush out sameness and inspire better solutions."*

**David Julian, illustrator and educator**

*"Two words: Vente Latte. Nothing inspires me like a good dose of caffeine. While I'm waiting for the coffee to kick in I read the New York Times, Pittsburgh Post-Gazette, USA Today, and wire stories on the Internet looking for a good topic."*

**Rob Rogers, editorial cartoonist**

## Chapter Objectives:

Discuss the beginnings of the process: how to generate ideas, and how to turn those ideas into illustration

Consider inspirations and influences and explore various components of the illustration process

Consider the abstract and intellectual illustration processes, including knowing "when to stop"

## Introduction

Where to begin? How to start? Good questions, and a great place to kick off any discussion about illustration—in both theory or practice. It is said of any challenging sport that to be a true champion, one must first master the mental game. It's the same with illustration.

## CONCEPT IS KING

The beginning of the illustration process means understanding and appreciating *concept*. It's really quite simple: concept dictates content and content determines composition. *Conceptually* what are you trying to do? What's the illustration about— what are you saying (see Figure 1–1)?

Figure | 1-1 |

What is William Ersland communicating in his sensitive illustration? What do *you* want to do *conceptually*—what are you trying to say? What is your illustration about? (© William C. Ersland)

Once we know where the concept is going, the underlying workings of the illustration—composition, line, value, color, pattern and texture, shape and form—combine with our artists' tools and toys to create what we call an individual process and a particular technique (see Figure 1–2).

## How to Generate Ideas

Before your incredible technique turns heads and grabs critical and public attention, you must think back a bit. Remember the pure joy you felt as a little kid when presented with just a box of crayons and a blank sheet of paper. Remember when one fat piece of chalk and the potential of the whole driveway were all it took to set your imagination and sense of artistic adventure soaring. This is still the mode you need to be in *now*.

### Inspiration and Influence

Where do your ideas come from? For me, it's anywhere and everywhere, actually. If I keep my eyes and ears open wide, concepts are universal. Of course, not everyone need work this

Figure | 1-2 |

An illustration that's *all* about process. I needed a promo to give to an artist's rep. Wanting something different yet familiar, I completely (and digitally) reworked a favorite flyer from the ground up. Gags were revamped and contact information updated. I reset type (the old promo was hand-lettered), and then redrew the entire piece—all new line art plus color—in Adobe Illustrator. I also was able to clean up some color and value issues nagging me from the first incarnation. (© Michael Fleishman 1999)

| TIP |

Keep a picture file, often called a morgue, where you can organize categories like kids, animals, fashion, interiors, and so on. I highly recommend this practice. Maintain and continually update your files—frequently tear out images from magazines (or newspapers and advertising) to add to this invaluable reference library.

"I look through my picture files for inspiration," Ali Douglass comments. The illustrator is careful to remind you to only use photo reference when necessary. "Use what you need from it," she says. "Then put it away and concentrate on making the drawing your own."

way—and time management may be an issue—but I say: *let the ideas come to you.* See Figure 1–3 and Figure 1–4 for some thoughts on inspiration.

Go to an art opening or take a trip to the museum. Spend afternoons at the bookstore. Pore over your illustration annuals and directories. Peruse the latest *How, Communication Arts,* or other industry publications. Relax at the library, loaf at the bookstore. Cruise the Internet, leaf through old and new sketchbooks. Then, and only then, *think about the job just a little.*

Go for a quick walk, take a long hike or short bike ride, exercise at the gym, have a swim, join the softball league, enjoy a weekend pickup game of any activity. Volunteer. Hang out with friends. Go to the movies. Watch a little television. Now, *think about the job some more.*

Read a good book while snuggled up in a favorite chair with a cup of coffee. Dance a little. Laugh a lot. Take a nice hot bath or shower. Play with the dog. Talk to some kids. Play with some kids. Have a meaningful dialogue with the cat. *Think more about the job.* Now, head over to the drawing board, and see what goes down. It's all good, *and it works.*

## Sketchbooks, Journals, and Diaries

Many illustrators carry a sketchbook wherever they go. Always handy, the collections become useful source books—everyday life, art for every day. Others maintain collections of what I call "artless art" and tap into these unpretentious compilations for inspiration or reference.

Many illustrators keep all their job sketches (as well as doodles or roughs for personal or uncommissioned art) in book form or on file. You never know when an orphan idea's time will come, or come again. Inventive recycling is no sin—it's the very nature of a recognizable style.

Illustrator Elwood Smith says, "I don't *do* sketchbooks, but when I'm on the phone I doodle—a kind of stream-of-consciousness thing. I select the ones I like, cut 'em out, and tape them in a sketchbook." Affixing the "little snipped out drawings" with transparent tape, Smith says that the mounting sometimes shows, but the drawings in the books have a wonderfully spontaneous quality.

Figure **1-3**

John Coulter finds he looks at many things for inspiration, but avoids simply mimicking his resource. "Never copy something outright," he says. "The more things you look at and put into your brain eventually just come out into your own style." Good point—his *Bongo Beatnik* is like, groovy, man. (© John Coulter)

Figure **1-4**

Hey—you're not in it alone; your art director can be a terrific source of inspiration. Produced for a billboard promoting the Los Angeles Zoo, illustrator Brian Zick credits art director Mikio Osaki on a distinctly collaborative effort. This splendid vulture was under-painted and then airbrushed with gouache on illustration board. The billboard itself used extension cut-outs, so the wings and head stuck out above the top edge of the board. (© Brian Zick 1998)

Some illustrators employ visual journals as a creative diary, an emotional release or intellectual steam valve. These volumes are sometimes shared, but I would think most are respected as true diaries, justifiably private and personal.

Still others create graphic travelogues—fascinating glimpses into the eye and mind of the correspondent, not to mention an introspective look at the port of call, and an intriguing revelation about the journey itself.

There are also those illustrators for whom the *act* of journaling is as important as the craft of preparing a page. Many volumes later, and still counting, there is no creative end in sight. There are worse addictions, to be sure.

There are those illustrators who journal to promote self-control ("I will draw every day"), and that's fine, if you need or want that discipline. But generally, I would say *don't force it*, and don't beat yourself up if it's not happening (or not for you). You must embrace both idea and act, if this intimate artistic process is to really work for you. I recommend doing sketchbooks, journals, or diaries, but it's such a personal thing that I couldn't assert that you must.

Some folks don't actually sketch in the sketchbooks themselves. Ali Douglass recycles the back of used computer paper or old fax cover sheets. "If something turns out great, I cut it out and tape it into my sketchbook," says the illustrator. "It's more spontaneous and less intimidating than a fresh page or nice piece of drawing paper."

| NOTE |

Many illustrators hit it hard from the very start—thinking immediately and *only* of the project at hand. I have heard this referred to as working "in the soup."

Figure | 1-5 |

You need to have a *vision* of a finished illustration that begins in your mind's eye. Here, Ilene Winn-Lederer's concept for *Jazz Dragon* is one step removed from her "personal image bank," and drawn with ballpoint on a yellow legal pad. (© Ilene Winn-Lederer 2003)

## How to Turn Those Ideas into Illustration

Before beginning an illustration, take a little mental stroll through your "personal image bank," try to arrive at a *vision* of the finished illustration. As that image comes to life on paper, work to stay faithful to the intensity of that original concept (see Figure 1–5). Imagine your drawing expressed as a metaphor of thought. In that regard, line work could be considered a phrase or sentence, and the resulting illustration becomes a complete conversation.

For instance, when doing a caricature, the first thing you may want to do is to gather as much information and picture reference as possible—via your client, at the library, or perhaps online. Such research helps the illustrator gain a special understanding of the subject and provides hints of that subject's personality—this can be an excellent starting point in the brainstorming process.

After reading a manuscript, consult with the art director for input, to possibly brainstorm, and to verify the client's preferences. Doing this at an early stage will avoid wasting time later. Now you can sketch ideas with a clear focus or goal in mind.

Reread the copy to pick up anything missed (or new visuals that spring out) from the first round. Look to the text to find the agenda, the priorities—the editorial angle. You must think: What does the *client* expect or want? What does your client have in mind for the art?

It is a great idea to find out if your art director has some definite approach he's after. I should mention here that an illustrator has more freedom in editorial art, but advertising concepts are likely to be presented to the client for approval. Even if you feel your approach to a problem is better, it's the client who makes the final decision.

Look to both colleagues and friends for critique as well as inspiration. Colleagues are other professionals who directly understand both concept and process. Your peers are tough critics who will help you raise the bar. The wise illustrator seeks the input of non-arty-types as well—your potential *audience* must "get the picture" or you haven't quite nailed it after all.

# THE ORDER OF THINGS

Let's discuss getting the job down and done—the real-world stuff as well as some philosophical and intellectual issues. To do so, we'll look at a sequence of events that start with simply *having fun*.

## Brainstorming

Brainstorming is the first step to the finish line of your illustration, and fun is what brainstorming is all about. How does one brainstorm? These usually loose, informal sessions are done solo, with a partner, or in small groups. Wordplay, brain teasers, free association, pencil games and puzzles, outlines, and charting are just a few basic constructs used to "rev up" your thinking and to get the creative juices flowing.

It's an enjoyable give-and-take of ideas and information, a creative connect-the-dots of productivity. The goal here is to identify what the job is really about, to establish the relationships that tie those elements together, and *start* to figure out how to express those relationships visually.

## The Raw Concept

Hollywood filmmakers talk about "high concept"—here, the point of the movie is so succinct, you can pitch it on the back of your business card. You won't have to jump this hoop, but you should be able to strip your idea down to its bare essence—the raw concept.

The raw concept will materialize out of all that brainstorming. It is here that the gem of the idea begins to shine. The concept is not polished or fully formed, but you can recognize it as something solid and real—you *can* pitch it, if you have to (but it still need not be on the back of your biz card). You can chat about the visuals—at whatever stage—in whole sentences; the premise of the illustration should make some sense to an outsider, as well as give you a good gut feeling.

## Concept Is Still King

I've been hammering the message home that if you duly consider your *concept,* content and composition will fall into place. Once we nail our raw concept, we can now begin to formalize line, color, value, and pattern as well as texture, shape, and form. To do this, I suggest starting small.

## Thumbnails

Thumbnails are where the ideas live. "Thumbs" are the initial loose and spontaneous products of your conscious (and unconscious) concept. They are the first doodles, so to speak, of the illustration process. A client may ask for, or be supplied, thumbnails as part of the review procedure for brainstorming, but often not.

A thumbnail may actually be the size of your thumbnail, but that's probably a bit too literal. This preliminary can actually be any size, but is most likely a smaller, and more immediate, first pass (see Figure 1–6).

The visual is just beginning to take shape, and anything goes. There are no "mistakes" here, no "right" (and definitely no "wrong") ideas yet, no

Figure **1-6**

A thumbnail of roughs—or a rough of thumbnails. This is a fabricated snapshot of different characters from a variety of my preliminaries. Even the frame is a thumbnail from a real job. Once I'm familiar with the assignment parameters, I often begin by simply immersing myself in line quality and characterization. Coincidentally, this drawing served as the thumbnail for my demo later in the book—see if you can find the central section that inspired the digital illustration done for Chapter 10. (© Michael Fleishman 2003)

Figure 1-7

I usually choose to refine my preliminaries—my roughs are seldom very *rough*. Though there were many pages of sketches that went into these collected spots, I'll only fax or e-mail my client the best of the bunch—the drawing that finally captures the concept, characterization, and line style of the assignment. (©Michael Fleishman 2003)

| NOTE |

Tracing is something artists have always done. If it's to serve the artist's pre-existing goal, that's fine, but as illustrator Gregory Nemec points out, "If it's due to physical or intellectual laziness, it's an offense."

"misdirections." You haven't thought the illustration through yet, but that's precisely the point—you're *starting* to work it out.

## The Rough

You refine and upgrade your thumbnails to create a rough (or sketch). Roughs can be any size, and are usually dictated by the dimensions of your illustration plus your general routine. My initial roughs go from thumbnails to about 1/4–1/2 page size relatively quickly. Developing and refining the sketch, I eventually get to a full-page rough. It just makes sense to work to size at this point.

And as I get closer to full-size, my roughs are not very *rough* (see Figure 1–7). The line art gets tighter and ultimately quite polished; you may not be able to distinguish this drawing from the final. This is my choice and the way I like it; my client knows what he is getting, and I am one step away from the actual final.

My color roughs, on the other hand, usually stay pretty loose. But there are various degrees of finish here as well. Again, this is usually dictated by the demands of the assignment plus your particular preferences and routine.

You will usually submit a rough (or roughs) for an initial review—you're working for a client, after all; it's best to keep him in the loop. This drawing is then art directed and adjustments are made—revisions are requested, corrections stipulated. You may even get the go-ahead, as is!

## The Comp

A comp (or comprehensive) could be considered a refined approximation of the final piece, close to a finish with some coarse edges to polish, sort of the diamond in the rough. "What you see is—just about—what you get."

You may be asked to do a comp—some clients will need to "have it spelled out" for them. Doing that comp may—or may not—be time (or

## STEP by STEP

# Daryll Collins

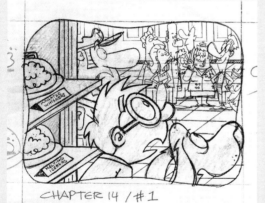

This progression succinctly documents how Daryll Collins developed one illustration for his book *The Stink Squad.*

### Step 1: The rough/conceptual sketch

"As I'm reading the manuscript, I jot down quick positional sketches of various scenes I want to highlight," says Collins. "Now I want to block in the composition and figure out the best camera angle. This is a planning step in the process, so I may draw a few sketches of certain scenes until I'm satisfied. I'll also make sidebar notes to myself about pertinent story specifics that bear on the illustration."

### Step 2: The tight sketch

"I create my working sketches in pencil on tracing paper," Collins continues. "I may redraw a sketch numerous times until I get it just right. At this point, I'm concerned with keeping the characters consistent (on-model) and that the perspective is correct. Since the finished art is black and white, I sometimes shade certain areas to show where I want to drop in the percentages of gray. Other times I'll make those decisions as I'm completing the digital finish."

### Step 3: Finished art

"I tape the tracing-paper sketch to the back of a piece of smooth bristol board," says Collins. "I ink the finished line with a variety of pen nibs over a light table. The finished line is scanned, converted in Adobe Streamline, and brought into Adobe Illustrator for final composition and application of halftones." (© Daryll Collins)

cost) efficient, but once again, this will be determined by job requirements and your way of working.

## The Finish

Toss your concepts of good or bad away for at least awhile. Think of a final illustration as either successful or unsuccessful.

You made it. The illustration is finished. It's a knock-out; one that will get in all the annuals; a guaranteed award-winner. Or perhaps you'll simply admire it and say, "Hey, *I* did this. I feel really good just looking at it; It felt great creating it. This is *mine, and I'm going to do all this again tomorrow.*"

# THE ZONE

Many illustrators (athletes and musicians, too) talk about "the Zone." The Zone is that place of intensive energy and extreme focus where you and your illustration are one and the same. For some, it is hard to get into, easy to slip out of, and (when distracted or interrupted) tougher yet to get back to (see Figure 1–8).

Figure | 1-8 |

In the Zone, your perception is keen, your skills are peaked. Time is fluid; an afterthought, if anything. Your head is clear; your hand and arm—if not all your muscles—are warmed and loose. Your whole *self* is in tune with the task. Indeed, it hardly seems like a task at all, even after long hours or extended application. Your labors may catch up to you later, but while you are in the Zone, you're drinking pure energy from a bottomless glass.

In the Zone, your deadline is merely a number, ever in focus, always in reach. The Zone is both mental and physical—a feeling of personal power and creative flow that is the state of *your* art. You may find yourself feeling strong, capable, confident—*in charge.* Or you may just feel *it's time to start.* It's at this point that true magic begins.

Here's Robert Saunders' melodious portrait of composer George Gershwin. Getting into the Zone, as Saunders succinctly puts it, means simply maintaining your vision. (© Robert Saunders 2003)

# DISTRACTIONS

If you're someone who cannot abide by interruptions or disturbances of any kind, at any point, you're a member of a big club. If you're a person who must attend to one task at any given time, you are hardly sideshow material.

But many illustrators can multitask. For these folks, the studio is hub of many projects, activities, and tasks merrily humming along. Ambient, outside, or simple background noise doesn't interfere with the artistic process one bit. Interruptions of any type don't curb the flow of creative juice at all.

Some illustrators can talk on the phone while they complete a sketch or even work on a final. The TV can drone on in the background, and just may provide a welcome diversion for the eyes. An eclectic mix of music can blare at loud volume, for hours (I know illustrators who say they put the tunes on *only* while doing the final). Talk radio may be the constant companion that stimulates the intellect or piques curiosity. Visitors come and go, and work still gets done.

But this is hardly a universal mindset. Company can kill concentration and clog the flow of energy (creative or otherwise). The telephone is another significant challenge to a workday and schedule. Some artists work late at night, expressly to prevent the interruption of phone calls. Still others screen their calls via the answering machine or other phone services.

At the initial concept stage, new ideas may pop into your head at odd times: watching TV, chatting on the phone, even taking a shower. But for many other illustrators, shepherding those concepts into the sketch stage (and beyond) is something else again. Here, concentration is the name of a very quiet game. Little or no distraction is what's needed to bring the sketch to life.

Where are you on all this? Each illustrator will develop his own system (Figure 1–9).

# OVERWORKING

On one hand, the course of an entire illustration is very simple. It can be stripped down to this: Draw. Draw again. Keep drawing until you get the illustration *just so*. Seasoned illustrators like Ilene Winn-Lederer realize that the self-discipline essential for artistic development simply means it is sometimes better to stop and start over again.

Figure | 1-9 |

Every illustrator will establish a personal rhythm—it's whatever works for *you*. If you don't know what works yet, *just keep working*. Your routine will be unique; when you hit the right combinations, you'll know. (© Michael Fleishman 2001)

Typically, the end result of *too much* scribbling takes on the character of processed food. Akin to that cuisine, what you have is seldom as vital as a newly prepared meal with fresh ingredients—the spontaneity, like so many essential vitamins, is too often cooked out.

Put another way: the technique steadily becomes too rigid; your concept looks forced; the entire piece begins to feel artificial. The fun factor is gone. It's *work* now and it shows—you're just correcting and changing, not creating.

Note that illustration done exclusively for decorative purposes will likely be judged on technical execution alone. However, even dazzling technical skills will never substitute for competent drawing ability. Illustration is the coordinated effort of eye, hand, and mind. The unique way in which you draw what *your* eye sees, *your* mind interprets, and *your* hand executes, defines who *you* are.

And your work is all about *you*. And in this instance, it's quite okay.

## When to Stop

How do you know when to stop? That's a good question. For me the answer has more than a few layers. Clock and calendar come into play when you must meet a deadline, but time investment isn't accurate at all. Thinking hourly only plays a minor role, so throw away your stopwatch—I believe knowing when to stop begins with a gut feeling that it's quitting time.

During the course of an illustration, I prop the piece up several times and really study it from the vantage point of my viewer. Is this a satisfying or compelling illustration from first glance to last—do I just like to *look* at it? Why? And if not, why?

Intellectually, does it challenge and/or stimulate, provoke or soothe (as appropriate)? Does it resonate with me at some level; or is it missing something?

At the same time, I think about the fundamentals of style and the basics of my process. I review the mechanics underlying the art—the artistic principles I intended to drive the visual—does it work visually; does it work academically?

I often seek out advice from objective, outside sources; folks whose eyes and opinions I trust. I do this because I may just be too close to an illustration—physically, mentally, and emotionally. At the same time, although I make the call, I welcome and enjoy the feedback (one reason why art school was so beneficial and so much fun).

Call it "done" based on what you know and what you were trying to do. Progress to the finish line with the reasonable assurance that you'll be in the studio tomorrow—every day and every illustration makes it easier to understand how to start and when to stop.

# PROFILES

## *Led Pants*

Illustrator Led Pants asserts that he must work his unique sensibilities into a drawing or that illustration always comes out too dry for his taste. Much of the Led Pants style, he says, is driven by personal ideology—it's what motivates the illustrator to keep drawing.

"People talk about style all the time," he says. "I'm not really interested in 'style.' What interests me about the visual arts is what people bring to it in terms of their politics—how they see society and all that. The stuff that enrages me is what gets me drawing. I really have to *react* to things."

Led works on a Mac—which he equates to the ultimate collage tool—and his technique has evolved with his digital prowess. He says that working in Adobe Illustrator means you will favor geometric shapes, precise curves, and sharp angles; it's a style really optimized for the computer, and exactly right for this artist.

Recently Led has been doing increasingly complex illustration. But he starts these elaborate visuals with a profoundly low-tech tool—Post-it notes.

The illustrator writes down a list of objects or scenes he wants to take place within the draw-

Illustrator Led Pants works on a Macintosh, and uses Adobe Illustrator almost exclusively. Led gets a number of high-tech clients and does a lot of stuff for kids. This obviously has much to do with his process—what he calls "that modern look"—as well as a sense of humor decidedly left-of-center. (© Led Pants)

ing. From here, Led doesn't sketch anything—he just draws the situations out one by one. When satisfied with the result, he fits it into the larger picture.

"I draw things pretty finalized and then move things around. In illustrations where there's a problem fitting elements together on one image, I draw pieces individually as separate files. I then group them, cut them out, and paste them into my original picture. I do the drawings and ultimately patch it all directly in the computer, right into the program."

## SUMMING IT UP

This chapter looked at the illustration process from start to finish—how to generate ideas, how to turn a bright idea into a bonafide illustration, and recognizing when to stop. We considered inspirations and influences, and broke down the various components of the procedure: brainstorming and the raw concept; sketchbooks, journals, and diaries; thumbnails, sketches, roughs, comps, and the finish. We acknowledged peripheral and abstract issues such as distractions, overworking, and "the Zone", as well.

## PROFILES

### *Ali Douglass*

© Ali Douglass

Ali Douglass says she uses some "pretty basic" stuff: HB and F pencils, tracing paper, white artists' tape, Fabrino Uno and Classico paper—140 and 300 lb. She recommends a good triangle and ruler, Sable brushes, Schmincke HKS designers gouache or Turner design gouache, and she raves about Masterson's Sta-Wet handy palette. "It's amazing," Douglass says, "your gouache can last weeks without drying up on your palette!"

This illustrator does her thumbnails on the backs of recycled office paper, and refines the sketch on tracing paper. She tries *not* to use reference, but if stuck will "look in the mirror, run back to my desk and draw it."

The illustrator scans this pencil sketch and e-mails it to the art director (and occasionally she'll take the scanned sketch, print it out, then do a quick gouache color rough over the print-out). When the sketch is approved she transfers it onto watercolor paper with non-photo blue transfer paper. "I blot the lines out until they are very faint; then come in with gouache and establish the background colors, or largest expanse of color. I next establish blacks, or the darkest colors, so I can work on contrast. Finally I work in smaller areas of color, details, linework, and pencil lines."

# PROFILES

## *Paul Melia*

To Paul Melia, the debate over generic versus brand name art supplies is not that pertinent. "It doesn't matter—to a degree," he says. "But I use the finest colors I can; I want to 'draw permanent.' I don't use any fugitive colors at all."

Melia uses Pelikan Permanent Inks. These pigmented inks are absolutely colorfast. They will not deteriorate with time or sunlight. "You may use a so-called permanent ink as a quick in and out—it goes before the camera and is done before it starts to fade—but I don't use anything like that on my work." With an eye to the future and the availability of these inks, Melia is also experimenting with acrylics for his base color rather than ink.

For Melia, inspiration comes from anything and everywhere— watching television, family-time, travel. On a particular trip to a ghost town in southern Ohio, Melia found an old gentleman at an ancient gas station. "It was like walking back into another age, and *ten years later* my painting *Sohio Man* sprang from that. I knew I wanted to do it, but I couldn't quite see *how,* so it sat in my idea file. I would come back to it occasionally and make some notations. Then one year it seemed appropriate, so I sat down in about three days and did it."

The artist relishes man-made objects and depicting architecture. "I do a lot of old houses," the illustrator tells us. "It feels like the spirits and the souls of the people are still kind of roaming around in these places—that they were once inhabited by people intrigues me.

"I do old houses with windows and people looking out to express the idea that the soul kind of lives on. It's that mysterious relationship of people to the places they inhabit. I also love graveyards, anything like that."

And when a hot idea kicks in—watch out. "I can't let it go," he smiles. "I must paint, even if it's into the wee hours of the morning, I have to stick with it. Once I am in there I'm like a demon, just get out of my way."

© Paul Melia

# PROFILES

*Stan Shaw*

"I like stuff that can take a beating," Stan Shaw insists. "#2 Kolinsky sable brushes, Pentel color brushes—I use those for a majority of my inking, along with crowquills and rapidographs. And I am very specific about the paper I use. I prefer Strathmore 500, three-ply, kid, or vellum finished—I like the texture of it. I need something that can handle a lot of abuse. This board is very well-sized, and tough.

"Lately I have started using the plate finish for some stuff that has to be a little more polished looking. This type of board doesn't give the brush line any character—the plate finish offers smooth strokes, very clean lines.

"Letramax board is a nice, bright white," the illustrator says. "It's great for doing black and white illustrations because there is more contrast. Plus, from my point of view, it's better for reproduction—I can really see the illustration when I am working on it.

"I use a lot of typing paper for sketches. It's cheap, I like the texture of it, and it

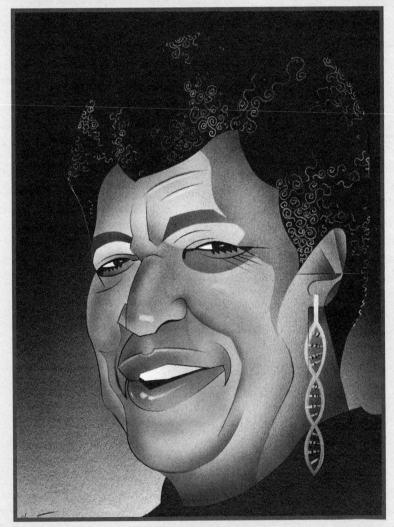

Stan Shaw knows his materials. He understands what supplies and tools work together to give him his best stuff—illustrations like this glowing portrait of writer Octavia Butler. (Illustrations © Stan Shaw 2002)

faxes and scans okay. It does limit you to a size that easily faxes and scans—8.5 × 11 or 11 × 14 inches—but here, you don't have to worry about making anything too large.

"Somebody could pick a different paper than what I have chosen, maybe they have a heavier hand, use a different brush. Perhaps they paint on Masonite. Maybe they stretch canvas simply because they want to feel that bounce. When you are working on the illustrations, it's just you, your materials and your concept. You want your supplies to act and react in a consistent way in which you're comfortable—you don't want to be battling those materials."

Shaw points out that technical concerns (cropping and/or reduction snafus, color shifts, lines filling in or blocking up, etc.) can and will affect your illustration. The illustrator must have a hand in (plus an understanding of) the reproduction process. "Otherwise," says Shaw, "You are illustrating in the dark. Not knowing how your art will make it through to print is akin to

working blind. The reproduced piece is arguably the actual illustration; and subtle or not so subtle changes ultimately impact how your work appears to the viewer."

Shaw believes that research, and seeing from the viewer's point ot view, plays an important role in developing your personal color systems. "The *world* is your laboratory. There is the traditional, tried and true method of color theory that can work with the everyday domain of color around you.

"All trees are not green," he continues. "Whatever 'green' is, is comprised of an infinite variety of tones and combinations. There are not 'tube colors' in nature, and thank goodness—it would be a boring work indeed."

The illustrator comments that *practical* theory reveals certain truisms. "Not all the colors around us offer the best combinations," Shaw states, "nor are all hypothetical color relationships perfect for how we *see* (and what we *feel*)."

## in review

1. What is *illustration*? How would you define this term? What is *fine art*? How would you classify this term? What is the difference between illustration and fine art? What do such labels mean to *you*?

2. What is the multi-level challenge illustrators face?

3. Define the term *concept*. Discuss why concept is so vital to the illustration process. Where do *your* ideas come from? What is a "raw concept?" How does brainstorming work? Why make thumbnails, or draw roughs and sketches? Are comps important?

4. What is "the Zone?" Do *you*/can *you* get into the Zone when you work? If so, describe your perspective of the Zone.

5. How do you know when to stop—when is an illustration "finished?"

## exercises

1. Do 25 pages of doodles in 5 days. (My numbers here are a bit arbitrary, and can certainly be adapted to your personal or class schedule. The assignment can be made easier or more challenging by simply adjusting the deadline and requirements.)

2. Maintain a *sketchbook* journal or visual diary for a specified period of time. Establish a regimen of one entry per day and stay with it. A diary is a most personal and private exercise, so no one need see this assignment—be as frank, open, or graphic as you wish. This project is all about discipline—can you keep up the routine?

3. Squiggle game. This is an exercise that perhaps works best with a partner. On separate sheets of paper (or on one larger sheet) draw a doodle for your partner, who now must create something out of this spontaneous line. Start with a simple squiggle, then make the doodles more complicated, if you wish. You can segué into two, then three (or more) squiggles.

   As you increase the number and/or complexity of your marks, the game becomes more interesting. But remember, you're trying to challenge your partner, not frustrate his creativity! Also, give your arm and wrist a chance to move freely—about five to ten doodle drawings (per partner) on one page.

4. Create a visual pun: pull your image out of the words themselves—for example: make a "cat" out of the word *dog. Draw* a short graphic novel in this manner.

5. Frankenstein drawing. You need a small group (3–4 minimum) for this exercise. Grab a piece of large paper—the bigger the better. Work vertically, not horizontally. Break down a basic figure into 8–12 (or more) segments; for instance: head, hair, eyes, nose, mouth, neck, shoulders, body, arms, hands, legs, feet. On the top right, write your name. On the top left, make a list of all the body parts. Put your name after the first item on the list.

   Now, render that first item and pass the drawing on to the person to your left. That person draws item No. 2, then passes the drawing on to the next person to his left. Make sure you sign your name to the "parts" list before you pass it on. Work down the list from head to toe, switch, and draw each body part. You can add or finish (or change, without erasing) anything you want, anytime your paper gets back to you. Whether you draw realistically, stylize, or mix and match, you end up with a marvelously eclectic figure of diverse proportions and unpredictable variety.

Building Blocks

2

*"Are we training cake decorators or visual commentators and communicators who enlighten and entertain in a meaningful way?"*

**William Jaynes, illustrator and educator**

*"I hate to be called a 'talented artist.' I was that from the get-go. What I am is a trained, educated, practiced, and skilled artist—and it didn't come easy, you betcha."*

**Jeanne de la Houssaye, trained, educated, practiced, and skilled illustrator**

*"When I was still a student struggling to find 'my style,' I met a very successful illustrator who told me to go home and start drawing as if I was a child. I filled a tray with assorted art supplies, and left it on my desk at all times. For about a year I just played with my art. This exercise was like an athlete running laps. By the end of the year I was so comfortable with my drawing, I had developed a style without really trying."*

**Robin Zingone, illustrator**

## Chapter Objectives:

Discuss six basic building blocks of illustration

Discuss the relationship of "looking" and "seeing" as well as the crucial connection between composition and concept

Examine line, value, and color in theory and practice

Relate pattern and texture and consider the correlation of shape with form

Look at peripheral challenges and design considerations for the illustrator

## Introduction

Foundations. Basics. Essentials. Details. Call them what you will, but all the words on your list will be synonymous with topics at the heart of every artistic endeavor. These are the core issues. For the illustrator, a solid, inherent sense of these rudiments, a dedication to the craft, plus a solid work ethic yield competence and distinction (See figure 2–1).

How does this proficiency come about? Where do you get it? Is it pure, dumb luck? The result of a good environment? Great genes? Art school?

There are credited illustrators who boast little or no formal academic training, but for my money, art school is indeed *the* best place to sort out the essential nuts and bolts. Saying that, I actually

BUILDING BLOCKS

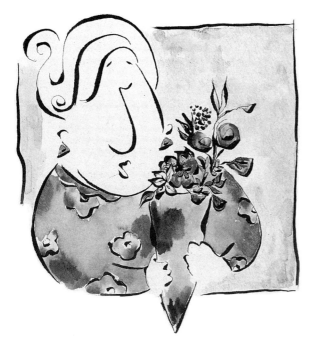

Figure **2-1**

Jacki Gelb's bubbly illustration sparkles because the illustrator solidly understands the relationship of the basic rudiments: concept and composition, line and shape, value and color, pattern and texture. (© Jacki Gelb www.gelbillustration.com)

Figure **2-2**

Ben Mahan's *Football Player* is oil wash, acrylic paint, and colored pencil on 3-ply bristol. But that's just the surface. Mahan's smart composition and concept takes full advantage of the basic illustration building blocks. (© Ben Mahan)

think—and many illustrators would agree—that it's an *art education* that is the key—even if you're self-taught.

Regardless of our gifts, we all start out at square one—you can learn the basics. Let's look at the ground rules as skewed toward the illustration process. To do so, we're going to discuss six primary building blocks:

- composition and concept

- line

- value

- color

- pattern and texture

- shape and form

These building blocks are easily recognizable in good illustrations, such as Ben Mahan's *Football Player* shown in Figure 2–2. When we do an illustration, we all go through a process, but we usually don't *think through* the steps. In this chapter we're going to talk about how to stack the blocks—we're actually going to think about those steps.

# COMPOSITION AND CONCEPT

How do we "look" at any image? There is some physiology involved. Great scholarly works have been written about such precepts as closure, sequence, eye movement, and visual flow. The study of after-image effects and the persistence of vision is rather fascinating science. But we don't have to get technical to make an important statement: The direction the eye travels and how we can direct that eye movement is essential to what illustration is all about.

And that, in direct relation, is what the building block of composition is all about.

Figure | 2-3 |

PJ Loughran's grasp of the fundamentals is strong, as he shows in this illustration for *Selling Power Magazine*. The article was about finding the best locations for business meetings. Loughran's lively, but ordered, arrangement of visual elements compels the viewer to consider concept, content, and message when exploring the piece. (© PJ Loughran)

## Seeing

In many ways, we are what we see. People perceive in diverse ways, based on where and how they live—on a personal level, locally or regionally, nationally and internationally. The experience and influence of culture and society can't be underestimated.

We can all visualize, but we don't often take it all in. And when we do, each of us does it differently, and to varying degrees. In other words, as illustrator Gregory Nemec puts it, "You must use your eyes, then comprehend." You could draw a parallel with the distinction between "hearing" and "listening." *Hearing* is passive (you *hear* the radio playing); *listening* is active (you *listen* to a song).

A commissioned illustration will hopefully be seen by a wide audience. The illustrator thus faces an interesting dual challenge: how do you want your illustration looked at in a *physical* sense? How do you want your illustration seen in the *intellectual* sense?

## All Things in the Right Place

A grasp of the fundamentals is universal across all artistic disciplines, and it's reasonable to argue that composition rules the roost. All artists deal with design—the ordered arrangement of visual elements within the picture plane. Yes, composition *is* putting the elements in the "right" place, arranging things in the "correct" order and establishing a "good" balance, but you must also discuss concept, content, and message at the same time. See Figure 2–3 for an example of an illustration that does just that.

## The View from Here

Conceptually what are we trying to do? What's the illustration about? What are we *saying* here? These sister concerns help to define "composition." You could also say that concept dictates content and content determines composition. The illustrator ultimately accepts the responsibility of conveying the message to complete the job.

Composition establishes the priority of elements in an illustration. An illustrator's prime directive should be to develop the concept. In a real sense, value, color, line, texture and pattern, and shape and form are *technical* aspects of craft, in the service of what an illustration must ultimately do: get a certain message across, tell a story, or "simply" decorate. At the very heart of any illustration worth the label is an image that *communicates something* to the audience.

Figure |2-4|

Composition. Concept. Message. Communication. Reproduction. Illustrators like Sarajo Frieden know that true process is a challenge on several levels. An illustration must stand on its own merits and be technically fit. (© Sarajo Frieden)

## Working on Many Levels

For illustrators, the design process is a challenge on several levels. First, and this is certainly important, the illustration must be able to stand on its own merits. However, one wild card for the illustrator is that his latest masterpiece needs to be *reproducible,* and as such, is required to be *technically* fit (see Figure 2–4). For example, if you don't choose web-safe colors, or if your lines are too thin to hold up when the drawing is reduced, your illustration has not done the complete job.

Following this thread, accurate reproduction of the illustration is another piece of the puzzle. Once the illustrator competently and professionally prepares the work, how faithful the printed piece is to that original illustration is often the ultimate issue.

For the sake of a rather loose argument, let's say that a "gallery artist" is not primarily concerned about her work *in print* (or on a monitor for that matter). Yes, accurate reproduction of the image is important for the gallery artist, but more from a promotional standpoint—to sell the work or showcase that artist.

And there's more. Illustrations exist as integral visual elements of a page layout. Whether the page is digital, on paper, or right up there on the screen is not the point; the pictorial and thematic match of illustration to "page" is what's important.

Yes, the image of the gallery piece may be employed as part of a page; but again, this is advertising, pure and simple. The image is being used in graphic design that promotes the artist, or discusses the piece. Perhaps that image announces an exhibition or an art sale. This is significant for sure, but a peripheral consideration, and not *why* the art was made.

# LINE

It's probably safe to say that most people think of "line" as a *straight line,* as in "a line is the meeting between two points." But often, the most interesting lines seem to have no specific direction or organization at all, and are decidedly *not* straight. The path is, or seems to be, random or chaotic; the sure stroke implied by our original definition is now replaced by nervous energy or disorderly activity (see Figure 2–5).

Figure | **2-5**

Great lines are not necessarily clean, straight lines! Notice the decided right-hand lean of the lines in *Model-T Wrecks.* Capitalizing on my natural wrist movement, I purposely tilted my pen to slightly catch the *side* of its point, working in short, quick bursts. The resulting scratchy, diagonal hits rode and skipped along the subtle tooth of the paper. I could also push or pull my strokes to gently smudge the lines, boosting the value range in select passages, too. (© Michael Fleishman)

You will find modern and historical art that completely depends on line, of course—Japanese, Chinese, and Arabic calligraphy, for instance. In these cultures the use of visuals may be limited or prohibited as dictated by centuries of tradition—the line is the thing, and the thing is a perfectly placed and exquisitely rendered line.

The same goes with prehistoric art. Our cave illustrators had a brilliant sense of line, not to mention a superb flair for narrative.

Figure **2-6**

One stroke or many, the joy of the line is very real—for both artist and audience. By varying line weight, in modulating control, spontaneity, speed, and power, Overton Loyd's flurry of lines cover a full range of motion—stops and starts plus directional cues. Like Loyd, be as passionate about line character as you are about the physical act of making those lines. (© Overton Loyd)

## The Power of One Line

Let's do a little exercise, as suggested by educator Melina Elum. Select a brush and grab a large piece of paper—any brush, any paper will do.

Dip the brush in paint or ink of your choice. Disregarding the edge of the paper, draw a long line across the page. Stop your stroke past the borders of the page.

For the sake of the game, we'll assume you drew your line on rough watercolor paper. Your brush held the ink irregularly. Notice that delightful little hop-skip and jump in the line that feathers back into a dense, smooth stroke? That was unexpected and interesting. See how your slight twist of the handle gracefully altered the tail-end of the line from thick to thin? When you slowed down in the middle of your arm movement, you applied a bit more pressure and notably textured the line character (Figure 2–6 shows how one artist uses line character effectively).

Wow, it's right there: variation in weight; both control *and* spontaneity; speed and power. Look closer: your line conveys a full range of motion, stops and starts plus directional cues. And this is all in *one* line. Think of what you can do with the flow and rhythm of multiple lines!

Am I exaggerating here to make my point? Try it and see. If you think you know everything about lines, maybe you've never stopped to think about just that—the line itself.

What a concept: a line in itself is its own piece of art—a classical example of pure illustration. And that is as it should be, for we are indeed virtuosos boasting a lifetime of preparation. How so? We daily manipulate lines and communicate concepts, *via the act of writing*. Writing thus represents a rather primal illustration experience, and is an essential part of our growth and learning curve. My whole point here is that, one way or another, *you know line; you're already good at it.*

Be impassioned about line for its own sake. Line is a strong, motivating force. As Elum says, "The beauty of one line is that one line can have it all."

## Life Along the Edge, or There Are No Meaningless Gestures

Gesture and contour drawing help you deal with mass and form. These types of marks quickly establish and strengthen spatial and shape relationships (part to part, part to whole), especially when figure drawing. Not everybody has the same understanding or definition of what makes for a gestural line or contour drawing.

You might be tempted to define a contour line as a glorified *outline.* But an outline is only the shell of the form—the outside. In contour drawing, we seek to establish the *whole form*—inside and out—by perceiving the *edges* of that subject matter.

Yes, gesture drawings also encompass the edge, but that's not where your process starts. In gesture drawing, you target the whole (*3-D*) form. A gesture study is not flat. Gesture drawing is not about vertical or diagonal lines. And like contour drawing, it is not about the shell. One way to look at gesture is to imagine your pencil actually laying down a length of yarn or wire, and you are wrapping these strands *around* the form you are drawing.

John Rutherford's portrait of John Madden is a fine example of a strong gestural line approach. (© John Rutherford)

# VALUE

*Value* is a relative degree of the darkness and lightness in color. Often called tone or shade, value is an extraordinarily powerful and expressive tool, particularly if you are working in black and white.

Every color beyond black and white has its own value as well. And in fact, there are different degrees of value within any one color. Take those beautifully rendered red apples in your

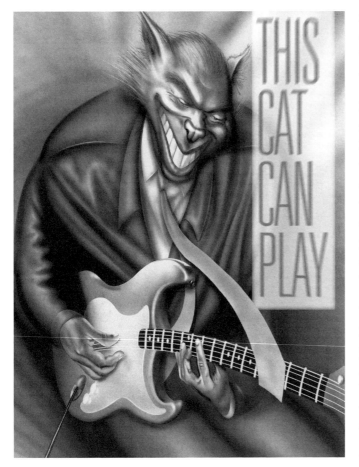

Figure **2-7**

Value is the relative degree of the darkness and lightness in color, and considered by many to be *the* most important building block. Illustrators like Randy Palmer understand and use value to tremendous effect. (© Randy Palmer/Dayton Daily News)

illustration. The side of the apple that catches the light holds a lighter tone of red. The opposite, shaded side of the apple has the darker tone of that same red.

Many illustrators regard value as *the* most important building block, for it certainly holds the key to great artistic power (see Figure 2–7 and Figure 2–8). Value creates form, and it closely relates to the principle of contrasting lights and darks. Light and dark creates weight, it anchors and pulls your eye one place or another. Value can quickly move the eye in or out, or slowly, subtly shift the focus back and forth in the picture plane.

Use value for compositional problem solving. If you understand value, you can literally push the picture plane around and achieve an acute sense of depth. Be interested in how far back a picture goes; for in a real sense, pictures are all about how close the action is to the viewer.

Value is also about the spaces in between, and creates both high and low drama. Indeed, a generous use of a dark value creates opportunities to increase contrast of light and mid tones. You can't ignore value. As illustrator Margaret Parker says, "An emphasis on value keeps your drawing honest."

It's very easy to get caught up in details, as we love to get to those details as soon as possible. We also want to make "nice drawings," maybe even a masterpiece right out of the box, every time. In attempting to do so, you can lose the underlying structure of the illustration, whether you are working in color or black and white.

As illustrators with a vested interest in precise reproduction, you need to see things very simply. For beginning illustrators, value is one of the keys, and exercising value prompts the illustrator to not only simplify, but see more clearly as well.

## THE BOOK ON COLORING

Color is a key concern, and in this era of millions of colors with just one click of the mouse, it's more crucial then ever. As artist and educator Carla Steiger-Meister points out, "Color in illus-

Figure | 2-8 |

Value is often called tone or shade. In the hands of illustrators like Ken Meyer, Jr., it is a dynamic and dramatic creative device. (© Ken Meyer, Jr. 2003)

tration establishes our sense of reality, and adds emotion or mood—to a viewer the art is more viscerally real." It is important to understand color theory—how color works and how our eye perceives it.

How does one learn about color? I know illustrators who consider color exercises or studies rather dull and boring. There are always folks impatiently looking for a shortcut to a pretty picture; some people never read a manual or bother with the rules.

But an understanding of color theories can really go a long way. Do lots of color mixing and blending. Analyze color relationships in general. Think and "do" color all the time.

Establish a color "tool box" so you're not out on a limb thinking every color is always available or that all colors automatically work together in peace and harmony.

Digital color means learning about, amongst other things, color gamuts (also called color spaces). A gamut is the range of colors available for print or display—like RGB and CMYK. Understand what perceived color is (traditionally this means color *apparent* to the human eye, as opposed to measurable color).

What are you trying to say with color, what are you trying to do with color relationships? Your choice of color (and the surface it's applied to), plus your decisions about color placement are of the essence. Color confidence should be a priority, and one of the first things to achieve before approaching any assignment.

## Where There's a Wheel, There's a Way

You can learn a lot about color by simply watching TV, going to the movies, flipping through magazines, or cruising through the mall. A hike in the woods, shopping for fresh vegetables, or sunset at the beach also qualify. But this is training by osmosis, of course. The real world *is* a wonderful classroom, and your own keen sense of observation is definitely a master teaching tool, so don't discount it.

*And, of course there is still basic color theory and practice.* We all know some color theory. Illustrators who know "some things" about color soon realize the need to know more. Likewise, if you practice, you understand the importance of *continued* practice.

Color terminology hasn't really changed over the years, and these things I know are true:

1. The name of a color is referred to as its hue.

2. The primary colors are now and forever red, blue, and yellow. Take these three colors, throw black and white

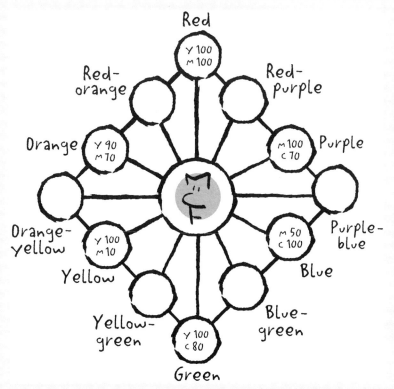

A color wheel without color? Well, why not? Every techniques textbook offers a perfunctory version of a color wheel. And we say we recognize all the common hues. We may even boast that we know the exact order. I'm going to put a spin on typical textbook practice by providing you with *only the chart and the names* (it's a basic chart, but it's in the right sequence). You provide the actual color yourself. Go ahead, color in the book—I dare ya! (© Michael Fleishman 2003)

# NOT JUST ON THE SURFACE—TEXTURE AND PATTERN

Both texture and pattern are important for providing visual interest beyond character development, color scheme, and composition (see Figure 2–9). Texture and pattern, as illustrator David Milgrim puts it, "give your work an extra nuance and help the eye linger."

into the mix at some point, and the proverbial rainbow is at your nimble fingertips.

3. Primaries can be mixed in pairs to become the secondary colors of purple, green, and orange.

4. A secondary mixed with a primary creates a tertiary—for example, yellow-green.

5. Tone. Also called value, this indicates the lightness or darkness of a color.

6. Intensity refers to the brightness of color. I've also heard such color brilliance labeled as saturation or chroma. The word "vivid" is often used to describe the intensity of color.

7. Color temperature deals with the relationship of colors and how such colors relate to blue (as the coolest extreme) and red-orange (the warmest). A color by itself has no "temperature"—temperature is a point of comparison.

8. Colors produced in the spectrum of pure light (*additive* color) interact differently than colors composed of pigment. Mixing red, green, and blue acrylic paint or inks (*subtractive* color) is *not* the same as combining red, green, and blue gels through a spotlight.

9. Color combinations collaborate to make various color harmonies. Hues grouped together are often called color families. On a color wheel these color families produce analogous harmonies. If you take one color only, and vary its values, you'll have monochromatic harmony. Opposites on the color wheel give you complementary colors. Mix in a complement to neutralize color. Adjoining complements create a visual vibration that can thrill or disturb. Three hues at equal distance on the color wheel form a triadic (or triad) harmony.

10. Playing with light/dark, thick/thin (also called lean to fat), warm/cool (also called hot/cold, or temperature), textured/flat, or bright/dull color contrasts opens up whole new worlds of exciting color relationships.

11. Place little teeny dabs or small strokes of two different colors—let's choose red and blue—against one another. Your eye will mix these color dots to make purple. This visual or optical mixing is called pointillism.

## Texture

Texture is more a manipulation of media (as in an impasto or scumbled painterly effect; the tooth of cold press paper under a wash of saturated watercolor strokes). It is about crushed cans, crumpled paper, mixed media, and other materials added to the illustration.

It can be about introducing additives to the media itself—sand, pottery shards, flecks of newsprint or gold leaf (and far more). In a real sense, texture can be as much about the tools as it is about the outcome of using those tools.

Figure **2-9**

Paul Melia is an absolute master of both texture and pattern, as demonstrated here with *Lady of the House,* and in *Rooftops,* (Figure 2–12). (© Paul Melia)

When I think about texture, a list of action words comes to mind: brush, smear, dash, splatter, scrub, drip, blow, wipe, roll, rub, dot, dab, squirt, dribble, spray, sponge, comb, flick, swipe. What's on your list?

## Pattern

Take a shape or a mark. Maybe cluster some different shapes together. Repeat it. If you keep repeating it, or repeat the groups, you'll create a pattern. This sounds like a compositional exercise; and indeed, pattern may be considered a subset of composition.

Pattern and texture often work together, and you can apply pattern and texture at the same time—by building up a pattern of thick, heavy brush strokes, for instance. Patterns often exist within patterns. The organization of pattern elements—frequency, number, size and space, contrast and similarity, and irregularity—is a working concern.

Man-made patterns are everywhere. Just look down to the kitchen floor, in your clothes closet, or at your tire treads. So are mechanical patterns (think gears and circuits). Of course, astonishing patterns (veining in leaves, rock strata, shells) occur naturally in the real world all around you.

| NOTE |

Don't confuse *real* (tactile) texture with texture created through the use of flat color and pure technique, or *implied* (simulated) texture.

## SHAPE AND FORM

Here's the quick, condensed definition: Shape is 2-D, form is 3-D. When discussing an illustration of Elvis Presley's '58 pink Cadillac, we might find it easier to talk about the shape of the car, even though we *really* mean its form. Same thing about the related principle of negative space: It's simpler to analyze the *shape* of the negative space, then move into the 3-D.

Continued definitions: shape has more to do with the overall visual perception of the parts of an image. Form, then, is the rendering of that organization (see Figure 2–10). "Shape can be big or small, and move back and forward," explains artist and educator Beth Holyoke, "but capturing the form is a bit of a trick. It's all about fooling the eye into thinking there's space there."

## 3-D or not 3-D—That Is the Question

Yes, you can talk a good game about depth and dimension. And maybe you *are* a fair hand at nailing these visual effects on paper. But at some point you need to actually look at and feel the *real* thing, whatever that real thing is.

If you dismiss this opportunity, you're missing out on the understanding that only comes when you dive below the surface of your paper or canvas. So work from the figure—do lots of life drawing; set up an actual still life, or simply draw right on the spot. You might even consider taking a sculpture class, building something, or even try making a pot.

And working from photographs doesn't count. Don't get me wrong. Photos are splendid reference tools. Indeed, photography and illustration are siblings at heart. It's no crime to work from photographs; but bad lighting or mediocre composition often block out true structure (the line of the nose, or accurate depth of field, for instance).

A photograph is not the real thing—it homogenizes and smoothes reality. Photos can also distort reality and misinform—especially the human figure. If you don't understand actual anatomy or real perspective, your illustration is only surface. You must study what's underneath; take that snapshot with your eyes instead.

Figure | 2-10 |

Understanding and working shape promotes visual organization and perception. Case in point: Stan Shaw's piercing portrait of author Walter Mosley, done as a conventional airbrush with black India ink. The powerful illustration doubles as a superb value exercise *and* sneaks a look at Shaw's hybrid airbrush look before he adds digital color. (© Stan Shaw 2002)

## Using Positive and Negative

One way to approach form is to concentrate on positive and negative shapes. If you get your negative space right, you'll nail the positive shapes of your composition. It's definitely a give and take situation: If the negative shapes aren't working, the positive shapes aren't working

Figure | 2-11 |

Think through and structure negative space. You'll easily sort out the positive shapes of your composition as a direct result, as Carla Bauer skillfully demonstrates with her beautiful woodcut, *Georgia O'Keefe*. (© Carla Bauer)

| TIP |

The face provides a wonderful vehicle for a little lesson in geometry. Here, a cheek can be indicated with a circular motion. The nose is a triangle, that mouth is really an oval. Keep studying— notice that the shape *connecting* these features is a rectangle with curved sides.

As you become increasingly aware, you'll see that these geometric shapes establish a syncopated rhythm. Clearly identified, you now transform the simple geometric shapes (and resulting spatial relationships) into rendered noses, eyes, cheeks, and so on. This promotes a likeness because once the basic stuff is down, you can then go back and look for the nuances that make that face a particular person.

either. Say you're drawing a portrait—just a face on a background—the outline of the shape of the head as it relates to the shape of the background is as important as the head itself.

It always sounds like an oxymoron, but defining negative space can give you as good a feel for a form as drawing the thing itself. While it may not be easy at first, keep drawing—you do improve and you will learn; the forms improve as the negative shapes around the form get better (see Figure 2–11).

## Geometry

Illustrator Paul Melia suggests you think and draw geometrically instead of organically (see Figure 2–12). Look for squares and rectangles, circles and ovals, triangles, and other geometric shapes within the structure of your illustration. Remember, you have to *see* them first to put them to use, so deliberately "pull out" the basic shapes that make up your subject.

You can also align picture elements in a geometric configuration. These arrangements don't have to be obvious; they could be multiple components or smaller parts that actually form invisible corner points to create a focal point.

Refer back to Melia's *Sohio Man* in Chapter 1. Notice how the illustrator works and plays with geometrics to create a stunning, smart visual and intellectual statement.

## STILL MORE CONSIDERATIONS

More principles come into play as we compose an illustration. There is no handy device guaranteed to help you work out better composition or your money back, but there are other subsets of our building block concepts—more tools that enable us to put our building blocks into play.

*Repetition* is one such principle. Repeating elements enhance and promote the flow of design, creating visual and intellectual links for the viewer.

Figure | 2-12 |

*Rooftops,* by Paul Melia, is a visual one-stop-shop of harmony, emphasis, and balance, as well as repetition, rhythm, and movement. (© Paul Melia)

Directly related to repetition is *rhythm*—the pace (or beat) of your compositional ingredients. Think spacing here.

Linked to rhythm is *movement.* Movement is the series of pictorial events captured in your illustration. This sequence (or progression) of visual matter ties right in with rhythm and repetition.

*Harmony* is the synchronization of design elements, how it all works together. We could also bring in the idea of *unity* here, as well—harmony only happens in unison.

There must be *emphasis*—dominant (and subordinate) design factors, and a variety of components. Without this range and diversity, your audience quickly moves on to something else; this is one of the hooks that brings a viewer in and keeps him there.

*Balance* means symmetry—a visual equilibrium that helps the viewer feel grounded. Without this comfort level, the eye will not linger. Scale enters in here, as well. The relative weight or size—by degree or in dimension—helps establish balance.

## SUMMING IT UP

A general understanding of the basics—line, value, color, pattern and texture, shape and form—is kicked off by considering the crucial relationship of composition and concept.

These building blocks preface production and reproduction considerations for illustrators, and are the first steps down our creative path.

# STEP by STEP

## Ken Meyer, Jr.

Ken Meyer, Jr. uses both Grumbacher and Winsor & Newton watercolors, and likes Pelikan Graphic White ink. He tells us that current wisdom points to his Winsor & Newton series 7 brushes as *the* brushes to use for comic book inking, but says, "I don't care too much one way or the other—it's whatever works."

On assignment, one to six sketches usually come first. He shoots photo reference or checks through his files, as necessary. Next, he stretches his paper, does the pencil work, then proceeds to painting. "I tend to layer my paint on in bits and pieces," he says, "working from light to dark."

Follow the accompanying visuals to see how Meyer puts it all together in this production sequence for his illustration *Atmos*.

Check out the reference photograph Ken shot himself and used for the main focus of the painting (Step 1). Note his changing of the gun style in the next image (Step 2) and look for pencils lightly showing through. For our purposes, the digital image is slightly darkened to pick out the pencil marks on the stretched 140lb Arches watercolor paper.

The first layers of paint (a combination of Alizarin Crimson and Cadmium Red) lead to added shadows of Dioxazine Violet, Payne's Gray, and Winsor Blue (Step 3). Meyer goes on to intensify the shadows, but leaves an area of exposed red around the alien's feet (Step 4).

He finesses the gun, lays the sky in quickly and loosely using Winsor Blue; you may even be able to see that the left side is still wet. Continued shadows and more details begin to lay the backdrop for the aliens (Step 5).

It all culminates in final details and refinements—including the moon background, alien figures, highlights (done with the Graphic White) in the hair and on the gun (Step 6 and 7).

Illustrations © Ken Meyer, Jr. 2003

**Step 1**

**Step 2**

**Step 3**

**Step 4**

**Step 7**

**Step 5**

**Step 6**

# PROFILES

*Bill Jaynes*

When asked about his process, Bill Jaynes begins with his favorite art supplies: "Winsor & Newton watercolors; Arches 300lb watercolor paper; generic, but high-quality, sable hair brushes. I really like the Dixon Ebony pencil—it's made a great comeback after being discontinued—this pencil gives you a nice black and mid-tone gray. Sometimes Higgins or Pelikan ink or Dr. Martin dyes—however these dyes give you a rather brilliant color that fades fast. Lately, my color sense has been a little bit more subdued, and these very bright, intense hues or stain colors are quite powerful.

"To do my thumbnails I use a ballpoint pen on tracing paper. I have to sort of let go of the *fear* of drawing. I saturate myself in whatever the story is—read it, think about it . . . the first conceptual ideas usually don't work out. Only when I start making the *connections* does it start to happen.

"So I tend to generate a lot of drawings, but you don't show the art director everything. Once a sketch has been approved, I tape the tracing paper to the back of the watercolor paper. Using a light table I try to recapture the *essence* of the sketch. At some point I will turn off the light box and finish.

"The watercolor process starts with picking a tone—a key color for the piece. I start building layers of washes in this color to set that tone—the mood—and tie all the color together. In the beginning it's a lot of really wet into wet—sloppy, happy accidents.

"You let that dry, and start building and developing both volume, and contrast. Because I am inking first, you lose much of that line beneath the washes, so I'll often go back and pull things out a bit. Here I use a waterproof uni-ball pen. The immediacy of drawing (as opposed to a very clean, polished line) is what I'm after now. Sometimes a ballpoint pen that bleeds a bit is kind of nice.

"There usually comes a point where the whole thing just looks like a mess and I put it away for a little while. Depending on the deadline, this can be an hour or a day. Eventually I look at the thing and decide what to push back and pull forward; what elements to play off of each other; what's really important about the drawing—what am I trying to communicate? What's the story about; what did I personally want to do?

"I then add focus by building shadow areas. Lately I have been using a grayed out ultramarine blue for shadow areas—it seems to work really well over an orange or yellow. Or if you put it over a *cool* color, it darkens that tone. This builds value and models the shadows. Painting for me is working that value structure."

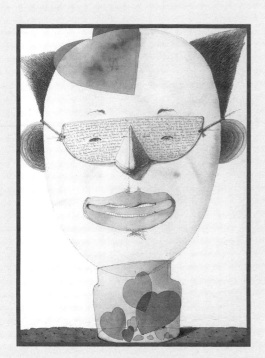

"Usually I'll have in front of me either a blank piece of paper or tracing paper," says Bill Jaynes. "I like using a ball point pen on tracing paper. But I usually have to sit there and sort of let go of the *fear* of drawing—the fear of that blank page.

"If it's for myself, my process tends to be more of a free association kind of drawing. If it is a piece for a client, I usually *just start*. Those first conceptual ideas usually don't work out. Some of this beginning stuff can be scattered and pretty weird.

"I try to surround myself with a lot of small, magical kind of objects to look at—other people might call them little shrines. I have a lot of little things—little Mexican folk art stuff, tiny wooden houses, bits of antiques that can stimulate the imagination and bring a nice spirit to your studio space. Then you start drawing; you just keep trying." (Illustrations © Bill Jaynes 2003)

"This was used by *American Showcase* to advertise their sourcebook to art directors," Jaynes tells us. "The idea behind the piece is that artist is a naturally introverted individual. However, to be commercially successful, the illustrator must open their mouth and tell the world of the wonder they can do."

# PROFILES

## *Overton Loyd*

The early 1970s found Overton Loyd apprenticing to Robert Grossman, who taught the artist what he calls the "Purist" approach to airbrushing. Here, no other tool touches the canvas. "We made sure that neither a pencil, a brush, nor X-acto knife purged the pristine surface," Loyd informs.

Grossman also instilled in the young illustrator the view that "your initial idea is usually the best." Approaching a job, Loyd will jot down the first thing that comes to mind. "I'll keep scribbling and free-associate, but that first idea usually wins—as in the case of Parliament's *Motor Booty Affair* cover. Then again, how can you not be inspired, listening to P-Funk?"

Segue to Loyd's tenure with funk star George Clinton of Parliament fame. The challenge and pulse of Clinton's primal art direction and mu-

A tight pencil drawing from a photo shoot was scanned into Painter, and then rendered with that application's tinting brush. The dark outline plus the flowers were carefully drawn with Painter's fine-point pen tool. That title? "Well, it basically means she's pretty darn versatile," says Loyd. The image was inspired by the work of Alfons Maria Mucha. (Illustrations © Overton Loyd)

sical vision did indeed inspire Loyd—as did working
with your standard Bic pen.
"They're cheap, accessible,
and I have yet to find a better quality of line," says
Loyd. "The best thing about
them is that I can draw at
the speed of sight, without
the ink skipping or drag-
ging."

The illustrator is also fond of
Tombow markers. "The best
brush tip around," comments
Loyd, "and the juiciest colors! They offer great line
variation—essential in the
art of caricature."

The 1980s found Loyd drawing caricatures for the television game show "Win Lose
or Draw." With his carica-

ture skills in such heavy rotation, Loyd attended
workshops to facilitate his speed and finesse.
He even turned to self-hypnosis and visualiza-
tion techniques to keep the gags coming!

Today Loyd explores both digital and traditional
techniques. His prolific creative energies embrace illustration and gallery arts. He is involved
in animation, cartoons, comics, and caricature,
of course. And he leaves you with this:

"My Mom took me to the Detroit Institute of Art
regularly as a kid. She also bought me an *Alice in
Wonderland* book because she knew I'd dig the
illustrations. Now I know this doesn't sound very
gangsterish, but I was totally hooked on Alice!

"I was literally weened on those exquisite
Lewis Tenniell renderings. His characters are
so 'true' that I was a little afraid of them. I was
convinced that they were actually alive on
some level. If I could give my stuff a pinch of
that vitality I'd consider myself successful.

"I guess I like to visually solve problems. I like
the 'aha!' of getting the idea, and the 'whew!' of
completing the execution.

"I also like the *mystical* part. If the work comes
to life for the viewer, then I've done my job. If
some aspect of the art magically appears that
the viewer wasn't readily aware of—then I've
*really* done my job."

# PROFILES

## A Conversation About the Basics with Mark Monlux

Mark Monlux layers objects to create depth; he takes advantage of both aerial and linear perspective while exercising a generous dollop of color theory.

As the illustrator tells us, "My color runs to the primaries, as these hues tend to 'bounce out.' Neutral colors can be tricky. Browns and grays are neutrals, and tend to knock back, but to pop a brown object off the page, you *don't* go with black linework—use a very thin *blue* line with another thin red outline layered against the blue edge.

"Learn about aerial perspective. Aerial perspective deals with how the eye perceives color. In the real world, colors that are up close are big, vibrant, solid, and very clear. You also have a nat-ural distortion through the atmosphere that grays everything out as you go back in space. Compositionally then, objects further back in the picture plane should get more gray.

"Value enters in here somewhat, as does texture. Use color to create texture—even texture your line. You can also create a texture that is purposely complex—too detailed. This overtly textured passage will gray out to the human eye and fade back.

"When all is said and done," he concludes, "have a critical eye—check your composition in a mirror. Reverse the piece to see if the color and design structure is holding up."

© Mark Monlux 2002

## in review

1. What are six basic building blocks of illustration as discussed in this chapter?

2. Which of the six basic building blocks of illustration is the most important, and why?

3. Use your observation and reasoning: is talent necessary to be a "successful" illustrator?

4. Like that between hearing and listening, is there a difference between "seeing" and "looking?"

5. Why and how is the design process a multi-level challenge for illustrators?

6. Name five other important design considerations you feel illustrators must know.

7. Class discussion and interaction: What is additive color? What is subtractive color? What do you get when you mix red, green, and blue acrylic paint together? What about cyan, magenta, and yellow inks? What do you get when you combine red, green, and blue lights?

8. People perceive in diverse ways, based on where and how they live—on a personal level, locally or regionally, nationally and internationally. Do you agree or disagree? Explain your answer.

9. Why and how are composition and concept related?

10. Exactly what are we referring to when we talk about positive /negative? What is figure/ground? What are we talking about when we discuss background foreground, and middle ground?

## exercises

1. Create a traditional 12-step color wheel. Consult your instructor, the sidebar in this chapter, or other resources for the correct sequence of hues. Now create a decidedly non-traditional color chart that still relates the hues in an organized, logical sequence. As with the color chart in this chapter, the word "wheel" can be completely conceptual, by the way. Your chart should be fun and dynamic. It need *not* be in a circular format with pie sections. Extra credit: research and do a color star and/or mixing wheel.

2. Do and repeat the line exercise as suggested by Melina Elum. You'll need a brush and a large piece of paper (any kind of brush or paper will do). To recap: dip the brush in paint or ink of your choice; draw a long line across the page. If you work on top of a backing piece, you can start and stop your stroke past the borders of the page. The idea is to see how your brush holds the ink, *how you hold the brush,* and how this interaction creates highly individual strokes. *Don't* try to repeat the *same* line, but do the exercise for a set period of time—say 30 minutes—or a set number of strokes (perhaps 25). You should see a spontaneous variation in the weight of your line, as well as the control, speed, and power of your stroke. This exercise is a good lesson in action and observation; your lines will convey a full range of stops and starts, motion and direction.

3. Do the line exercise again, but play with the flow and rhythm of *multiple* lines.

4. A fun exercise to get you to explore form is to make a gesture *sculpture.* Create your rough model out of clay or tinfoil (rolled up newspaper works great, too) and then cover and finesse this armature with plaster permeated bandages (which will dry faster and stiffer than papier mache). Like a gesture drawing, this sculptural variation is supposed to be immediate and intuitive. Work quickly, and right from your gut. Don't overthink the problem, and definitely get your hands dirty! That's the whole point—as your fingers work the structure you should get new insights into capturing that form on paper.

5. Geometric Opaques. Draw a group of figures composed only of varied, multi-sized, and opaque geometric shapes. Media is open. Shade the shapes to reflect volume and mass, as well as to promote lighting effects. Or you might use the shading to simply practice gradation.

6. Geometric Transparency. Instead of shading, overlap "transparent" shapes. Every overlap must now be a different value and/or color. Variation 1: Pure black and white only. Every overlap must now be black against white, white against black. Variation 2: Outlines only. Establish spatial relationships or perspective by using varying line weights. Can you also create a sense of weight and mass through line weight only? Variation 3: Texture and Pattern. Every overlap must now be a different texture and/or pattern. Can you create a sense of space through this mix and contrast of texture and/or pattern? And can you come up with a readable design that is not overtly chaotic or overly busy?

## notes

© Michael Fleishman

The Subject Matters

3

*"Illustration is done for a common denominator—the 'average person.' Push and pull—both technically and conceptually—but don't stretch so far that the audience doesn't get it . . . this defeats the whole purpose of the illustration."*

**Stan Shaw, illustrator and educator**

*"I'm most motivated by a need to create images that have some sort of idea to communicate. It doesn't matter much whether it's a print, painting, or illustration. The impulse is always there to make pictures that tell, or at least, 'imply' a story."*

**Steve Dininno, illustrator**

*"My work has a journalistic edge—I interview people, draw on location, and relate the world I experience with the larger world of current events. Surprise is a critical component of my process—if I can imagine the finished piece before I begin, I'm not interested in pursuing the idea."*

**Lauren Redniss, illustrator**

## *Chapter Objectives:*

Evaluate the general range of subject matter and venues

Study portrait and figure, exteriors and interiors

Discuss conceptual and narrative

Consider the venues of editorial and advertising, technical illustration, children's books, and the gallery arts

Examine collage, montage, and assemblage

Explore the genres of fringe and grunge, science fiction, horror, fantasy and the fantastic, cartoon and caricature

## *Introduction*

What do we mean by "subject matter?" Classical definitions certainly suffice: You *study* a subject; you *discuss* a subject—subject matter thus becomes the objective of these examinations. It is, after all, what the illustration is really about—the principal theme of the illustration hinges on the subject matter (see Figure 3–1).

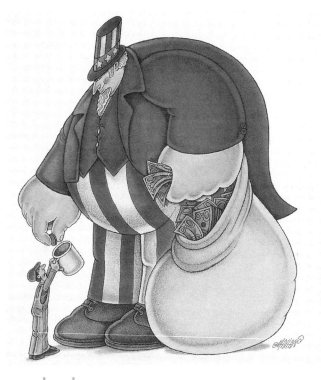

Figure | 3-1 |

Whether you're peddling tires or condemning corrupt government practices, there is *subject matter* to deal with. This piece by illustrator Benton Mahan resonates on many levels, and has been sold several times. (© Benton Mahan)

Subject matter doesn't necessarily have to be all true facts and accurate figures trotted out as a straight, dry report. Whether you're a tested professional or weekend Norman Rockwell, subject matter is about your planning and your audience's perception. Shortchange or skip subject matter and an artist's work—no matter how casual—will appear unfocused at worst, or, well, *abstract,* at best.

Abstract art—non-objective work—is always up for interpretation. Illustration can certainly be interpretive—visually providing the meaning or promoting a better, or just different, understanding. However, non-objective art is not subject to the standards of *representation* that illustrations are.

A non-objective (non-representational) piece can exist completely on its own terms: as a physical exercise ("hey, this is fun"), or a declaration of the intellect ("what did we learn from this?"). In that sense, non-objective art can even exist as a complete disaster ("well, at least I learned something not to do").

But illustration can't afford those relative luxuries, for at the end of that same day, an illustration just might have to sell a can of orange juice or make a hard-hitting point about foreign policy. In other words: there's *subject matter* to deal with.

## THE FACE AND FIGURE

The representation of the face and figure may arguably be the most prevalent of the subject concerns we will look at in this section. We seek to express ourselves through our art; thus the foremost object of that artistic expression *will be ourselves.*

The rich language of capturing a likeness or nailing a pose is as diverse as the figures and faces we depict (see Figures 3–2 and 3–3). The act of rendering that likeness (and this could be a physical, emotional, or psychological likeness) and capturing the human form is generic to most every artistic activity.

Form may be the hardest thing to see, and portraiture and figure the most difficult of artistic challenges. "The figure is the great teacher," says illustrator Paul Melia. How true. Working from

Figure | 3-2 |

When we think "portrait," we may immediately visualize a very realistic and stiffly posed studio sitting. But why? Carla Bauer's *Homeless in New York* is a gritty *portrait* of a hard life on mean streets. (© Carla Bauer)

the figure trains your eye to really *see* shape and form, and sharpens that all important mind-eye-hand coordination (see Figure 3–4).

# EDITORIAL AND ADVERTISING

While content may be one wild card, both the editorial and advertising markets offer wonderful creative opportunities for the illustrator. For our purposes, I'll group ad agencies and public relations firms under the general category of *advertising,* while lumping magazine, book, and newspaper illustration within the *editorial* category (it wouldn't be a stretch to throw the greeting card field in here, as well). Let's break it down a bit further.

## Advertising

Advertising agencies solve a client's marketing problems by communicating what that client wants (and needs) her market to know. To meet this goal, ad agencies develop and sell these concepts in magazines and newspapers. They produce television and movie commercials, conceive billboards, and direct mail campaigns. Most produce literature, sales brochures, and other such collateral material. You'll find the larger agencies doing public rela-

Figure | 3-3 |

In *The Thrill of Victory,* James Bennett stops the clock and literally transports us to another place. Bennett deftly "freeze-frames" every nuance in this *portrait* of a contest lost in time (but won in the upper deck). (© James Bennett)

tions. These days, agencies also create interactive, multimedia, and website accounts.

All of this promotion and marketing is often complemented, if not substantially driven, by illustration. See Figure 3–5 for an example of just how big illustration in advertising can be.

Public relations firms assist clients by increasing awareness of their clients' existence, presenting a new image, or even polishing a tarnished reputation. Keeping a client in the limelight is the task at hand, and when the task involves visual imagery (in print or on screen), illustration may come into play.

## Editorial

Whether it's the *New York Times* or the *National Enquirer*, the primary function of any newspaper is to report news. Within the pages of any newspaper, different types of illustration help get that news across (see Figure 3–6).

Figure | 3-4 |

The joys (for the viewer) and benefits (for the artist) of knowing the human figure are huge—as shown in this potent illustration, done in oils by Greg Manchess. (© Gregory Manchess)

You will find neighborhood newsletters, local and regional newspapers, big city newspapers with a national circulation, newspapers with a national scope, tabloids, plus general or special interest newspapers.

Look for magazines in the following categories: local and regional; trade journals; general audience or consumer periodicals; special interest magazines; and in-house or company publications.

Each will be directed to a particular reader. Therefore, different periodicals require different kinds of artwork. Many magazines will offer an eclectic mix of illustration styles within any issue.

Every magazine has its individual editorial tone and visual tenor. It's a safe bet you won't find bizarre illustration in a magazine like *The Saturday Evening Post;* it just wouldn't mesh with the magazine's conservative audience.

The book market offers illustrators rich artistic rewards. There are the trade books—sold at retail stores, and appealing to a select audience. They can be scholarly works or professional titles, special interest books, instructional manuals, biographies, serious or humorous fiction,

Figure | 3-5 |

Mike Quon says this was the biggest *actual size* illustration he has ever done. The art was 15 stories tall—150 feet high! Smack in the middle of Times Square (perhaps the splashiest place to be seen in the country), the advertising kicked off the NFL season (including a big party with celebrities, rock stars, and national TV coverage), and ran for over a month. The client was Verizon. (© Mike Quon 2003)

Figure | 3-6 |

Lauren Redniss' delightful illustration about urban chess and streetwise strategy is an info piece about the game, as well as a perceptive portrait of the players. The illustration was done for the *New York Times* op-ed page. (© Lauren Redniss)

larger format coffee table items, cookbooks, and juveniles (with or without a teaching motive). These texts are intended for the general public and marketed through bookstores and to libraries.

You'll find textbooks—educational materials sold directly to educational institutions (but frequently found in or ordered through a bookstore)—manuals of instruction, and books used for the study of a particular subject.

Mass-market books are more commercial looking (think: "hey, no dust jacket!") and are created to appeal to a large audience. These books are sold at newsstands, bookstores, and other retail outlets. They are produced in high volume at less cost, and hopefully generate big sales. Mysteries, spy novels, gothics, fantasy and science fiction, plus historical and modern romance novels all fall into the mass-market category.

## CONCEPTUAL AND NARRATIVE

Conceptual illustration, a revolutionary trend for illustration in the 1950s, is still a major direction today. You might say that the realm of conceptual illustration is a viewer's head and heart, as well as eyes. Metaphor and symbolism, surrealism and illusion, wit and satire, representational expressionism (and impressionism)—virtually all of the generic vocabulary of "modern" illustration—took root in this period.

The rise (and staying power) of conceptual illustration means that illustrators are free to pictorially analyze complex attitudes, strut intense personal opinion, or depict moral, mental, and emotional conundrums. The states of your mind, head, and heart are fair game, as are all the critical issues of the day (and the players).

Narrative is illustration that literally tells a story, or visually recounts the story it accompanies. Good books immerse the reader with lucid description and powerful prose. Narrative illustration does the same, engaging the viewer with a vivid pictorial account or description. Conceptual illustration may make us "read between the lines," but narrative compels you to comprehensively "read the text."

Another aspect of narrative illustration is combining words and visuals to, as illustrator Elwood H. Smith says, "Enhance and/or further the assigned story." Yes, we might be talking about cartooning and comics, but not necessarily.

"I don't really do cartoons," Smith continues, "but I have added words to my illustrations for many years." While Smith grew up on a steady diet of two of the best narrative comic strips, *Krazy Kat* and *Pogo*, he cites Saul Steinberg as a great narrative illustrator. Mixing in some narrative along with your drawings may seem as perfectly natural for you as it does for Smith, who tells us, "I'd do more of it if clients would let me."

Many illustrators use ongoing visual imagery in their work. Perhaps the most famous and classic example of this is Al Hirschfeld stealthily slipping his daughter Nina's name into a given illustration. A tiny number next to Hirschfield's signature tips the viewer off to the number of times the artist has hidden the name.

Elwood Smith maintains a recurring cast of characters who not only heighten the drama (or humor) in a given picture, but give the illustrator a chance to draw his favorite images, as well.

Artist David Julian also incorporates a personal icon into his visuals. If you look closely at his work, you will frequently find the image of an ant. The ant reflects Julian's tenure as an entomologist and represents the illustrator's ongoing relationship with his personal history. The ant changes with each picture, but ties together Julian's illustrative past and illustrating present. See Figure 3–7 for an example of Julian's work.

Figure **3-7**

David Julian's evocative *Eugenics (The Legacy of Lynchburg)* is a conceptual illustration that confronts the viewer on many levels—eyes, heart, head, and gut. The back story is indeed about eugenics in Lynchburg, Virginia, circa 1930. Julian was asked to depict the sterilization of children due to their "undesirable properties," and the illustration was created from 11 separate photographs and props. By juxtaposing certain familiar objects, these routine items take on a new meaning, and the photographic realism is very convincing on a visceral level. (© David Julian www.davidjulian.com)

## OUTSIDE THE LINES

In this section, we're going to do an overview of some varied opportunities an illustrator may choose. If you are intrigued by a particular methodology or venue, you'll want to know more. There are entire websites devoted to, and whole books written on, the following artistic possibilities; these resources offer further examination of whatever resonates within you.

# Illustrating The Story of Ruth

Margaret Parker understood the difficulties in taking on the story of Ruth, a well known and often illustrated biblical tale. Working in close collaboration with a biblical scholar writing a new translation, the artist felt that the most important factor in creating these images was to create a narrative—a commentary in visual form that paralleled the translator's written commentary (the subtitle of their book is: *Reading Ruth through Image and Text*).

Her challenge was to explore the text, and she quotes Matisse here, "as it really is." Parker asserts that the story of Ruth is not the conventional romantic idyll depicted by many illustrators, but a tale of suffering and loss redeemed by steadfast faithfulness. The story ends on a note of joy and hope, but is neither carefree nor light.

In what ways did this understanding of the story shape Parker's illustrations? What other factors informed the images? Her first decision was to create the images as woodcut prints.

"Woodcut is among the simplest and most direct of printmaking techniques," she says. In its most basic form, a woodcut image is limited to black and white. The medium is characterized by a sobriety, even starkness, of expression—qualities that make it suitable for Parker's reading of Ruth as a dramatically serious tale.

Parker also decided to create a "running narrative" of images—a scene-by-scene exploration of the story. This mandated a closer reading of the text and required that Parker pay sharp attention to both individual anecdotal elements and the "trajectory" of the entire tale.

In addition to thematic concerns large and small, Parker also addressed the practical considerations of consistency in dress and appearance. Ultimately, she examined the entire set of images, searching for inconsistencies. The illustrator found that each character took on dimensions and characteristics illuminated by her understanding of the story.

Case in point: "We first see Naomi bereft of husband and sons," says Parker. "Her head is bowed; she clasps her arm across her breast as though closing herself off from any hope of comfort. Later, when Naomi sends Ruth out to encounter Boaz on the threshing floor, her whole stance is different, more open and confident. In our final glimpse, her head is bowed once again, but her arms have been filled; she is looking down tenderly at the child in her embrace."

Aware that the figure "tells" a person's story, Parker worked to orchestrate gesture and facial expression. She understood that even minute shifts in the angle of a shoulder or chin can lift a character from despair into hope. (© Margaret Adams Parker. Image and text taken from *Who Are You, My Daughter? Reading Ruth Through Image and Text*, Westminster John Knox Press, Louisville, Kentucky 2003.)

## Collage/Montage

Collage—from the French, literally (according to Webster's) meaning *gluing*—"An artistic composition made of various materials (as paper, cloth, or wood) glued on a surface."

To quote the late Carol Wald: "The collage medium offers . . . the opportunity to arrange and rearrange tones and forms until the most satisfying solution emerges. When the final juxtaposition of elements is properly balanced in a beautiful environment, I always feel the thrill of accomplishment."

This neatly sums up the heart and soul of any collage—a visually rewarding mix and match of diverse academic elements or pictorial fragments. The assembled artwork is one thing; when we intellectually associate these varied pieces we also come up with what is labeled a collage of ideas (see Figure 3–8).

Figure | 3-8 |

Tom Nick Cocotos' sharp collage portrait of Anna Nicole Smith was commissioned for an article about Ms. Smith and her allergies to peanut butter. Now I ask you—what illustration textbook would be complete without a shot of Anna Nicole eating pb and j? (© Tom Nick Cocotos 2003)

The term *montage* is used to describe a literary, cinematic, musical, or artistic composite picture, made by *combining* several separate images *side by side*—often a quick series of images depicting the *relationship* of ideas.

Sisters they are, but a montage is not a collage. The succession of imagery—one after another, and/or side by side—*plus* combining and associating those pictures makes the difference.

# CARTOON AND COMIC ART

Highbrow or lowbrow—illustrators working under this umbrella are a creative workforce quite deserving of praise and recognition. Like any next-big-thing, there is a rush to join the ranks, and we find ourselves in a true golden age of cartoons and comic art.

# STEP by STEP

## *Drawassic Park! With Scott Jarrard*

Before Scott Jarrard begins an illustration, he likes to sit down and take a few minutes to doodle and brainstorm. Scott's two sons love dinosaurs, so when he started to think about what to draw for *Exploring Illustration,* he had two requests: make a dinosaur, and make him scary. "Well, it didn't turn out too scary," he laughs, "but they were still happy with the final illustration." And so are we. The illustrations in this box show how the character developed.

Even while going for a scary look on his subjects' faces, Jarrard is hoping for a happy look on viewers' faces. "This is the way I feel about my illustration," says Jarrard, "I want to make people smile. The added bonus is that I'm having fun doing what I love to do. I come up with a cool, crazy character that is fresh and new—to see the smile on someone's face when they get it, or when a client becomes excited over an illustration that I've done for them . . . *I absolutely love it.*

**Step 1:**
Jarrard does a series of sketches and focuses on one. Here's his choice, but he tells us, "I have no idea *why* this big dino wants to crush the last innocent flower on earth; but I thought it was kind of funny—so I went with it."

**Step 2:**
The next step is a basic color layout. Jarrard uses flat colors to capture the general shapes of the image.

"Here's a true story: My wife and I are in Yellowstone National Park. We go to a chuck wagon dinner in Jackson, Wyoming one night. While visiting with some of the other guests, a kid (named Ben) traveling with his grandparents starts talking to me about how much he's into video games. I tell him that I've worked on some of the characters he's talking about, and the little guy gets very psyched.

"He asks me to do a picture for him. So I pull out a pen and start scribbling on a napkin—I draw a picture of Ben playing a video game with a giant monster com-

ing out of the the television and attacking him. I entitle it 'Ben's last videogame,' which delights him.

"I then draw an action scene of him in a spacesuit, on the moon, shooting a creepy creature. He really goes for this one too. His grandparents carefully put the napkins in their bags and Ben promises me he'll keep in touch.

"Just seeing his smile when I gave him those napkins was *so* cool. I entertained all of the people around us for a while. It's a treat brightening someone's day with my art."

**Step 3:**
He then goes in and figures out lighting and the general dimensions of the creature.

**Step 4:**
He adds detail and places a basic background. Check out the final as Figure 13 in the color insert. You will see how Jarrard tweaked the dino, painted the frightened flower, and fine-tuned both sky and ground. (Illustrations © Scott Jarrard 2003)

© PETER KUPER  www.peterkuper.cor

Figure **3-9**

Peter Kuper's comic strip *Eye of the Beholder* was the first comic strip to ever appear in the *New York Times*. Kuper later self-syndicated the strip to alternative papers. This is scratchboard and is entitled *A Brief History of Education.* (© Peter Kuper)

One only needs to cruise channels on the TV (at all hours these days), go to the movies, or hit the video store. Scan the bookshelves at any bookstore—not even a so-called "comic book" store—or flip through the magazine racks at your local library to see for yourself.

The talent pool is deep and business is booming. The field benefits from an influx of artists bringing high energy, big ability, and better production skills to the drawing table. Comics are historically tough to break into, but if this is your niche, persevere.

The fan and product base for both adult and juvenile animation (for television, in the cinema, and on the Web), cartoon books, graphic novels, and video games has taken off. These avenues—plus the traditional outlets of newspaper cartoons, comic strips, and comic books, along with advertising and editorial humorous illustration—are showcases of prodigious talent and remarkable concepts. See Figure 3–9 for an example of comic strip illustration.

## CARICATURE

Most of us probably first learned about caricature on a trip to the amusement park as a youngster. There, our parents sat us down across from a caricature artist (usually working in marker and/or pastel) who created the keepsake that is probably *still* up on the wall of your folks' house.

As an older kid, you may have noticed political cartoons in the newspaper, the covers of *Mad* magazine, the contents page illustration in *Rolling Stone,* or even courtroom drawings on the evening news. You began to see caricature in a new and varied light.

That golden age of cartoons and comics mentioned earlier must also embrace the art of caricature. Caricature is currently very alive and well; the venerable art form has been viable for literally centuries. See Figure 3–10 for two modern artists' views of caricatures.

Websites, newspapers, magazines, books, and advertising—all these venues employ caricatures as part of the design mix. College art majors still draw long hours every summer at theme parks everywhere. Many seasoned caricaturists make a good living, nationally (even internationally) touring a circuit of shows, parks, conventions, and private parties. Of course, editorial carica-

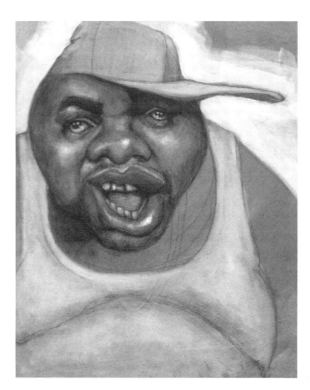

Figure |3-10|

Both of these illustrators do sly, astute caricatures. Akiko Stehrenberger says her work—like this caricature of performer Biz Markie—is the end result of "a lot of ball point pen, gesso, and acrylics." Jeanne de la Houssaye's caricatures are "rendered with Design markers on a regular card stock." (© Akiko Stehrenberger, left, and Jeanne de la Houssaye, right)

turists still mercilessly skewer politicians today, just as they did in the heyday of Honoré Daumier or Thomas Nast.

As with all current artistic pursuits, modern tools and materials have impacted the medium. Digital (and 3-D) caricatures are making inroads, but the art of capturing that essence of character and deftly playing with a likeness has not changed.

## CHILDREN'S BOOKS

Another rich mine of creative opportunity is children's books (see Figure 3–11). Illustrators working in every style and media have a shot in the juvenile market. The superb art thus produced is a primary reason this literature enjoys such popularity.

This has perennially been a fine market for illustrators, but the field hasn't always been looked at with such high regard. It seems that everyone wants to draw children's books these days—and for good reason. While not tremendously lucrative, the challenging format offers fun assignments that usually boast remarkable creative freedom for illustrators. So, the pool of talent is great and the benchmark of quality is *very* high.

Figure |3-11|

These vivid illustrations are from two children's books illustrated by Loren Long: *My Dog, My Hero,* by Betsy Byars, and *I Dream of Trains,* by Angela Johnson. Loren has also illustrated *The Day the Animals Came,* by Frances Ward Weller, and *The Wonders of Donal O'Donnell,* by Gary Schmidt. The illustrator really enjoys working in this genre. "I find the art of creating a picture book an exciting and creatively fulfilling art form," he tells us. (© Loren Long)

# TECHNICAL ILLUSTRATION

If you have a keen eye for detail and the knack for rendering a heightened realism, technical illustration will give you the opportunity to exercise those proficiencies (see Figure 3–12).

Technical illustrators work for advertising, editorial, and educational venues; in books and magazines, brochures, guides and manuals, and on the Web and video, as well.

No, the artist does not have carte blanche or license to alter a technical illustration to taste or to let the mind's eye run wild with a schematic or diagram. But good technical illustration shows no loss of creativity or lack of skills.

And yes, technical illustration can be an exercise of the imagination! My favorite examples of this: the movie *Star Wars* has generated fascinating books of profoundly detailed technical blow-ups and cut-aways. This technology *doesn't exist;* yet these im-

Figure |3-12|

Greg Maxson's crisp, clean technical illustration of a Ryobi jig saw accurately conveys a wealth of information about the product. The artist employs strong positive/negative contrast and a variation of line weight that demonstrates both artistry and craftsmanship. (© Maxson Illustration, all rights reserved, 2003. From *The Complete Technical Illustrator* by Jon Duff and Greg Maxson.)

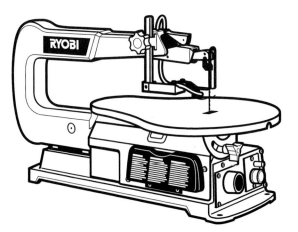

ages look just as plausible as the drawings in the manual that came with our Honda (which at times also feels like unfathomable technology).

## Automotive Art

Many regard the automobile as rolling sculpture. Cars are often vehicles (literally and figuratively) for editorial, advertising, and self-expression. More than just a sub-genre of technical illustration, car art is as old as the auto itself.

Illustrators have been depicting the car in decades of advertisements. Cars are not manufactured without a concept drawing that must drive off the paper or screen; and of course, somebody, somewhere draws it. The market for the art of the automobile is also strong—in both editorial and fine art (see Figure 3–13).

## 3-D Illustration

Sculpture complements painting and drawing, it does not oppose. 3-D illustration is a wonderful and harmonious alternative to working flat (see Figure 3–14). By and large, 3-D work

Figure | 3-13 |

As a teen with sports car fever for both of these automobiles, Ken Smith's fine illustrations of a 1960s era Mini-Cooper and Triumph TR4 brought all the nostalgia and yearning right back. Look for Smith's sweet '63 Corvette as Figure 22 in the color insert. (© Ken Smith 2002)

Figure | 3-14 |

*The End of the Line.* Bob Selby's wonderful 3-D self-promo is papier mache, and was the runner-up in the Society of Illustrators 3-D Biennial Salon, 2003. (© Bob Selby 2003)

must still be photographed or digitized for the page, but the world of pop-up books and paper engineering is an inventive and fascinating hybrid of both worlds.

If you are an illustrator whose ideas figuratively cry out for more dimension, you are in good company. There is no reason you cannot *assemble* an illustration, and nothing to stop you from *building* your concept; so keep *crafting* that technique.

## SCIENCE-FICTION, HORROR, FANTASY

In this genre (and whether it be for books and magazines, movies, video games, or game cards), the illustrator has free license to roam the reaches of imagination. Here, an artist can stare into the eyes of true horror, test the limits of science, defy the occult, and challenge reality. Look for Douglas Klauba's work later in this chapter to make this point.

Exploring the art of the fantastic is another centuries old pursuit. We may think we are pushing the envelope, but you only have to check out Hieronymus Bosch's *Garden of Earthly Delights* (about 1500 A.D.) to realize otherwise.

Figure | 3-15 |

The splendid lighting makes Linda Crockett's *Ringside Seat for Life* a brooding, atmospheric interior. The illustration won an Editorial Gold Medal from the Society of Illustrators, who knew a good thing when they saw it. (© Linda Crockett)

## EXTERIORS AND INTERIORS

I made the previous assertion that portraiture and the figure may be the most prevalent of our subject concerns. My logic here was straightforward: When we artistically express ourselves, the main focus of this expression will be *ourselves*. But we don't live (or illustrate) in a vacuum, do we? Our sense of physical space—our *place*—is unmistakably, undeniably *real*. Thus, I'll take my reasoning a step further: When we artistically express ourselves, we also seek to express ourselves *in our environment*—we put ourselves in our place, as it were.

Which brings us to our place—the landscape (and by extension, interiors—see Figure 3–15) and also to still life—the objects of that

Figure 3-16

Ali Douglass' *Steeple* and *Parakeet* are sweetly stylized, nicely focused cityscapes. (© Ali Douglass)

place. To put it another way, it's where we are, and all our stuff. The general category of land-scapes can be broken down into two clear-cut components: urban—the landscape of the city (see Figure 3–16)—and rural (or country) landscapes.

You'll hear talk about a so-called "landscape of the mind." While I have heard this phrase used as another simile for the imagination, a "landscape of the mind" may also mean an interpretive or introspective terrain—landscape as a *state of mind*. The artist tries to project feelings or perceptions into the colors, textures, and topography of an environment—a natural world whose elements act as metaphors for emotion or morale.

# ORGANIC/MECHANICAL

One might simply sum up this genre by employing the label *animal, vegetable, mineral, or thing.* It is a bit of a category *at-large,* and would include food and product illustration (good illustrators of chocolate are always in demand, by the way) plus scientific illustration (an airbrush rendering of your wiggly, squiggly DNA, for instance) and architectural rendering. Lumped in

(a)

(b)

Figure | 3-17 |

Animals are popular subject matter, and many artists specialize in such illustration. Here we present pieces by Marti McGinnis (a) and Wendy Christensen (b). These two illustrations are indeed opposite sides of the coin, but it's a big world, with room for both the yin and the yang. (© Marti McGinnis, left, and Wendy Christensen, 2003, all rights reserved, right)

this category would also be medical illustration; maps, charts, diagrams, and informational graphics; and animal portraiture and illustration (see Figure 3–17).

# ALTERNATIVE

Call it "New" or "New wave," "cutting edge," "fringe," "grunge," or "free-style," but there is always illustration that deviates from the mainstream (see Figure 3–18).

Such imagery challenges our safe conceptions of "good" art. Thus, this genre has been called "outsider art," or "renegade style." Critics who don't quite understand it rush to the easy judgements: "this is ugly," "how naïve," or "rather primitive." Practitioners—including stellar lights from Turner and Van Gogh to Picasso—are often labeled as amateur, lazy, or both.

Let's be frank. There *is* illustration that warrants these labels, and artists who fit that bill. There are also artists working in new or different directions that aren't readily classified, but effortlessly pigeonholed.

In years past, this imagery may also have been labeled "modern art," for that matter. But in actuality, every era boasts "modern art." The cave paintings at Lascaux were modern for that time. Impressionism was "modern" during its day, but not universally loved.

Figure | 3-18 |

Alternative. New wave. Cutting edge. Renegade style. "Modern" art. And those just might be the *polite* labels! Illustration done on the fringe is not safe, but definitely not sorry. Plus, your vision can have stylistic grit and still be pretty—pretty exciting! My *One Wild Hair* is on the left, Lisa Ferlic's *Cha-Cha-Cha* to the right. (© Michael Fleishman 2003, left, and Lisa Ferlic 2002, right)

In fact, all the art done during a specific time period could actually be labeled "modern art," so this is a term that is problematic at best.

The labels can be sticky. This art may not be "pretty," but beauty is relative. It is certainly not a "safe" (and definitely not the easy) answer. This style may very well create trends and set standards, but it will almost certainly fly in the face of convention at its beginning. As such, initial acceptance may prove to be a professional and personal stumbling block.

This illustration is usually associated with young artists, but age has nothing to do with thinking differently or creating to suit your tastes and rhythms. Young artists have no monopoly on innovation and inventive personal expression. Indeed, both younger and older illustrators are capable of making derivative, stale art that is decidedly pedestrian—both safe and sorry.

# GALLERY ARTS

Is illustration "art?" Is illustration *fine* art? Can fine art be used as "illustration?" If we get hung up in binding definitions and restrictive labels, no. True—such labels and definitions can affect sales and marketability, and the great art versus illustration debate continues to rear its ugly little head.

We live in the real world and it's easy to fall into the pigeonholes, but brands and categories don't have to be self-imposed. N. C. Wyeth, a virtuoso illustrator, lamented that he was—*by his own estimation*—"merely" an illustrator. Today, we recognize him simply as one of our masters, and his oils are considered not only milestones of book "illustration," but great works of "art," as well (see Figure 3–19).

Figure |3-19|

The pigeonholes and labels imposed (or self-imposed) on our art are all relative. N. C. Wyeth, a master *artist* in the true sense of the word, took illustration to new heights, but was troubled and conflicted by the dichotomy between his commercial and non-commercial work. (Courtesy of the Society of Illustrators)

Labels and definitions don't legitimize your work, and mean nothing in the long run. I think you can be both artist and illustrator, and I use the terms concurrently. Although there are those who split hairs regarding this terminology, I find the titles interchangeable.

Humorous illustrator (and *Mad Magazine* art director) Sam Viviano dislikes the label *fine art*. Viviano says: "It's as if the commercial arts are not particularly fine—in the sense of meaning good—and that the fine arts are not particularly commercial. Unfortunately, the public in general, and too many artists, buy into this." Instead, Viviano uses the terms "graphic" and "gallery" arts. "What's really different is whether one's art hangs on a wall or is intended for reproduction," he comments.

You can, of course, make a distinction and separate art done for reproduction from art produced for the gallery wall. But these days, illustration, comics, and cartoon originals (and limited editions) are both collectable and a viable commodity—there is both an audience *and* a market for what is called "illustration" or alleged as "art".

## SUMMING IT UP

The range of subject matter represents the very topography of the illustration process, and examining specific venues—from the classical study of portrait and figure to alternative fringe and grunge, gives you a real lay of that land.

# PROFILES

## *David McGlynn*

As a photo-illustrator, David McGlynn's list of supplies *starts out* sounding very photographic. "Most of my materials are readily available," McGlynn admits." A 35mm camera, color film, lights, props, and models. Post-production is when the magic happens, and all through simple "one-hour-photo" prints, scissors, X-acto knives, and plenty of tape!

"The most satisfying part." McGlynn reflects, "is that photo collage injects spontaneity into an otherwise stilted creative process—still photography—so-called 'normal' photography."

A session itself resembles a typical photo shoot—"Except for me," laughs McGlynn. "I'm usually running all over the set, up on a chair or ladder, shooting dozens to hundreds of pictures. Then I process the film, and edit the prints. And here's where the fun begins!"

McGlynn lays out as many pictures as possible, slowly building the collage, moving and shifting, cutting and trimming, and temporarily taping. He continually steps back (or up on a ladder looking down) to evaluate the work in progress. "I'll do my preliminary, and take a break (usually overnight). When I return, it's easy to spot what to correct or improve.

"Once I am confident it is done, I delicately flip the collage over and tape it together from behind. I then pack that baby up, ship it out, or send a disc."

McGlynn says that part of the charm of a photo collage is how the disparate pictures (or parts) look a little different from one another, often as the result of inconsistent "one-hour-photo" printing. "As the labs get better and better at what they do, I find that I am asking them to 'screw things up a bit' just to get the variation I need!

"There is still a strong attraction to the 'hands on' look and feel of an 'old-fashioned' hand-made photo collage. I hold the belief that to make the switch, digital has to offer two of three key advantages: It should be cheaper, easier, and faster. We're getting there."

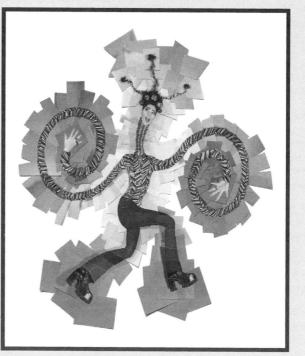

*Monica* by David McGlynn. "I make very basic pencil sketches," McGlynn says, "always keeping in mind that I still have to create what I draw from actual photographs." (© David McGlynn)

# PROFILES

## *Douglas Klauba*

When asked about supplies, Douglas Klauba makes his list: "Staedtler Mars Lumograph graphite pencils—5B, 2B, B, HB, and sometimes an H. I sketch on any available copier bond paper and Hunt Layout pads for larger sketches and drawings.

"I use Crescent 110 Illustration Board kid finish, with or without a gessoed surface. For work scanned on a drum for reproduction, I use Strathmore Bristol Board 5-ply, kid finish.

"I like Liquitex Acrylic Gesso to prime the working surface. Liquitex Acrylics in tubes or jars and the Winsor & Newton Acrylics in tubes. Prismacolor and Derwent Artists color pencils. Princeton Art Brushes and Strathmore Kolinsky Brushes. My handy Iwata HP-C airbrush is my loyal partner. I use it to put down acrylic color. It's easy to maintain and simple to use because the paint cup is right at the top."

Klauba counts on consistent quality. "I've used cheaper Bristol Board or illustration boards in a time crunch," he says, "but these off-brands never performed as well. So I stick to what works for me—what I know and I am happiest with. For that reason, I feel brand names are pretty important."

This is a man who loves to draw. And he draws upon what interests him for subject matter—art nouveau, perhaps a 1930s pulp magazine illustration, and the movies. "I think cinematically in terms of composition, design, color, shadows, and light," Klauba explains. "I go for a desired effect and then 'cast' my characters accordingly."

"Creating ideas on paper with pencil is the most enjoyable part of my day in the studio," the illustrator maintains. "Drawing is very important, as it motivates the end result of a painting. If there is no fun in the drawing, the finished painting won't be as fresh." Klauba thus considers the drawing and the finished illustration two separate pieces of work that inspire each on their own.

Klauba feels this sketching and concepting is not only the most challenging process (in producing an effective image) but also key to the piece. He knows that working out any problems early on enables the rest of the job to run smoothly. Conceptually he says that all thoughts are laid out during the sketch/concept period in the form of doodles and notes, inspirations, and color ideas.

Douglas Klauba's cinematic concept—and luminous rendering—of Dr. Jeckyll and Mr. Hyde was a calendar image for the Scottish Tourism Board. "I wanted to capture the duality of the soul during the classic transformation of Dr. Jeckyll—that would be the 'meat' of my concept," says Klauba, "but I didn't want it too disturbing to the viewer who had to see this illustration for the next thirty days on their calendar. If my memory is correct, the buildings took about four days of drawing and painting; the split figure took about 5 hours. The title may be Jeckyll and Hyde, but I feel the real star of the painting is the buildings." (© Douglas Klauba 2000)

After about 3–7 hours of drawing the image on the board, the entire paint process ranges from 12–40 hours (over a period of a few days), depending upon the illustration. Klauba starts painting with the background and works towards the foreground, going from light to dark.

He saves any focal point for last. After the air-brushed acrylic phase is done, he roughs in opaque colored pencil over the paint. Klauba then brushes opaque acrylics and adds darks through a glazing technique that blends in with the airbrushed look. "I tweak color harmony and tonal value until the painting is complete."

# PROFILES

## *Joe Murray*

Joe Murray says he is always inspired by a challenge; especially if an art director isn't afraid to go out on a limb, or if the job doesn't show an immediate solution. Here, Murray takes a beat. "As far as finding answers to creative problems, all I can say is, the universe works in weird ways.

"A little competitive spirit inspires me, as well. If I see someone has really raised the bar, I respond to that. And if a client or an art director has a lot of respect for what an illustrator brings to the party, that's tremendously motivating."

On assignment, Murray starts with roughs that go back and forth with the client. "I prefer to develop my own concepts rather than have an art director tell me their idea," he points out, but he is careful to also note: "It's commissioned work, of course; so I obviously value the input of that art director or client. As much as I have my ego

at stake, they are paying for the job, so it has to work for their needs."

After a rough is chosen, he tapes the sketch to his Strathmore board (and leaves it there through the painting process). "I'll transfer this sketch with transfer paper, then begin laying in blocks of color. I leave the rough there because previous lines may get painted over, and I may need to transfer lines back."

He does the same when working on a book. "I may occasionally (but seldom) scan the rough into PhotoShop and work out a color problem. Most of the time I just start painting and 'use the force.' Drawing comes really easy to me," he says with a pause, "but painting does not."

When he paints for a show, or for himself, Murray forgoes the rough. "I just start slapping paint down," he smiles. "It's a lot more fun; but still a struggle, and just as messy.

"I am able to draw and paint for a living," Murray says in summary. "Not that it's been easy—just very rewarding. Except for mowing lawns and having a paper route, I've always made money from my art. And I feel very fortunate and lucky for that.

"I once voiced my financial concerns to a very wise art director, who kind of took me under his

Joe Murray, the creator of *Rocko's Modern Life*, brings an animator's wild perspective to his illustration for the printed page. This very animated illustration is from Murray's book *The Enormous Mister Schmupsle*. (© Joe Murray Studio Inc.)

wing. He told me that I would worry for a bit, but then forget about it, because I would find my bills getting paid.

"And he was right. I didn't always have what I wanted, but I had what I needed. So, I say go for it. And, oh—don't keep pens in your back pocket."

## in review

1. Define, then relate these terms: non-objective/representational; conceptual/narrative; advertising/editorial; collage/montage/assemblage; comics/cartoons/caricature.

2. In your estimation, what is the most relevant subject matter concern? The most prevalent? What venue or genre appeals to you least?

3. What classifies "alternative," "new wave," "cutting edge," "fringe," and "grunge" for you?

4. Name some examples of illustration you find extreme.

5. What is "modern" art?

6. Discuss and debate the labels "fine art" and "illustration." What do these tags mean for you professionally and to you personally?

## exercises

1. Choose a topic and develop a specific theme. Work from a live model. Find appropriate props. Pose your subject and set the scene. Create a conceptual illustration from this staged scene.

2. Pick an old cliché and do a fresh, dynamic, conceptual interpretation of that old saying. In the same vein: work up a fast moving montage about something considered excruciatingly slow and mundane (paint drying, a snail in motion, etc.) Another variation on this theme: create an exciting book cover illustration for a rather boring book.

3. Do a series of portraits of family and friends or do a series of self-portraits over a specific period of time (one hour, one day, one week, one month, one semester, one year). Variation: use one media only. Variation: vary the media with every piece.

4. Do a collage self-portrait that involves no personal, private imagery or artifacts. Use only outside, found elements.

5. Create something mechanical by nature, but organic at heart (or vice versa).

6. Choose a topic or celebrity. Create a fully-color illustration of this subject as it might be commissioned for (a) a stylistically conservative publication and (b) a stylistically cutting edge magazine.

7. Take a walk; do 10 random caricatures of people on the street.

8. Paint a landscape of a real location only accessible after a long, arduous journey. Draw a landscape of an imaginary place only minutes away by foot.

9. Do an illustration your grandmother wouldn't understand. Do an illustration of which your parents wouldn't approve.

© Paul Giovanopoulos

*"I've learned something from just about every period in the history of art and illustration."*

**Ilene Winn-Lederer, illustrator**

*I can't remember a time when I wasn't crawling across, looking at, and, finally, reading the Sunday comics. My fat baby knee bones were smudged with images of Krazy Kat, Pogo, Mickey, Popeye, Barney Google, Snuffy Smith, and the Katzenjammer Kids—they seeped into my bloodstream."*

**Elwood H. Smith, illustrator**

*"Pablo Picasso has been a great inspiration for me; not only from his artwork, but how he was able to change throughout his lifetime. And he broke the rules. Andy Warhol influenced my attitude towards art. His dissolving of the barrier between art and commerce is just one example. And he broke the rest of the rules that Picasso missed."*

**David McGlynn, illustrator**

## Chapter Objectives:

Study general directions and summarize American illustration history

Examine illustration schools, genres, and styles

Discuss cross-cultural, ethnic, and international references and resources

Consider the influence and dictates of taste

Explore visionaries, role models, heroes, and peers

## Introduction

It's necessary to look at the thread of the past to unravel the present or to consider the general direction of the future. Any student of history knows that current events provide the fascinating background for what's going to happen *tomorrow*.

The field of illustration, the craft of illustrating, and the art itself has evolved from just such an interesting back story, complete with a great cast of characters, a rich catalog of images, and a wide range of influences.

It is important for you, as a professional, to appreciate your illustration family tree, as we are truly the flower of those roots. As a student, you can gain much from heeding the lessons hard-learned by our elders; the ongoing *experience* of illustration is cumulative.

History itself is not boring (but the *presentation* of history is something else again). *History is us,* on *rewind;* and it answers the very important questions of "who, what, when, where, and why."

# THE TIES THAT BIND

There have always been "illustrators" and "illustration." *Visual* communication is older and more universal than language itself; and as such, directly affects one's *primal* understanding of the world.

Early man was compelled to paint on cave walls. Intricate symbols decorate Egyptian scrolls and sarcophagi (the Mayans employed this picture-writing—called hieroglyphs—as well). Medieval texts were "illuminated" by sumptuous, full-color, hand-painted visuals and elaborate lettering. In various mid-eastern cultures, beautifully executed, richly calligraphic—and perfectly legal—marriage contracts have literally been "drawn up" for centuries.

But this is the counterpoint of illustration for multiple reproduction. As far as mass communications were concerned, bonafide, *literal* replication of an image—an *exact* rendering on the printed page, on a grand scale—was a problem.

| **NOTE** |

Engravers work *in reverse,* and particularly close to a piece, thus the "big picture" of lighting, depth perception, and perspective can be tricky.

"Modern" illustration, as we might recognize it, has its origins with Gutenberg and the invention of printing via movable type in the fifteenth century. But as the old crafts gave way to new technology, the learning curve of a different discipline (and resulting limitations) became quite apparent.

Visuals would now be incised into wood blocks or metal plates, then fit directly with the movable type. It was "what-you-see-is-what-you-get" technology in its earliest form; but if the artist lacked those skills, an intermediary—the engraver—redrew the picture to the plate or block. So what you got was not *really* what the *artist* saw (or rendered). Skilled engravers (and there were major talents) could get close, but it wasn't the original image.

The relationship between the artist and the engraver was always a bit of a balancing act. As printing technology developed over the next centuries, this situation improved. The new and exciting lithography process, as well as innovative engraving techniques, offered larger print runs plus better reproduction (and some absolutely lovely art as a result). But it wasn't until the turn of the nineteenth century that we saw reproductions of drawings and paintings created with unprecedented fidelity to an original source.

| **NOTE** |

If you examine a lithograph or engraving closely, you may see two signatures; that of the artist on the left and the engraver/lithographer's signature on the right.

This extraordinary breakthrough was the photo-halftone process. Developed at the end of the 1800s, this method combined photography and halftone engraving. Along with better and faster printing presses (we're talking steam power here, folks), plus a growing audience with a huge appetite for product, photo-halftone precipitated what was labeled the "Golden Age of Illustration."

# SCHOOLS, GENRES, AND STYLES: AMERICAN ILLUSTRATION

Let's take a light look at history and trends in American illustration over the years. A note here: this section can only be a mere overview. Obviously, the body of work by (and creative impact of) the illustrators mentioned crosses over a lifetime, and spans many creative decades. And, of course, careers don't start and stop on a 10-year cycle. This is a synopsis; written with a personal resonance, and to provide a backdrop for our later discussion of illustration process.

Space considerations and certain priorities meant many relevant illustrators, trends, and events were regretfully omitted in my rather general discussion. I tip my hat to all our heroes and inspirations everywhere; without them there would be no history of illustration.

## The Early Nineteenth Century

The early nineteenth century saw American illustration in its infancy. A dialogue about this era should mention a number of worthy and representative illustrators. One, whose name may now be somewhat forgotten, is Felix Darley (1822–1888), actually considered America's first great illustrator of note. An outstanding talent, and self-taught, this artist was a prolific force in early American illustration for a good half-century.

World famous in his lifetime, and the namesake of an organization that thrives to this day, John James Audubon (1785–1851) traveled extensively and documented bird and animal life throughout the New World of America.

You've likely heard of Currier and Ives (see Figure 4–1). If your eyes are open around Christmas time, you'll see a Currier and Ives print somewhere; the once immensely popular nineteenth-century lithographs are immortal icons of vanished Americana.

Figure | 4-1

Nathaniel Currier opened up shop in 1835. Teaming with James Merritt Ives in 1857, he established a company that chronicled their times and entertained the masses. Almost 170 years later, the names of Currier and Ives prevail, and their work is still highly regarded today.

## | NOTE |

Currier and Ives staff artist Frances "Fanny" Flora Bond Palmer was the only woman lithographer (and one of the best in her field). Skilled and savvy, she was the innovator of the background tint, and even improved on the basic tool of her trade, the litho crayon.

The prints depicted breaking news events or simply celebrated daily life. Litho—a new process in the 1800s—could be turned around relatively easily and quickly. Reproductions were pumped out and sold on street corners in vast numbers.

Viewed today, Currier and Ives imagery may be dubbed kitschy Americana in certain sectors, and you may snicker at the artistic merit of such illustration. But for Currier and Ives, there was nowhere to go but up. With fame and financial success came the means to hire better artists and offer art that boasted both authenticity and quality for an eager market. Thus, when we define *nostalgia* today, Currier and Ives live on.

## The Middle Years of the Nineteenth Century

For most of the nineteenth century, there were not many venues for illustration, nor was there any pressing *need* for art, beyond the regional or personal level. The war between the states changed everything.

As the Civil War loomed, steady advances in printing technology, supplies, and materials resulted in the creation of illustrated weekly and monthly magazines. A market was growing.

The great conflict profoundly impacted *all* Americans, and an information-hungry public wanted news about the turbulent current events that were reshaping their daily lives. Words were not quite enough; and with photography still new, too inefficient and quite slow, pictorial reporting helped satisfy America's need to know.

Pictures were in demand. Pictures were a *necessity*. And publications like *Frank Leslie's Illustrated Newspaper* and *Harper's Weekly* were ready (even before the first shots were fired).

Winslow Homer and Thomas Nast are perhaps the two most famous names connected with the war artist-reporters. Homer went on to become one of America's most revered artists. Nast, of course, is the legendary and prototype political cartoonist and caricaturist.

When the war was over, magazines began to publish diverse articles that needed illustration. The market was beginning to boom. Freelance illustrators found work, and publishing houses established staffs of artists and engravers at this time.

Pictorial reporting continued in a variety of forms as the nation mended, rebuilt, and expanded towards the Pacific. To name just a few, George Catlin (considered a premier Western artist), Charles Schreyvogel, and the Moran brothers had been chronicling the frontier for years. Later counterparts like Frederic Remington and Charles M. Russell continued to docu-

Figure | 4-2 |

Well-known illustrator Winslow Homer
became one of America's icons of painting.
(Courtesy of the Society of Illustrators)

ment the last days of the old and glorious American west. Eventually the *wild* west of the nineteenth century was tamed, but the scenic beauty remains; as does the current market for Western art—still an extremely viable venue in our twenty-first century.

With no real native tradition *as yet,* American illustrators looked to Europe for inspiration and example, and particularly to British illustration. England was also enjoying an artistic renaissance at the end of the nineteenth century. Magazines like *Good Words* and *Once a Week,* showcasing artists such as Arthur Boyd Houghton and Charles Keene, were big influences on their opposite number "over the pond."

English illustrators often visited America; some even covered the Civil War, or explored the West like their American counterparts. In turn, Americans traveled to and studied (some even taught) in Europe; eventually returning stateside to work, teach, and further distill the European influence back home.

Other European illustrators, such as Daniel Vierge (Spanish, but working in Paris), and Gustave Doré of France, had a significant influence on American illustrators.

Publishing houses began to form staffs of artists and engravers. Toward the end of the century, the photo-mechanical process of halftone reproduction revolutionized the world of publishing, as well as the business and art of illustration.

Figure | 4-3 |

Accomplished illustrator Thomas Nast is
the prototypical political cartoonist.
(Courtesy of the Society of Illustrators)

Figure | 4-4 |

The influential Charles Dana Gibson—a legendary illustrator of the late nineteenth century. (Courtesy of the Society of Illustrators)

## The Late 1800s

Edwin Austin Abbey, A. B. Frost. Edward Henry Potthast and Childe Hassam (both important American impressionists painters). Poster artists Will H. Bradley and Edward Penfield. The great Western artist Frederic Remington. These are just some of the name artists working in the late 1880s.

Posters were popular. Illustrators enjoyed fame and fortune. We saw a "Golden Age of Illustration" that flourished until the advent of World War I. English illustrators, like Aubrey Beardsley and Phil May, continued to be popular and influential. Among the most notables of this period:

- Charles Dana Gibson, whose superb pen and ink work defined his era both then and now—the Gibson Girl is an immortal American icon (see Figure 4–4). Gibson's prodigious technique spawned many imitators and inspired James Montgomery Flagg. (creator of the legendary World War I recruiting poster of Uncle Sam demanding "I Want You").

- Howard Pyle, often considered the father of American illustration, is one of the field's most revered figures and was the preeminent illustrator of his day (see Figure 4–5). An artist of immense talent, he was also a superb role model and master teacher with a decidedly *American* perspective.

Figure | 4-5 |

Howard Pyle is widely deemed the father of American Illustration.

During this period, newspapers dominated the markets. Staff artist-reporters had a new conflict, the Spanish-American War, to document. The first comic strips appeared. Illustration was hitting its stride.

## The Twentieth Century, 1900–1920

In these decades, color-halftone printing revolutionized the industry. Magazine covers, formerly just glorified tables of contents, were *illustrated*. Page, poster, and advertising illustration boomed, and so did salaries; illustrators continued to enjoy hefty earnings and continued prestige.

Howard Pyle's students were, by this time, professionals, and they stamped a lasting mark on the early years of this era (and beyond). The role of women in illustration increased as family and women's markets grew, and Pyle's female students like Jessie Willcox Smith, Elizabeth Shippen Green, and Violet Oakley were prominent.

Some significant illustrators working in this era were Joseph Clement Coll, a true master of pen and ink, pioneer animator Winsor McCay, the creator of the landmark comic strip *Little Nemo in Slumberland;* Arthur G. Dove, also a pioneer abstract painter; critically acclaimed painter George Bellows; the renowned N. C. Wyeth and Maxfield Parrish, both Pyle graduates; and the virtuoso western artist Charles Marion Russell. In addition, the prolific Henry Patrick Raleigh, J. C. Leyendecker, and C. Coles Phillips all help set the pace and raise the bar for a very productive era.

One of my personal all-time favorites, Franklin Booth, worked in this period. The great, classic story about Booth is that he taught himself to draw by examining the pictures from available publications of the later nineteenth century. The young Booth meticulously studied and developed his incredibly chiseled line character from this reference, never realizing that his resources were actually steel or wood *engravings,* and not pen and ink *drawings* at all.

## 1920–1930

In this decade the call for illustration surged as advertising, book, and magazine venues grew. Richly talented artists like May Wilson Preston, Neysa Moran McMein, and Saul Tepper enjoyed active careers. Dean Cornwell was a dominant force in the field and in the classroom and remained so for years to come. A strong Chicago style emerged. But when discussing the 1920s, two names come immediately to mind: John Held, Jr. and Norman Rockwell.

| NOTE |

Howard Pyle's university teaching and later classes at his Brandywine School trained such stellar illustrator-educators as Frank Schoonover, Harvey Dunn, and many others. These pupils in turn passed on the Pyle method, philosophy, and wisdom to the next generation of talents. The Brandywine tradition continues to influence to this day—Andrew Wyeth and his son Jamie are two such keepers of the flame.

| NOTE |

Of interest in this period is the derisively labeled (but ultimately and extremely influential) "Ashcan school" of art. This maverick organization of painters boasted illustrators like William Glackens, Everett Shinn, and John Sloan.

Also called "The Eight," the group's center was painter/teacher Robert Henri. Henri's classic text *The Art Spirit* was published in 1923 and is still required reading in many art schools.

Held's stylized, oh-so-thin line style was wildly popular, and his illustration immortalized the flapper. The artist's work was the visual manifestation of "wild youth," the very personification of the jazz age itself. His cast of characters embodied this era just as the Gibson Girl did in decades past.

If you ask a random stranger to name one famous illustrator, chances are they may cite Norman Rockwell, arguably the most beloved of American illustrators. His sly humor and folksy take on America was every bit as indelible as Held's jazzy vision. Rockwell, of course, chronicled the American way of life for decades to come.

It was a heady time for illustration, but just around the corner at the end of the decade lay the Great Depression.

## 1930–1940

Easy come. Easy go. The stock market crashed in 1929, and so went the arts in general. Although some magazines prove durable (*Esquire, The New Yorker, Fortune*), the domino effect was devastating: The economy collapsed; many publications (and businesses in general) went under; publishing and advertising budgets were slashed; assignments were cut back or disappeared; fees plummeted. Hard times.

Uncle Sam pitched in with the Works Progress Administration, commissioning murals for government and public buildings. Americans (and illustrators) learned to barter. People escaped to the movies to hang in there, and many illustrators escaped to cheap pulp fiction just to hang on. Some definitions: *cheap* as in small fees; *pulp* as in the low-grade paper stock used to print a rag that sold for ten cents; *fiction* as in the sensationalist, provocative subject matter (pulps were not known for quality, but were all about excess).

Franklin D. Roosevelt's New Deal put the American economy back on track, as we geared up for war. Some illustrators to know in this decade: E. Simms Campbell, a pioneering and prolific cartoonist of color, and one of the foremost humorists of his era; the controversial and distinguished Rockwell Kent; John LaGatta and Mead Schaeffer; Haddon Sundblom, at the forefront of the Chicago illustration scene; Boris Artzybasheff, who deftly melded the organic and mechanical in his illustration (and was a prolific *Time* magazine cover artist); brothers Benton and Matt Clark; fashion illustrator Carl Oscar August Erickson (who signed off as "Eric"); vivid colorist R. John Holmgren; Frances Tipton Hunter, and Theodor Seuss Geisel—yes, *the* Dr. Seuss!

## 1940–1950

This decade encompasses the war years and after. As war loomed, America prepared for the epic clash and pulled itself out of the Depression, and illustrators were there. Many, of course, served in the Armed Forces. Other artists generated educational and motivational material, as well as propaganda and morale-boosting graphics and illustration. The artist-reporter never really went away, but the war provided a global canvas of monster proportions for the illustrator-correspondent.

Some of the notable artists working in this decade: master illustrators like Al Parker and Robert Fawcett; Chesley Bonestell, Stevan Dohanos, and Albert Dorne (who also was the founder-director of the Famous Artist's Schools); John Gannam, Tom Lovell, René Bouché, and Noel Sickles (a ground-breaking comic strip artist, too).

We find one of my personal favorites—painter, illustrator, and educator Ben Shahn—working in this period. Amongst others, illustrators Harold Von Schmidt (primarily known for his western art, and a spiritual descendant of Russell and Remington), Alberto Vargas, Lynd Ward, and Jon Whitcomb all made their mark, as well.

During the war, magazine fiction targeted the women in the audience, and you could find men in uniform all over the printed page (as in real life). The Atomic era was ushered in, but a publishing explosion hit when the conflict was over—magazines grew in numbers, size, and page count; need and demand for more housing and goods skyrocketed. The boys were back home, and the subsequent Baby Boom rejuvenated the flagging children's book market. Like the upcoming jet age, illustration was taking off.

The artists whose work is shown in Figures 4–6 to 4–17 are all representative of the gifted illustrators working in every era during the twentieth century.

Figure | 4-6 |

*Coles Phillips* blended figure and background and came up with his signature compositional effect called the "Fadeaway Girl." (Courtesy of the Society of Illustrators)

Figure | 4-7 |

The distinctively chiseled, wonderfully decorative line quality of *Franklin Booth.* (Courtesy of the Society of Illustrators)

Figure | 4-8 |

A student of Harvey Dunn, *Dean Cornwell* was a prevailing force in illustration. His preliminary studies are considered as stunning and dynamic as the paintings that followed. (Courtesy of the Society of Illustrators)

Figure | 4-9 |

The rich, atmospheric work of *Saul Tepper.* Tepper was a productive (and well-recorded) songwriter, as well! (Courtesy of the Society of Illustrators)

Figure | **4-10** |

A master of the female form, the sought-after *John LaGatta* earned a popular reputation as a painter of beautiful women. (Courtesy of the Society of Illustrators)

Figure | **4-11** |

The brilliant, versatile and eclectic *Al Parker* was a true original who set the pace for illustration during his distinguished career. (Courtesy of the Society of Illustrators)

Figure | **4-12** |

"Most people have never heard of *Joe Bowler*," says Sam Viviano. "He did these luscious oil paintings in the fifties and sixties. His work so awe-inspiring and special to me. I still have stuff of his that I tore out of magazines from 30, 40 years ago." (Courtesy of the Society of Illustrators)

Figure | 4-13 |

Inventive, experimental, and in-demand, the award-winning *Bob Peak* was a prolific editorial and advertising juggernaut. (Courtesy of the Society of Illustrators)

Figure | 4-14 |

The finely nuanced linework and delicately crafted illustration of *Paul Giovanopoulos*. (© Paul Giovanopoulos)

Figure | 4-15 |

The rambunctious and rollicking illustration style of *Reynold Ruffins*. (© Reynold Ruffins)

Figure | 4-16 |

When I think about *Guy Billout's* illustration, these words come to mind: very subtle, tremendously clever, just plain interesting (and so well done). (© Guy Billout)

Figure | 4-17 |

*Sam Viviano's* pitch-perfect caricatures are a not-so-odd coupling of great concepts and exceptional drawing skills. (© Sam Viviano 2002)

## 1950–1960

Illustration meant big budgets and illustrators enjoyed big business during this decade. Freelancers thrived big time, and it was also the age of the big art studios. Big is the word, but eventually, there came big changes.

Television drew advertisers away from the magazines, and offered a different and riveting medium to tell (and take in) a story. Illustrators, out of necessity, rose to the occasion.

Innovation became the order of a new day. The idea of conceptual illustration was one such revolutionary direction for illustration. The rise of conceptual illustration gave illustrators the opportunity to fully explore abstract and representational expressionism. This generation of illustrators deftly employed wit and satire, and mines the rich and eclectic veins of modern, primitive, and comic art; boldly playing with the very metaphor and symbolism rejected by their predecessors.

But the tide was turning and more and more markets vanished. Smaller magazines held on, and illustrators sought other opportunities—finding safer havens in paperback books and other venues.

The talent was still there, of course. You'll find big names like M. Coburn (Coby) Whitmore, Joe Bowler and Austin Briggs, Al Hirschfeld (who literally defines caricature, to many minds), and the gifted David Stone Martin, whose wonderfully calligraphic line work was oft-imitated (Martin was a Ben Shahn disciple, by the way).

## 1960–1980

The 1960s was the period where I blossomed as a young artist. I was in art school during the 1970s. These were formative creative years for me, and I look back at these decades with more than a touch of nostalgia and wonder. I was cognizant of illustrators as *working* artists, and not just names in an art history book; I enjoyed their craft on a daily basis; they created the defining images of my day.

Looking back, it feels like Bernard Fuchs, Bart Forbes, Brad Holland, and Mark English had an illustration in every magazine I ever read (and Holland's op/ed images for the *New York Times* had a sweeping impact).

My dad owned a movie theater and you could just about wallpaper the entire lobby with Bob Peak film posters. Milton Glaser and his Push Pin Studio colleagues (like Seymour Chwast and Paul Davis) were a fountain of original concepts and fresh technique. We all had Glaser's poster from *Bob Dylan's Greatest Hits, Vol. 1,* taped on our bedroom walls.

During the 1960s, photography and crafts were strong. Pop art was *everywhere.* Andy Warhol's "15 minutes of fame" played out much longer, and Peter Max's images were seemingly on *everything.* I first saw the innovative and influential work of Bob Ziering, Murray Tinkelman, Edward Gorey, and David Levine in the 1970s.

*The New Yorker* without Saul Steinberg's covers was a bit of an oxymoron, and where *was* that Patrick Nagel illustration in the new issue of *Playboy?* I own a sizable collection of children's books that probably began with Maurice Sendak's wonderful *Where the Wild Things Are.*

Look for Gilbert Stone, James McMullan, Alan Cober, and John Collier illustrations in this era. Reynold Ruffins, Ken Dallison, Mark English, and Jerry Pinkney were also working at that time, as well as one of my all-time illustration heroes, Paul Giovanopoulos.

Many major, national magazines (and their audiences) came and went during these decades—even the *Saturday Evening Post* was discontinued in 1969. Smaller circulation, specialty magazines popped up. Paperback book sales were huge; in fact, paperback cover assignments literally saved the careers of many illustrators.

Movie poster art was big, and illustrators became an important part of the production team on many films. Phonograph album cover art (not to mention inside sleeve material) was happening. As a teenage record buyer, the first actual album cover illustration I was personally aware of was for the Beatles' *Revolver* album. Robert Crumb's cover for Big Brother and the Holding Company's *Cheap Thrills* is another true classic of this genre. For an adolescent artist, it seemed that "suddenly," illustration was all over the record racks.

Comic books got hot, comics-style illustration got hotter (and both still sizzle today). Even my parents knew the Marvel and DC brands (but the juicy underground comics I had to sneak into the house). Jack Kirby, Jim Steranko, Marie Severin, Neal Adams, and Joe Kubert are just a sampling of the incredible talent working in what's called the "silver age of comics." So many comic books; so little time!

In these years, retro was back, psychedelic art flared brightly, and the Western genre continued to grow. The imagery, influence, mysticism, and spirituality of the East—the *far* East—was also coming into vogue. Momentous social and cultural changes in America were reflected in all of the arts, and the field of illustration was no exception.

Illustrators, through associations like the Graphic Artist's Guild, begin to organize and fight for copyright and other due legal and ethical rights.

## 1980–Present

I began working in the field during this period, and this section feels more like current events than history. The 1980s have been labeled the time of a so-called "New Illustration." But from where I stand, a careful look at illustration through the years points out that every era has its "new illustrators."

This is not to shortchange the creative juices, technological achievements, and forward thinking of our era—we live in remarkable times, to be sure. It just strikes me that all periods boast rebels and innovators whose attitude, concepts, and technique fly against what is then considered the more conservative establishment.

For instance, Norman Rockwell was arguably king of the hill from the 1930s to the 1950s. These were decades of great illustration, by any standards. The Rockwell influence was pervasive, and his imitators were legion. Eventually, the Rockwell manner was watered down. His style was then considered visually boring and thematically stale—much too conventional, way too safe. Besides, television was "The Next Big Thing," and print was fighting an uphill battle for an audience. So, in the 1950s, conceptual illustration ascended to counter the old school and shake it up. No more "snap shot illustration," as it were; *interpretation* was the word.

In every era, the "new illustrators" went on to actually *become the establishment.* If not part of a status quo, this now old guard at least paved the way for another crop of upstart iconoclasts to reject, rethink, and reshape illustration *du jour.*

# Influences

It was fun and educational to collect this inventory of visionaries, role models, and heroes. Most illustrators offer long lists of personal favorites, major and minor generic influences (plus recognized and underrated champions of the cause). This collection of luminaries could actually be a book in itself, but for now, we'll take a look at the "short list."

It was interesting to see just how many of the same names kept coming up throughout the individual lists (so the following is somewhat edited for overlaps and repeats).

**Akiko Stehrenberger:** Gustave Klimt; Egon Scheile; Modigliani; Anita Kunz; Mark Ryden; Philip Burke; Sebastien Krueger. "My classmates at Art Center. Never competitive, they were always there for encouragement, and still are now."

**Loren Long:** "Certainly Thomas Hart Benton, Grant Wood, and John Steuart Curry—the fathers of American Regionalism. Paul Sample, James Chapin, Howard Cook, Fletcher Martin, and Paul Cadmus. I also love Edward Hopper, George Bellows, and John Sloan from the Ashcan school. The Harlem Renaissance produced some wonderful painters such as Hale Woodruff and Archibald Motley. I have to mention Frederick Remington, Charles Russell, and Maynard Dixon, western painters. And I can't leave out Winslow Homer.

**Robert Saunders:** Political cartoonists Herb Block and Paul Szep. Peter Arno; Roland Topor; Eugene Mihaesco; Saul Steinberg. Steven Guarnaccia; Ross Macdonald. Local pals Mark Fisher; Richard A. Goldberg; Marc Rosenthal. Henri Toulouse-Lautrec; Ernst Ludwig Kirchner.

**Ilene Winn-Lederer:** Howard Pyle; Violet Oakley, Leonard Baskin; Edward Hopper. Moebius; Alan Cober; Mary Cassatt; Kathe Kollwitz. The original Push Pin Studio crew.

**Led Pants:** John Hersey; Dan Clowes; Chris Ware; Charles Burns; Hieronymous Bosch; Georges Grosz; Dr. Suess; Shel Silverstein; Mercer Mayer; J. Otto. *Asterix; Tin-Tin; Heavy Metal.* David Kirk.

**Phillip Mowery:** David Lance Goines; Michael Schwab; Roy Lichtenstein; Maxfield Parrish. "Andy Warhol and pop art culture are also obvious influences on my style."

Other recurring (and related) trends in our epoch are retro, homage, and parody. We all know the clichés: What goes around comes around; there's nothing new under the sun. To a degree (and more so in select eras—like our time frame, perhaps) this is quite true. Study Walt Reed's *The Illustrator in America.* Leaf through a cross section of illustration annuals and creative directories to see for yourself. If you keep your old clothes long enough, as it's said, they come back in style eventually.

The Graphic Artist's Guild continues the fight for copyright education and reform (as well as other legal, ethical, and business issues). And make no mistake, this is particularly important in an age of immediate global access and instant opportunity via both Internet and the computer. The Illustrators Partnership of America was formed in the last half of the 1990s.

**Gregory Nemec:** Comic books, Ray Harryhausen movies, *Star Wars,* Michelangelo, *Mad* magazine. Winsor McCay; Lynd Ward; Fritz Eichenberg, M. C. Escher; Rockwell Kent; Will Eisner; Robert Crumb; Guy Billout; and David Suter.

**Peter Kuper:** Sue Coe; Norman Rockwell; Jack Kirby, Harvey Kurtzman, Gerald Scarfe; the German expressionists; Romare Beardon; Jacob Lawrence. "Illustration is a little too narrow. My influences crisscross into comics, fine art, and my travels, as well."

**PJ Loughran:** Frank Miller; Dave Mazzucchelli; Jean-Michel Basquiat. Ralph Steadman and Ronald Searle. Cy Twombley, Robert Rauchenberg ("A huge step forward for me—where I first saw assemblage and collage being used"), Paul Klee; Jackson Pollock; Joan Mitchell. Warren Lynn. Peter de Sève; C. F. Payne, Carter Goodrich; Edward Gorey.

**Sam Viviano:** Al Hirschfeld; David Levine; Carmine Infantino; Jack Davis and Mort Drucker. Joe Kubert, Gil Kane, Wally Wood. David Stone Martin and Burt Silverman. Michaelangelo; Rembrandt.

**Michael Wertz:** Peter Max; Gary Panter; *Love and Rockets* (the Brothers Hernandez); Raymond Pettibon; Cezanne; "My teachers and friends: (amongst them) Bud Peen, Susan Gross, Vivienne Flesher, Marcos Sorenson."

**Overton Loyd:** Rick Rogers, William Stout. Corky McCoy, Pedro Bell and Ronald "Stozo" Edwards. Robert Grossman. "When it comes to fine art: Degas; John Otterbridge—he founded the Watt's Festival in South Central Los Angeles. His words of wisdom are always encouraging." Robin Strayhorn; Larry Gluck; Jerome Gestaldi.

**Robert Zimmerman:** "I have no idea who my favorite illustrators are. Every professional is there because they have something valuable to offer the marketplace. I appreciate them all for what they have to offer and don't draw much of a distinction. Commercial art is like that in my mind. A professional fills a needed place and is successful because they fill that spot very well."

Some illustrators to note (and names you may know): Richard Amsel and Drew Struzan; Gary Kelley, Gregory Manchess, and C. F. Payne; Yvonne Buchanan and Kinuko Craft; Anita Kunz, Barbara Nessim, and Nancy Stahl; James Bennett and Mark Summers. Also: Guy Billout, Etienne Delessert, and Henrik Drescher; Kyle Baker, Chris Ware, Lynda Barry, and David Mazzucchelli; Brian Ajhar and Peter de Sève; Joe Ciardiello, Lane Smith, Art Spiegelman, and James Yang; Arnold Roth, Randall Enos, Hal Mayforth, and Simms Taback.

As in the decades past, venues continue to wane. Illustrators branch off or out into other alternatives. We see the first viable computer illustration in the 1980s, the subsequent rise of digital technologies, and the resulting conundrums of this momentous breakthrough: Is the computer the holy grail, or is it deviously thinning the gene pool of skilled illustrators? Is digital production

> ## My List
>
> Here are the author's essential illustrators/artists—my personal creative influences and inspirations (in brief, and in no real order).
>
> Stuart Davis, Jules Pascin, Ben Shahn, Al Hirschfeld, Milton Glaser, Richard Diebenkorn, and Ward Schumaker. Vermeer, Franklin Booth; Picasso and Braque (and almost any Cubist painter, for that matter). Paul Giovanopoulos, George Herriman, John Held, Jr., Fritz Scholder, Rick Griffin, and Franz Kline.
>
> I must mention that the Art Department at Indiana University of Pennsylvania boasted many fine teachers, but my design, drawing, and painting teachers—Paul Ben-Zvi, Robert Cronauer, Jim Innes, Joanne Lovette, Robert Seelhorst—set me on a lifelong career and journey. Also at IUP: Jim Capone—to my mind, the best of the best of my student colleagues (and the benchmark was high).

and reproduction simply changing and challenging our industry as we know it, or actually methodically killing it off? Doom and gloom? Fight or flight? Stay tuned. Don't touch that dial; it's only going to get more interesting—if you leave now, you're going to miss the most exciting part.

## CROSS-CULTURAL REFERENCES, ETHNIC INFLUENCES

As society continues the work of embracing diversity, we should note that there have always been fine illustrators of color. But chances are you may not be aware of them.

There's a depth of talent—both historical and contemporary—throughout the venues. You'll find such names as Aaron Douglas (and the wonderful artists of the Harlem Renaissance); Thomas Blackshear II, E. Simms Campbell (see Figure 4–18), Ashley Bryan, Susan Guevara, Donald Crews, George Perez, Tom Feelings, and The Brothers Hernandez.

Look for Angel de Cora, Yuyi Morales, and Brian Pinkney; John Steptoe, Leo Dillon (working with Diane Dillon), Ted Shearer, Jose Ortega, Miguel Covarubbias, and Camille Rose Garcia.

You'll see James Ransome, Antonio Prohias, Terrance Cummings, Milton Knight, Pat Cummings, Sergio Aragones, Carole Byard, Morrie Turner, Maya Christina González, and more.

Illustrator Ezra Jack Keats was not black. Nonetheless, his award winning books feature blacks as the main characters and not just incidental cast. He turned the world of children's publishing upside down, and opened doors for black illustrators in the process.

Jacob Lawrence and Romare Beardon are not illustrators per se, but their artistic influence is strong for many illustrators who cite these artists as a source of inspiration. Include Jean-Michel Basquiat and Gronk in this category as well.

It is a matter of debate and carefully worded biographies, but facts point to George Herriman, creator of the enduring and legendary *Krazy Kat,* as being an artist of color. It is a sad commentary about his life and times, but there are no existing photos of Herriman *without a hat on*—thus, his hair texture could not be noted, and intolerant readers of his day (circa 1913) would not reject the comic strip.

More than a few artists are taken with ethnic and cross-cultural art, incorporating or referencing such resources throughout their work. For instance, Picasso was particularly keen on African masks. If you look at his groundbreaking work, you'll see that this influence pervades his imagery. So, if you're influenced at all by Picasso—or by the many illustrators who creatively nod in his direction—you have an indirect, but very real link to African art forms.

## THE INFLUENCE OF CULTURE AND THE DICTATES OF TASTE

Figure |4-18|

In a time of both rampant and insidious segregation, E. Simms Campbell was the first acknowledged black cartoonist illustrating for many top national publications. Working from the 1930s through the 1950s, you could find his illustrations in magazines like *Esquire, Playboy, Cosmopolitan, Saturday Evening Post, Redbook,* and *The New Yorker.* He eventually was syndicated in over 140 newspapers, as well. (Courtesy of the Society of Illustrators)

Reflected in both advertising and editorial, illustration is literally history—subjective and objective. Illustration is a graphic testimonial to the moral tenor and spirit of the times, as well as the events, of an era.

Illustrators have long both influenced and been influenced by cultural and social phenomena. We strongly identify particular eras with certain visual icons. To cite some examples: you'll find that the stunning Gibson Girl and her handsome suitor literally defined beauty and sophistication in the late 1890s. Flagg's Uncle Sam has endured long after World War I; the Held flapper was the epitome of the 1920s jazz age.

George Petty's pin-ups of the 1930s became the Varga girl in the 1940s. She, along with Norman Rockwell's stalwart Rosie the Riveter and Bill Mauldin's war-weary but resolute GIs, are all famous 1940s images. The 1960s had the ubiquitous Peter Max, Glaser's image of Dylan, and Crumb's Mr. Natural. They're still ripping off Steinberg's "view of the world from New York City" map concept. I got your smiley face right here—and Snoopy, Mickey, Garfield, and Homer (to name just a few of those characters) are everywhere.

# THE BORROWERS

Everyone has personal illustration heroes, both historical and contemporary. We all borrow in varying degrees from the masters and our mentors, consciously and unconsciously. If your eyes are open, it's probably impossible to *not* be influenced. As the old saying goes: "It's all been done before," right?

Well, yes; and according to that other old saying, "there's the rub." This basic template of influence must be moderated by personal inspiration. If you appropriate or adapt other concepts and methods without putting your own obvious, personal spin on it, you are only demonstrating *your* distinct lack of imagination.

Sure, everything can be considered subject matter, but copying somebody's ideas or drawing approach can only be labeled as poor form. Illustrator Robert Zimmerman points out that the commercial art world is actually a rather small place, and art directors *will* recognize when an illustrator is lifting someone's stuff. "Create a unique place for yourself, and add to the experience of the audience," he soundly advises.

It's a non-issue if you borrow *in the service* of your vision. Coming up with a concept, doing a rough sketch, and then finding existing imagery as *reference* is one thing (do it); but looking for an old photo and building the entire image around such a "swipe" is something else again (don't do it).

Even Norman Rockwell appropriated from classical art, but did so in a smart, clever way. Find Rockwell's 1940s era "Rosie the Riveter" piece, then study the illustrator's reference point. He doesn't try to hide the fact that Rosie is really a Sistine Chapel figure dressed as a 1940s factory worker—in fact, that's the point.

There is also the chunky issue of professional imitators—artists who ape the style of another artist. Some even change their style to "evolve" along with their source! While there is a market for these folks (successful artists can't take every job, after all), this practice is an ethically and aesthetically shady area—at best, a soul-deadening way to make art.

# A BRIEF DISCUSSION OF THE FUTURE

This discussion will be very brief—it's dangerous to speculate (you just might be wrong). And after all, if I could predict the future of anything—the field of illustration no exception—I myself would be downright dangerous (and, I hope, rich).

As I've said previously, I'm not a fortune teller. But my earlier educated guesses still apply. The future looks even more digital from this corner. Software will be very sharp, hardware will be really cool. I think there will also be a noticeable return to non-digital techniques—"traditional" will be the "new Retro." Copyright will be a hotbed issue in the digital age. Controversies of originality, and debates about the levels of standards will be the norm. The Mac will survive, and remain the platform of choice for illustrators and designers.

If I *am* wrong about all this, you'll tell me. If I'm right about any of it, we'll both know, but tell me anyway.

# PROFILES

## *Daryll Collins*

Daryll Collins feels his work is directly descended from early to mid 1960s Hanna-Barbara and Jay Ward Studio cartoons (as well as other studios producing cartoons for television in this era). Boris and Natasha, and Fred, Wilma and the bunch serve as elemental inspiration for this illustrator. "The product and character design from these studios, in those years, was just great. I can still see it in my style to this day." Nothin' up his sleeve, Rock—see the connection? (© Daryll Collins)

As a kid, most of Daryll Collins' influences were not really illustrators; he found his heroes in the likes of the old Hanna-Barbara cartoons and Jay Ward Studio. The look of those characters really grabbed him.

Collins makes no apologies for what's often labeled "limited animation." "There was a wonderful design sense to the way these characters were put together," he comments. "I love that limited animation look from the early to mid 1960s; and I still love the stuff now."

When an editorial job arrives, "I normally start reading and then grab a pencil, tablet, or sketch pad to do quick positional doodles or gesture drawings," Collins says. "Whatever comes out of my head—whatever I think works. If these thumbnails look good to me, I'll develop it from there."

The small but important thumbs are drawn proportionate to actual layout size. After the illustrator gets these roughs—and the basic concept—down, he renders a drawing at about 150 to 200 percent up. Collins keeps this sketch rather tight, so the decision makers know exactly what he's thinking. "No surprises . . . art directors don't have to decipher a scribble or put missing parts together," Collins explains. "If they can see a fully realized sketch, they may just send me right to the finish; or go to finish with minimal changes."

With the okay, the illustrator transfers the line work onto smooth Bristol, and scans this drawing into Adobe Streamline. The result will read precisely like his hard copy—Collins notices no difference from an inked piece to its digital incarnation, and a printout is exactly the same.

From here he brings the drawing into Adobe Illustrator, with the sketch often on a separate layer and sent to the back as reference. The final line art is on top, and Collins builds layers of color, detail, and background from the sketch up. The finished job is usually sent out as an EPS file. "This works pretty well," the artist comments, "Clients can manipulate the size, and the files don't lose any resolution.

"Working in Illustrator also means that you are basically working in flat color and gradients," says Collins. "I'll have color gradients in the backgrounds, but foreground characters are usually left as flat color—I try to make my illustration look like a little snapshot of an animated cartoon!"

## PROFILES

*Elwood H. Smith*

You'll usually find Elwood H. Smith's zany dogs hanging around television sets, his grumpy cats draped over sofa backs, and more than a few startled bunnies peering out from behind hills and bushes. They are usually reacting (or overreacting) to the situation Elwood has created for them. Smith finds that this cast of characters not only adds to the drama, but gives the illustrator a chance to draw his favorite images.

For most of his career Smith has depended upon Arches 90 lb. cold-pressed watercolor paper. "I loved the way my paint laid flat on the surface. The texture was ideal for my Pelikan #120 fountain pen," he reminisces. But Smith now finds the quality of this paper too uneven—random sections of the sheet will blot, sucking up the watercolor in a splotchy, uneven pattern.

To compound the problem, Smith's favorite pen has also been discontinued from the Pelikan line. "And it is nearly impossible to find a Kolin-sky sable brush with a consistent, tapering point," he comments. "My trusty FW waterproof India ink is currently manufactured with an unacceptable acrylic formula—when my old ink stash is depleted, I guess it'll be time to grow and learn a new medium."

Before you mistakenly get the idea that Smith has been associating with those disgruntled felines too long, let me say that this seasoned pro only represents the many illustrators who feel "they just don't make 'em like they used to." But one difference is that after 40 years in the biz, Smith also advises you to remain as open and flexible as you can. "Stay true to yourself," he says, "but dodge the mummification process whenever it looms over your drawing table (or computer screen). Everything is changing more quickly than ever before (trust me, I was there back then), and freezing up creatively is a one-way trip to Endsville."

Smith eludes all that on a daily basis, although he doesn't claim to succeed 100 percent of the time. "It is easy to become cynical and crank out second-rate work," he reflects. "But I advise keeping a tight grip on your optimism—muck about in the creative soup of your pure creative self as much as possible. Endure those lackluster assignments that enable you to buy shoes for the dog, but remain vigilant, keeping the creative fires tended."

## SUMMING IT UP

Our casual jaunt through the history of American illustration helps us better understand and appreciate current illustration schools, genres, and styles. To be truly informed illustrators, we must consider cross-cultural, ethnic, and international references; look at our role models, heroes and peers; plus weigh social influence and the dictates of cultural taste, as well.

These three pieces show how Smith's style has evolved in over 40 years of picture making. The first piece is from the late 1970s, when Elwood's work was still very much influenced by Rube Goldberg and Billy DeBeck (creator of Barney Google). The characterization has the trademark big feet, big nose, and big props of that nostalgic period. The second piece is a transitional piece—a precursor to Smith's current style. You'll find smaller feet and Smith moving even further from actual human proportions. The final piece represents where Elwood's style is today: Now his characters are more influenced by design considerations than anatomy. (Illustrations © Elwood H. Smith)

In 2003, and just shy of 100 years of age, Al Hirschfeld passed away. I mention this to acknowledge the awesome challenge and passion that is uniquely your gift for hopefully, a long, long life. Perhaps long enough to be a source of inspiration for the next generation of illustrators.

# PROFILES

## *Loren Long*

Loren Long paints mostly with acrylics, on either canvas or masonite panels. His brand of choice is Golden or Winsor & Newton. He also likes Daniel Smith acrylic gloss medium. "I've tried many acrylic mediums and find that I like Daniel Smith's the best," Long comments. "It's crystal clear, and seems fuller bodied and less plastic-like than the others. It gives my paintings a rich oil painting quality. Implementing the medium into my painting process has shaped the way I approach my work.

"It's mostly based on painting wet over dry," he explains. "With a build-up of washes and glazes over and over, working from transparent to opaque; back and forth. This prohibits the use of oils; but it always comes as a compliment when someone assumes I paint with oils."

Long first strives to take a subject and develop an interesting composition. "Here, I always refer to N. C. Wyeth—not only a wonderful draftsman and dramatic painter, but an absolutely brilliant designer. Stand in front of a Wyeth painting, and you'll see the accomplished rendering of figures, plus the beautiful color and brushwork.

"But when you walk back across the room 25 feet away, the painting has power and interest on another level. The strong overall design of the composition becomes more of an abstract form with powerful lights and darks, and clear shapes."

You can do this exercise when looking at art in a book, by squinting your eyes and reducing the image to rudimentary graphic shapes. Long believes that this compelling sense of design and abstract form in a representational piece of art is what makes it appealing—even if the viewer doesn't recognize (or even care) about it. "It's what many refer to as the *grand design* of a picture—the big elements," says Long.

"Your light source is very important, and essential in creating that overall abstract strength. A cast shadow may become a shape, so I draw with form, not just line. An artist that sketches in line may have a completely different opinion about this than I do, however."

Loren Long has always been drawn to the WPA muralists and the American scene painters of the 1920s and 1930s. "These artists had a certain simplicity to their work, it all felt handmade and home-grown," he says. "They weren't all consummate draftsmen or colorists, but they had *soul*. I'm drawn to that. It certainly has helped shape my own painting." (Illustrations © Loren Long)

Summing up, Long says, "I believe that if a picture is strong at 1 or 2 inches, then it will be strong at 2 or 3 feet, or for that matter at 20 or 30 feet. If a picture has good black and white value, then it can be effective in any color."

## in review

1. Why is it necessary to look at illustration history? What does illustration history mean for your generation of illustrators? What does illustration history mean for you *personally*?

2. What was/is the halftone process, and what is its significance for illustrators and publishing in general? What is color-halftone?

3. Research and reference: In your estimation, choose the most influential illustrator from each era and briefly discuss why you made that choice.

4. What kind of impact did television have on illustration in the 1950s?

5. What is the Graphic Artists Guild? Why is this organization—or others like it—important?

6. What is the "New Illustration?" What does "New Illustration" mean to you? Are you a "New Illustrator?"

## exercises

1. Reasoning and application: in a written paper, or in oral discussion, compare and contrast two eras of illustration. Choose time periods from adjacent decades or pick two periods separated by many decades. The key words here are *compare* and *contrast*. How are these eras similar? How are they different? Discuss media, style, and technique as well as the personalities of the illustrators and the character of the times.

2. Who are your favorite modern illustrators and why? Who are your favorite historical illustrators and why? Pick one illustrator and do an illustration in the style of that illustrator. Don't simply copy an existing piece, create a new illustration in the manner of your selected artist.

3. Choose a particular era (the 1970s, for instance). Research the events of that day, look at the cultural, social, and political climate of the times. Create a visual portrait of that era in *your* style, in the technique and media of your choice. Something to ponder: If you were doing this illustration in that particular era (a self-portrait of the era), would your drawing look the same? What would a self-portrait of our era look like?

4. Research an historical product. Do a product illustration for this item in a modern style. Find a modern day product. Do a product illustration for this item in an historical style.

5. Choose and study a past event; create an illustration about this historical event in a modern style. Choose and study a current event; create an illustration about this current event in an historical style. This exercise can also work as a conceptual piece.

© C.F. Payne

PART

## A VISIBLE MEANS OF SUPPORT

As a kid, you may have gone out on a dark evening with a flashlight. Whipping your arm about quickly, you drew trails of light in the air—a fast flurry of lines making a drawing that is there for only an instant, and then gone forever.

Well, maybe. There is a famous slow-shutter photograph of Picasso creating just such a "light drawing" in a studio situation. Captured on film, this document of Picasso's drawing is "in print," so to speak.

Drawing on air is a most esoteric surface, indeed (and a fun exercise), but we are going to discuss supports and surfaces that are not as rarefied (please see Figure II-1). The blank sheet has tantalized and tormented artists for time immemorial. It offers a pristine creative opportunity that tickles the fingers and excites the mind's eye; it gives you the chance to (literally) make your mark.

Confronting that clean piece of paper or newly primed canvas is both a bit scary *and* exhilarating. The opportunity for thrills or frustration is all right there. Whatever the outcome, it's your level of commitment to that blank slate that gets you back to the drawing board the next day.

We're going to begin our examination of illustration techniques by first addressing the base level of any process—the paper or support surface you're working on.

## PULP FICTION

First, I'd like to dispel a vicious rumor. It is the myth that you absolutely must have high-priced and precious art supplies to make "good art." Yes, the so-called "cheap stuff" could mean inferior quality. Sure, you can certainly get exactly what you pay for. I agree, there may be archival concerns and issues about durability. Red flags on handling, or cautions on the compatibilities of low-grade materials, are very real.

But saying that, it's a tactical mistake to let only your wallet dictate the illustration supplies you buy. This works both ways; it's a trap for the frugal as well as the spendthrift. Rather, you must buy absolutely the best supplies and materials you can afford—you must work with the right resources to get the job done well.

And towards that goal, you must recognize value. There is an understanding of cost to performance ratios (the "hey, it's worth it," as well as "what an incredible bargain" factors). There is technical savvy—knowing your tools and materials and how they perform; realizing what you *need* to get a particular job done. Combine this expertise with astute shopping, and you will be truly dangerous at the art store.

Figure | II-1 |

An illustrator can work on classic surfaces and supports (here, Tad Suzuki's *Barbershop at Sunset (San Diego)* is acrylic paint on stretched canvas). But you can also explore more humble, or specialized, even unusual options—and that's the beauty of it. (© Tad Suzuki 2003)

## The Ream Goes on Forever

Paper and board weights, textures, and colors vary; you have quite a choice on all these counts. You can buy supports in many formats, from one shots to packs to rolls. Papers and boards are found with various surface textures—such as hot pressed (smooth), cold pressed (with some tooth; sometimes called "Not"), and rough (lots of texture) watercolor paper. Supports boast various grains, patterns, and opacities; come in a variety of weights (which can affect tooth), plies, or layers; and are found in many, many sizes. Edges can be cut clean or ragged (aka "deckled" when discussing watercolor paper).

There are supports designated for particular media (for instance: pastel paper) There are supports earmarked for other functions (like masonite). Supports can be machine, mold, and handmade; of natural composition, synthetic, or natural/synthetic blends.

| NOTE |

Paper is usually designated in what's called *imperial* measurement, in pounds per ream. Thus, a 90lb watercolor sheet means that 500 sheets (a ream) of this 22 × 30 in. paper weigh 90 pounds. You'll also see paper designated by grams per square meter. 90lb paper translates to an 180gsm sheet, so 500 sheets of 56 × 76 cm paper weigh 180gsm.

## ALL PAPERS AND ALL THINGS

Esoteric supplies are part and parcel of the technical process for a good number of illustrators. But by that same token, a big part of illustration practice for many of us is the continual search for new ways of working with common materials.

Illustrators working in collage, for instance, are always on the prowl for papers. These artists revel in the combination of paper textures like cardboards, foils, and tapes. Illustrator Tom Garrett finds that tissue papers with stamped bronze and copper centers and torn and cut bits of metallics for backgrounds or edging are ideal for his artistic vision. He also seeks out more obscure materials or mundane items—cheap, pulp, or throwaway papers are prized as much as top drawing papers. It all adds just the right punch to the mix.

## Just Common Sense

Not to contradict the "anything goes" theory of materials and production—especially if you consider that there will be inevitable trade-offs in the name of artistic exploration—but if you want your work to endure, use acid-free papers, and archival-safe, conservation-quality supplies and materials (including adhesives and tapes, lightfast, waterproof, and permanent inks and paints). See Figure II-2.

Figure **II-2**

*Snail's Pace* (circa 1975) will hopefully stand the test of time. This little illustration is holding up quite nicely. The paper is not yellowing; line work remains crisp, and the ink has not discolored. I like to think that we will creatively persevere today, and that museum curators of the twenty-sixth century won't curse us for a lack of foresight and preparation. (© Michael Fleishman 2003)

Dry Media

*I spent the mid-1970s working with George Clinton. He only wanted raw, rough, funky sketches. Pen and ink or my handy Bic; add a touch of magic marker—it was done. During the 1980s I drew caricatures for "Win Lose or Draw." Luckily, I attended some workshops on Renaissance techniques and learned a vine charcoal process that allowed me to capture likenesses much faster than my normal hit or miss method—sometimes, I'd have to knock out up to 24 heads per week!"*

**Overton Loyd, illustrator**

*"Draw all the time. This is old advice, but still true. My younger brother wanted to become an artist for a day or two, but when he realized he wouldn't become as good as I am—and I have a long way to go—he gave it up. Look at everything, draw everything; find your medium, find your style."*

**Ken Meyer, Jr., illustrator**

*"There is nothing like sitting down with that #2 pencil and just drawing, because everything else after that is just finishing."*

**Sam Viviano, illustrator**

## Chapter Objectives:

Examine charcoal and Conté

Explore pastel, oil pastel, and related media

Discuss various types of pencils—including graphite, water soluble pencil, colored pencil, and watercolor pencil

Consider combinations and mixed media

Look at the trimmings—drawing accessories

## Introduction

Drawing, in it's seemingly infinite variety, is at the heart of most visual arts—especially illustration. We're going to continue to explore illustration by examining assorted dry media and the application of these materials.

Figure | 5-1 |

John Rutherford's fine character study was done in graphite pencil with oil glazes. (© John Rutherford)

# CHARCOAL

Actually burned wood, charcoal is typically soft and chunky, rather powdery and flaky. And by that very nature, it's delightfully messy. Take care—charcoal can be inadvertently rubbed off as easily as it is deliberately rubbed-in. It can be accidentally smeared instead of artfully smudged. Brittle charcoal wears down quickly; it easily breaks just as fast.

But due to those same physical characteristics, the medium is feather-light, extremely portable, and absolutely simple to apply. Charcoal emphatically marks a range of surfaces (but a paper with some tooth works best). It blends and gradates superbly, while giving up a great range of line quality, values, and textures with minimal effort.

You will commonly see willow and vine charcoals readily available, but you can also find other wood types (such as beech or poplar). Charcoal comes in many shapes and forms: pencils; as pointed, squared or rounded sticks; actual twigs, or in powder form (compressed charcoal, by the way, is actually charcoal powder mixed with a binder and cut into solid sticks).

Like a graphite pencil (see Figure 5–1, done with graphite pencil), you can choose varying levels of both thickness and hardness. And like graphite pencil, charcoal is one of the most generic illustration tools—a fixture in nearly all drawing classes, and the staple of any basic course. An ideal tool for a novice, charcoal is also a mainstay for the practicing professional. See Figure 5–2 for two examples of charcoal illustration.

# PASTEL

Chalks and pastels are similar. Actually, pastels are made by mixing ground pigment with water, *and* chalk or clay (plus a gum binder). Like chalk, pastels are rather soft and powdery—a bit fragile; they can break and crumble (or smudge) relatively easily.

More chalk base and/or adding white pigment produces tints, and certainly one of the hallmarks of this wonderful medium is the grand array of tints and shades available. The revered and time-honored pastel technique is quite famous for luminous colors and a silky sheen (see Figure 5–3). Blending is almost effortless; painterly effects are very easy to achieve.

figure | 1 |

"I operate under what I call the Small Chunk Theory of Relativity: business, creativity, promotion/marketing, studio-time. It's all relative. A job (especially a big job or a number of jobs that come in at the same time) can be overwhelming and intimidating if I look at the entire task as a whole. But if I break the task(s) down into small chunks, doing something every day, any job is manageable. Hours invested are variable, so the buzzwords are 'constant' and 'consistent.' It takes discipline and focus, but it keeps me from hitting the panic button." (© Michael Fleishman 2003)
**Michael Fleishman**

figure | 2 |

"In my work, my inspiration comes from the urban subjects themselves that I paint. I shoot photos on location, maybe combine them in my sketchbook and write my comments and impressions, etc. After awhile, I pick a canvas that fits the image in my mind . . . and I paint. All kinds of things motivate me: the technical challenge, an upcoming solo exhibition, a book publication with my image on the cover, competitive juried shows, or my growing portfolio." (© Tad Suzuki 2003)
**Tad Suzuki**

figure | 3 |

"My advice for up and coming artists? Get everything in writing, signed, up front, before sharpening your pencil. Business advice? Get everything in writing, signed, up front, before sharpening your pencil." (© Brian Zick 1998)
**Brian Zick**

figure | 4 |

"Technical concerns (cropping and/or reduction snafus, color shifts, lines filling in or blocking up, etc.) can—and will—affect the end result. You must have a hand in (plus an understanding of) the reproduction process. Otherwise, you are illustrating in the dark. Not knowing how your art will make it through to print is akin to working blind. The reproduced piece is arguably the actual illustration; any subtle or not so subtle changes ultimately impact how your work appears to the viewer." (© Stan Shaw 2002)
**Stan Shaw**

(a)

(b)

figure | 5a and 5b |

**Ali Douglass**

"Your individual visual translation cannot be matched. Art directors want us for how we look at things, conceptually and stylistically. So be unique, they like that. It's okay." (© Ali Douglass)

"You can do it without art school, but the daily interaction of students and teachers, that whole experience of goofing off hard and working even harder is a big part of the training." (© Paul Melia)
**Paul Melia**

"Illustrators are people who really like to paint and draw—who know how to paint and draw. Everyone that comes to art school is born with talent, but the difference is if you're willing to make that commitment to practice and learn." (© Benton Mahan)
**Ben Mahan**

figure  8

"Go to work. Be your own worst critic. Get to work." (© Robert Zimmerman)
**Robert Zimmerman**

figure 9

"I think it is important to have other illustrator and/or artist friends to talk about projects and get a feeling for changes that might be happening in the market. Because the work at times can be isolating, I usually hook up with another illustrator once a week for coffee and talk on the phone a couple of times a week with other illustrator friends." (© Tom Garrett)
**Tom Garrett**

"At first I found the move from one way of working to another rather upsetting; I learned kind of by way of monkey see, monkey do. But I must confess that having made the move to digital, I have not looked back since." (© Chris Spollen)
**Chris Spollen**

I may burn in Hell—in that the art that I am currently creating does not reflect a solution to an art director's problem. Rather, I am shamelessly illustrating more and more of my own visions and concepts. A lot of water under my professional bridge has sort of made this possible.

I'm even jotting down bits of story ideas and playing with developing a couple of characters to run around my futuristic fantasies.

I am sort of on automatic pilot, and I guess years of professional assignments have made this part of my career possible. (© Chris Spollen)
**Chris Spollen**

figure | 11 |

"We are all influenced, directly or indirectly, by other artists' work and by everything that has come before. But the idea is to take all that influences you and do your own unique spin on it. What the world doesn't need more of is sameness and mediocrity." (© Sarajo Frieden)
**Sarajo Frieden**

figure | 12 |

"I try to keep organic as much as possible. New technology has always helped me, but I have been really stubborn with sticking to traditional methods when it comes to process." (© Akiko Stehrenberger)
**Akiko Stehrenberger**

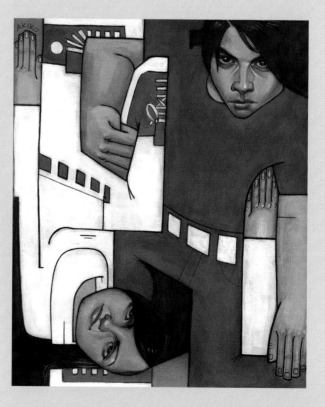

figure | 13 |

"I love to hear criticism, because I know that whenever someone gives me their opinion it will only make my work that much stronger." (© Scott Jarrard 2003)
**Scott Jarrard**

figure | 14 |

"The original transparency on this was an accidental exposure of daylight film with tungsten (indoor) light from the modeling lights on the flash equipment I use. The result—although not appropriate for the client I was working with—was interesting enough to keep for many years. I later scanned it and eventually used it as you see it here." (© David Bishop/ San Francisco)
**David Bishop**

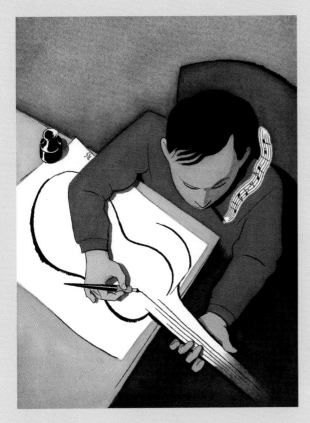

"There are cases where inborn talent is an option, not a requirement, for success. A steady effort and commitment to a vision can indeed earn you a noted career. Many at first glance might conclude a particular illustrator can't draw because his work seems to flout academic rules of form, shading, or realism. But it's the sensibility he or she has uniquely developed and refined that is the achievement, and this may be perfectly suited to expression. It is a creative, engaging response to the tyranny of the conventional—which in fact, obeys tenets of content, balance, compositional emphasis, texture, and detail. It's an economy of means."
(© Robert Saunders 2003)
**Robert Saunders**

"These days, you truly have throwaway art, or art on command! Most of the business (clients included) assumed that the computer would destroy the need or desire for analog art—which in fact, hastened this demise. Artists by the droves dumped what they were doing to jump on the digital bandwagon, so they wouldn't be left behind in the twenty-first century. Now, many of these artists are returning to traditional media because the computer—although versatile, fast, and cheap—leaves one without an original piece. Clients who want something real are always willing to pay for that quality." (© Gregory Manchess)
**Gregory Manchess**

figure | 17a and 17b |

"Because of new technology, an illustrator can finish a piece in a fraction of the time compared to working in traditional mediums. Art buyers in many cases have reduced the time allotted for assignments. These quick turnarounds have bred a burgeoning stock-art industry, where art buyers can buy existing imagery within minutes.

"This new avenue is quite controversial, and has polarized illustrators. There are those who welcome stock as a way to generate income from older work. Others see it as a threat to commissioned assignments. How this (and other challenges brought on by new technologies) will play out is very much up in the air." (© Steve Dininno)
**Steve Dininno**

(a)

(b)

figure | 18 |

"Artistic expression is a visual language we use to give shape to our imagination. Just as it is necessary to speak clearly in conversation, we should work toward clarity in our visual statements." (© Ilene Winn-Lederer 2003)
**Ilene Winn-Lederer**

figure | 19 |

"Ideally, the criticism directed at your work is motivated by a desire to help you perfect something. It's no different from the urge one might have to remove the flashing around the edges of little plastic toys, or trim that one rogue leaf sticking oddly out of the topiary elephant. In other words, just making things look better. Isn't that what artists do? The craft has gone out of so many things in life, this is an opportunity to do good work; to know that you must work and learn, and keep at it forever. And hopefully all these things will lead you to a form of self-expression that satisfies the artist and the audience, and that bridges the gap between what you see in your mind's eye and what's on the paper. Be receptive to the criticisms about small details, as opposed to your overall vision—the leaf, not the elephant." (© Gregory Nemec)
**Gregory Nemec**

figure | 20 |

"Seeing or hearing the delight from someone I've done a piece for— being able to draw for a living—that's a pretty big thing." (© Ken Meyer, Jr. 2003)
**Ken Meyer, Jr.**

figure | 21 |

"I like to stand up when I paint and draw; you get your whole arm and body involved in the entire process—you work your whole physical self—you immerse yourself—into your piece, into your art. Time sort of expands. You're there with the painting and in that moment. This space is just really nice to be in." (© Bill Jaynes)
**Bill Jaynes**

figure | 22 |

"As you go through life, always listen to that little voice inside you. No, no, not the one that says: 'Doesn't anybody pay on time? My parents were right. I should have majored in something safe.' The other voice." (© Ken Smith 2002)
**Ken Smith**

figure | 23 |

"My subject for a calendar was Haley's Comet and I was stumped. Ultimately, I remembered myself as a little kid interested in space exploration and I flashed back to the outer-space heroes of yesteryear like Buck Rogers and Flash Gordon. Now, I had my concept in mind and my hero viewing the foreboding meteor image on a futuristic video screen—vintage 1940s imagination.

"The painting was later reused as promotional advertising for The Chicago Fantastic Film Festival. I was then given the opportunity to illustrate the commemorative poster for that event and produced a companion piece—a space woman standing in front of some 1940s style rocketships."(© Douglas Klauba 2001)
**Douglas Klauba**

figure | 24 |

"Pastel on paper . . . this art accompanied a feature on the singer-songwriter in *Rolling Stone* magazine (the art director was Fred Woodward). The style, edge, and angularity were somewhat dictated by the features in her face." (© Gary Kelley)
**Gary Kelley**

figure | 25 |

"I do a lot of work for the kids market, which means vibrant color. One of the great things about my years in greeting cards is that I got to work with color all the time. A lot of cartoonists and humorous illustrators start out exclusively in black and white, but I constantly had to be aware of color and color trends. These color predictions change a little bit every year, but I add on to my basic color look by knowing what the current directions are." (© Daryll Collins)

**Daryll Collins**

figure | 26 |

"My cats are my muses, in the deepest and most elemental way. They offer unstintingly their uniquely feline gift of observation—a generous sharing in their fresh, relaxed and deep perception of the world. Too often, in the rush of busy-ness and deadlines, I'm tempted to brush those furry tails off my drawing board, push aside those paws, ignore the sweet tickle of whisker-kisses.

"But the cat insists, gently. 'Stop. Notice me. Look into my eyes. See the wild beauty there. Observe how the afternoon sun sparkles tiny rainbows in the glistening fur of my throat.'

"My cats' most precious gift is this new way of seeing, of perceiving their wild loveliness. Accepting this gift in the spirit given makes me a better artist." (© Wendy Christensen, 2003. All rights reserved)

**Wendy Christensen**

figure | 27 |

"My small studio has the 'typical' array of art supplies. There are a variety of pencils, paper and erasers. Illustration and fine art books are around for inspiration. You could say all the prep supplies are of no particular brand; but when I get to the supplies for producing the real things—finished artwork like oil paintings or pastel drawings—the items become slightly more specific." (© Brian Shellito)
**Brian Shellito**

figure | 28 |

"When they called me to try out for Spy vs. Spy, I figured if I was going to do it, I was going to make it my own thing. So I decided to do it in stencils; if they don't like it, then I'm not the right guy for the job anyway. I really didn't want to mimic Antonio Prohias (who created the strip for Mad in 1961)—I didn't want to be just a ghost artist. It was interesting because I wasn't anxious to have this job. It wasn't something I was ever expecting to find myself doing. But when I sat down to work on it, I suddenly realized what an influence Prohias' work had on me (because I do a lot of wordless comics). It turned out to be a nice fit, and they were open to the idea of having somebody come in and update it that way. I felt like I was not betraying where I was headed with my own work, as well." (© Peter Kuper)
**Peter Kuper**

"If your art is your bliss, you will find a way of making it work." (© Joe Murray Studio, Inc.)
**Joe Murray**

figure | 30

"One dark and stormy night, as I sat at my drawing table, alone, unwashed, and speaking in puns, Lou Brooks, disguised as a rodent, appeared at my door, a horse blanket slung over his shoulder. Lou unwrapped the well-drawn blanket to reveal the contents: several Tom Waits LPs, a beaten up hardcover of Rube Goldberg cartoons, two brandy snifters, and a bottle of vintage India ink.

"The next day, the morning sun peeped through the cabbie haze. 'Cabbie haze?' Lou said, a big smile on his ink-stained face, 'You're gonna be okay, kid!' " (© Elwood H. Smith)
**Elwood H. Smith**

figure | 31

"I love to be out in nature, but it is people and the things they make that I want to draw. We were all taught the same principles, but it is amazing, isn't it—that artists can be so different—blows me away."
(© Jeanne de la Houssaye)
**Jeanne de la Houssaye**

figure | 32 |

"To paraphrase Gilbert and Sullivan: Let the art fit the assignment; don't expect the assignment to fit the art—at least not until you become famous!" (© Mary Thelen 2003)
**Mary Thelen**

figure | 33 |

"I find myself talking to so many people—especially younger people—about the computer as the means to create a finished product very quickly. It's kind of a quick way to get to something that looks somewhat professional. Many kids coming up are really against taking drawing and painting classes, because they have such a command over the computer. They feel it's not really necessary to learn traditional tools, because they can get the results working digitally.

"I still think there is something crucial about having drawing and painting skills. Make room for those things . . . spend time looking; try experimenting with (and mixing) colors; learn about line and form, lighting and perspective. Even if you suck, even if your drawings are terrible, at least spend the time working through that. Even if it doesn't come out well on the other end—or you're never going to draw again—I think that time is valuable." (© PJ Loughran 2003)
**PJ Loughran**

figure | 34 |

"Someone once told me my work had a sarcastic style. I'm still trying to figure that one out." (© Lori Osiecki)
**Lori Osiecki**

figure | 35 a and b |

"I believe very strongly in not hammering yourself in front of your computer, trying to think up ideas. I believe passionately in mentally cross training— go to an art gallery, take a walk, or do whatever your sport is. In my case I kyack and run, so I have a number of ways to relax and channel my mind. You have to put yourself in a different place to come back. Saying that, I understand that some people can simply go to sleep and wake up knowing what they want to do." (© David Julian 2003 www.davidjulian.com)
**David Julian**

(a)

(b)

figure | 36

"Lately, I've been fascinated with metallic fabrics. Usually what I do is build up a body of fabrics and then experiment—like establishing a color palette. I don't know if this direction would have much of a commercial connection, because I'm not sure it would really relate to any commercial assignment. But I am interested, so I buy a yard of fabric here and there, and keep adding to this palette of colors and textures. It's all just sort of waiting for me to get time to do it. It is like a body of things that will help me later." (© Margaret Cusack)
**Margaret Cusack**

figure | 37

"What I love most is the journey. Who wouldn't love getting paid to create? What's my motivation? I'm a workaholic. Do I practice? Not too often—I don't have the time, I'm usually working. If you don't have the energy to work long hours, if you can go to a museum and not be inspired, if you can look at a set of paints and not want to pick them up—you'd better find a day job. If art is in your blood—you'll know it; it's an obsession." (© Robin Zingone 2003)
**Robin Zingone**

figure | 38 |

"When I graduated from college and returned to Yellow Springs, I got a commission from the local Frisbee team to do their team tee shirts. My first paying gig! There are still some Frisbee players around who have those tee shirts." (© Robin Zimmerman)
**Robin Zimmerman**

figure | 39 |

"Our business is changing; and the greatest change is one of perception. New technology has made parts of the process faster and cheaper, and that can be good. But I believe it has skewed our expectations of what art can and should be. Looking at images on a computer screen is no match for looking at a finely printed piece— or original art for that matter." (© David McGlynn)
**David McGlynn**

figure | 40 |

"Building up layers of paint adds thickness and texture. I scratch through the wet paint to reveal whatever color is under the wet layer—working into it with my brush end, then smearing and blending it with my fingers. I continue adding texture and pattern with added smears and splotches of color, then more scraping and sgrafitto. It's easy to spot bits of Klee and Miro in my pictures—I'm very fond of many early to mid-20th century painters." (© Jim Dryden)
**Jim Dryden**

figure | 41 |

C-21

"I did caricatures for the TV show *Win, Lose, or Draw*. I'd spend anywhere from a few hours to a few days working out a likeness on a 30 × 40 in. pad. Once the likeness was solid, I'd lay it on a light-box and trace over it with a very light grey (Tombow #81) brush marker. The juicy pointed tip makes a clean line.

"I'd then go over the line with a slightly darker grey (Tombow #77). This darker tone makes it possible to correct some of the line work because it literally cancels out the lighter grey. I'd next go over that line with a slightly darker grey (Tombow #45), refining the drawing even more. Then I'd use the solid black (Tombow #15) to finesse the almost completed line work.

"At this point I'd add some gray pastels to flesh out the face. Finally, I'd use a fat Magnum 44 Permanent Marker to create a bold outline around the figure so that it 'pops' on the TV monitor.

"Today, I mix media using a program called Painter. It's a virtual art store loaded with mediums from chalks to oil paints. I scan a pencil or ballpoint pen drawing into Painter and paint it with the watercolor tool. I usually end up tweaking the colors in Photoshop." (© Overton Loyd)
**Overton Loyd**

figure | 42 |

"I think the best thing for me is turn off the phone or work in the evening when things slow down in the outside world. If I have to stop for some reason or other—hey, this is real life and things don't always go as planned—I usually accept that and get on with it." (© John Jinks 2003)
**John Jinks**

figure | 43 |

"There is no such thing as a 'pure,' original concept—I think all art is an adaptation, dilution, or enhancement of other artists' work." (© Linda Crockett)
**Linda Crockett**

figure | 44 |

"The most important thing is the idea. The technique and the idea together is what it's all about. Solving the conceptual problem is the first thing." (© David Milgrim)
**David Milgrim**

figure | 45 |

"Though the magazine article involved acid rain in the U.S. and Canada, the focus was a study area on Camel's Hump Mountain in Vermont. The article stated clearly that the destruction of the forest by acid rain was so gradual it was virtually imperceptible visually and had to be measured in other ways. Illustration was employed in this case because it could provide a visual element where photographs just wouldn't work. The 'conceptual' and the 'iconic' are two ways that illustration can communicate a complex idea that is difficult to get across any other way.' (© *Providence Journal* 1986)
**Bob Selby**

figure | 46 |

"I'm not a snob about the kind of art supplies I use. Almost anything will do. I've been using styrofoam takeout containers and trash from the street in order to make my prints. I like the random glitches you get from using styrofoam." (© Michael Wertz 2003)
**Michael Wertz**

"I always work from the outside in. I start with a very broad concept then think composition, mood, and finally details. I've always found that the failure and success of a piece of art usually comes back to those first stages of broad ideas." (© James Bennett)
**James Bennett**

"Joe Bowler did these luscious oil paintings in the fifties and sixties. My art was nothing like his—which is precisely what made his work so awe-inspiring and special to me. I still have stuff of his that I tore out of magazines from 30, 40 years ago." (© Sam Viviano 2002)
**Sam Viviano**

figure | 49a |

"This was for a greeting card design. I was trying to picture a card that a woman might want to get for her significant other that was cute, but a little bit saucy too." (© Allport Editions 2003)
**John Coulter**

figure | 49b |

"It is said that imagination is the window to the soul, a divine attribute that lets one retreat from the real world to create a world for oneself—a world inhabited by fairies, rocketships, and angels. A place where I choose to dwell whenever possible." (© Chris Spollen, www.spollen.com)
**Chris Spollen**

figure | 50a |

"My greatest inspiration usually occurs in the sketch process. I'll do anything: I'll doodle; look at a blank piece of paper and see what I can visualize. If I have an idea—particularly if it seems like an odd one—I'll force myself to say, "why not," and try to draw it. It's important to get myself to relax and get my arm moving. I try to introduce errant lines (and lines of varying widths and textures) into a drawing and deal with them." (© Tom Bachtell 2003)
**Tom Bachtell**

(a)

figure | 50b |

"This is called *Margharita Diver.* I want to make it clear that I'm not advocating drinking for swimmers; I just loved the idea of one of those bathing-capped beauties from the 1950's diving into a big cocktail. Although the way things are going, it looks as though she's going to bang her head . . . "(© Tom Bachtell 2003)
**Tom Bachtell**

(b)

figure | 51 |

"I love the process. Have passion for what you want to do and stay curious. This can help empower you to overcome just about anything." (© Mark Braught 2003)
**Mark Braught**

figure | 52 |

Randy Palmer's illustrations, graphics, and page designs for the Dayton Daily News have won awards from the Society of News Design, the Associated Press, Print Magazine, the Society of Illustrators, and more. (© Randy Palmer/Dayton Daily News)
**Randy Palmer**

figure | 53 |

"Whatta babe! Everyone should hang out with a big blue ox. This illustration was done for *Babe's Blue Christmas,* a folk tale. In the story Babe has awakened after eighty-five years of slumber. Machines have replaced lumberjacks and oxen, and Babe becomes even more blue over the lack of forests. Paul is awakened by her mournful bellowing and pulls down the moon from the sky to set atop a huge pine tree to cheer Babe's holiday." The artwork here illustrates a passage where lumberjacks are skating with torches on the frozen river, much to Paul's delight. (© William C. Ersland)
**William Ersland**

figure | 54 |

"I enjoy the aspect of using watercolor that insists I don't have control over the medium. I like to control things, and I think I unconsciously chose watercolor because you're asked to let go, and trust what emerges from your hand, and heart—that it's just right to be there.

"I see my purpose in life as bringing more warmth and connectedness to the earth . . . and my art and writing are my way of doing that. I like the idea that my art makes people feel good inside. I don't have a lot of training. While I feel insecure at times because I don't draw things like they're 'supposed to' look, I think there's something about letting your insides guide and direct you that offers an essence that's very strong." (© Jacki Gelb www.gelbillustration.com)
**Jacki Gelb**

figure | 55 |

"Sometimes, the client will give me reference. I keep a whole file of reference myself. I can always find things online, but usually not stuff I can collage with—I have to recreate it. I used to do more caricatures where I tried to re-create the face with nothing of the original person, but I've actually gotten away from that. I find if I use a few features of the actual person, it lets me distort the face more. If I include some well-known characteristics, I can fool with the rest of the face more, and you still know who it is.

"If it's a portrait of somebody specific, I want to get more than just a likeness; I want to reveal a glimpse of the personality. I want something that hopefully reveals more than you would see in a straight photograph of that person. Do I ever get stumped? Oh, yes." (© Tom Nick Cocotos 2003)
**Tom Nick Cocotos**

figure | 56 |

"I think that every artist, to a certain extent, uses or borrows aspects from other artists' work. This does not mean outright copying or appropriating, but to absorb and transform the influences into your own visual language." (© Jud Guitteau)
**Jud Guitteau**

figure | 57 |

Marti McGinnis' illustration is actually a travelogue to a land of fancy and fascination. (© Marti McGinnis 2003)
**Marti McGinnis**

figure  58

Guy Billout's work tickles the intellect and teases the eye. (© Guy Billout)
**Guy Billout**

figure | 59 |

"I use gloss medium as part my process and as a final coat. It makes the darks darker and the lights lighter. It makes the colors richer—and if it makes it look like an oil painting? Then I'll take that as a compliment."
(© Loren Long)
**Loren Long**

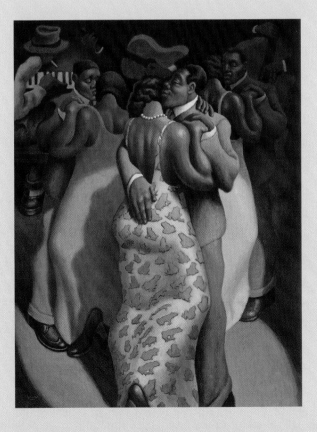

figure | 60 |

"Draw what you want to draw, and how you want to draw it. Your style will appeal to someone. Maybe not to a lot of someones, but at least to yourself." (© Phillip Mowery)
**Phillip Mowery**

figure | 62 |

"I love to draw and paint pictures. It really isn't anything more or less complicated than that. The actual process of looking, observing, drawing and mixing of stuff is what makes a picture tell a story. It is what I love to do, period." (© C.F. Payne)
**C.F. Payne**

figure | 61 |

"What I love about digital art and what inspires me all goes back to John Hersey, the first and greatest computer illustrator. Hersey's work covers the gamut of what is possible with computers." (© Led Pants)
**Led Pants**

(a)

figure | 63a and 63b |

(b)

"I have always had a fear of falling into a creative trench—doing things the same way, every time. So I vary techniques to keep it interesting. Yes, use the right tool for the job, but that can also slow the process down—learning and searching anew each time.

"Most of my work is acrylic on Bristol or cardboard primed with gesso (I sand the surface to give it texture and imperfections to add interest). Or, I draw in pen and ink on watercolor paper and add watercolor washes. Ideas are initiated from lots of sources: sketchbook drawings, notes and doodles while working on large paper, digital sketching, personal photos, picture files, or gallery shows.

"Then I move to pencil sketches and revisions on tracing paper. I photocopy and transfer the drawing to my painting surface via opaque projector using regular or colored pencil. With the acrylics, I build up the values with a very limited palette and gesso. The gesso gives it a dry, almost chalky surface which is good for additional pencil line. Gradually, I add more color, sometimes sanding the surface between layers.

"Sometimes, I will create a complete painting traditionally. More often, I work the painting to about 75% complete, then scan and finish in Photoshop, punching up color and adding details." (© John Dykes)

**John Dykes**

figure | 64 |

"One of the things I love to do is volunteer services to a worthy cause. What's cool is that they've all been real fun projects, and totally within my style parameters." (© Tuko Fujisaki 2000)
**Tuko Fujisaki**

figure | 65 |

"Questions of ethics, morals, and legalities are no-brainers. At these junctures, NO becomes the biggest word in your vocabulary. Beyond that, sometimes you must say NO to get to YES. Frequently, it's better to say NO and walk away. Occasionally, it's wise to hear NO and walk away. And, of course, you can just say YES.

"And if you say 'Personal life? What personal life?' It is definitely time to rethink things. 'Success' and 'quality' are relative, somewhat nebulous terms. In the long run, I want to be a successful person more than a successful illustrator. I want to be a great dad more than a great designer. I want to be a good husband and life partner more than a good businessman. There are trade-offs and consequences, and it's not an easy juggle. Understand. Prepare. Know why you do what you do. Live with the results, or make it better or different." (© Michael Fleishman 2003)
**Michael Fleishman**

You buy pastels in stick form, thick and thin; in singles or by the set. Boxed sets usually number from 12 to 144, and prices vary. You'll find *soft* pastels and *hard* pastels. Handy pastel pencils—a nice, "best of both worlds"—are also available.

The more popular soft pastels are usually found in a cylinder shape. Think less binder and more pigment. Hard pastels are formulated with less pigment and more binder, and come as squares or rectangles.

## OIL PASTEL

Oil pastels are made by combining oil, animal fat, or wax with chalk and powdered colors. Like water-formulated pastels, you can purchase this medium in boxes or by the stick. Again, prices vary and there is a wide range of set sizes available.

Oil pastels—even the cheaper choices—are very sumptuous and rich. Thicker, harder, and *greasier*, oil pastels are not as fragile as their soft pastel sisters. Because of this viscosity, they blend *in their own way*—in more of a creamy smear—but I wouldn't say they blend *better*.

It does takes a bit more effort to blend oil pastels, and the chunky or stubby sticks won't give you the detail and gradation of soft pastels. On the other hand, you can really work the surface quite energetically, and oil pastels are noted for concentrated color. This is a satisfying medium that offers exciting results that really smack of *oil-paint* effects (see Figure 5–4).

Figure | **5-2** |

Two of Mark Braught's delightful charcoal illustrations for *Cosmo's Moon,* by Devin Scillian (Sleeping Bear Press). Braught's initial drawings were such an instant hit with his publisher, they asked him to work more into the book. (© Mark Braught 2003)

Mark Braught's captivating pastel illustration was done for *Cosmo's Moon,* by Devin Scillian (Sleeping Bear Press). (© Mark Braught 2003)

Figure 5-4

Oil pastel is a great media that offers a very tactile response, vibrant color, and real paint quality. But there is absolutely no paint nor brush work on *City 1* and *City 2.* Pure oil pastel is rubbed in, scrubbed off, manipulated and blended with only my fingers. I did brush on a final coat of acrylic varnish to protect and seal the surface. (© Michael Fleishman 2003)

# CHALK AND CRAYON

Plain ol' simple crayons and chalk! Simply two good illustration tools found in a sly professional's art box, chalk and crayon have never been "just for kids." Of course, these drawing tools are probably all young artists' first creative media, but my guess is that both wax crayons and some form of chalk are probably somewhere in your studio (or should be). Perhaps you even have that classic coffee can of stubs and nubs you just can't throw away.

You can find both anywhere and everywhere. Putting it mildly, there is a wide range of size sets and a great variety of colors available. You don't have to spend a lot of money to find decent chalk or crayons.

I use both of these tools as part of my mixed media when drawing or painting traditionally (and always have). Both make marks that are bold and distinctive—never lowly, maybe humble—instantly, universally, and historically recognized. Thus, you will also find some digital variation of these utensils in most paint or natural-media applications (for either juveniles or adults).

# CONTÉ

The graphite pencil, as we know it, was invented by Nicolas-Jacques Conté during the eighteenth century. Conté crayons (and pencils) are an interesting option to working in charcoal. Definitely not as fugitive as charcoal, some consider the harder Conté crayons not quite as vibrant a media. But your results will certainly vary—try this very viable alternative for yourself and compare.

Bind color and graphite with gum and grease and you have a medium that is often referred to as hard pastel. Modern Conté comes in various grades, and in a complete spectrum of colors, but the traditional tones of black, brown, red, and white are often preferred (see Figure 5–5).

Figure | **5-5** |

*Irma.* Jeanne de la Houssaye draws caricatures on the scene. She uses white and sanguine (a red earth tone) Conté over black colored pencil to lay down her tone. Conté, chalk and crayon are all splendid drawing options. Consider these alternatives when looking for strong line, as well as a good value range. (© Jeanne de la Houssaye)

A detail from a lovely pencil study by Paul Melia. (© Paul Melia)

# GRAPHITE PENCIL

2B or not 2B—that is the question. The common pencil. The glorious pencil. It comes in several grades, ranging from "H," (hard) to "B" (soft). Something like an 8H pencil would be very hard, indeed, and makes more of a gray line. An 8B is rather soft and leaves a decidedly black mark. And, yes, you're right—this means an HB would be right in the middle of the scale.

In the right hands (like yours), one pencil within any grade can produce an impressive and extensive range of both line and tonal quality (see Figure 5–6). But many illustrators will mix and match, simultaneously using various grades to achieve their maximum results.

## Get the Lead Out: What You Have to Work with

Graphite comes in many forms, including:

- Round and hexagonal pencils: your "garden-variety," all-around standard pencil—don't leave home without it.

- Sketching and carpenter's pencils: ovular or rectangular. Use a knife to customize the wider lead. Thick and thin—thick to thin with just a turn of the point.

- Pure graphite pencil: just unadulterated lead. Comes in square, uncoated sticks or as coated and uncoated round pencils. Absolutely great for shading.

- Mechanical pencils. Click the release mechanism to get more lead. No sharpening for some varieties, others require special sharpeners or sandpaper to create a point.

- Powder: Rubbing graphite powder gives you soft, velvety tones. Probably will be a base for, or the complement to, line work to come. You'll need a rag or tortillon (a rolled paper rubbing stick), or just use one of the best drawing tools available: your fingers.

- Water soluble graphite pencil: It may seem funny to mention this in the "dry" chapter, but water soluble graphite pencils are a good way to introduce wash effects to your line and tone, without the fuss of watercolor or ink.

## Pencil Envy

Basically cleaner than charcoal, this equally light, portable medium is simple to use and comes in many sizes, thicknesses and shapes. Pencils can be sharpened in many ways, to a variety of points, and are capable of producing many effects: smooth blends and gradations, myriad textures, plus delicious line quality and variation. Subtle shading or striking contrasts of tone are all easily accomplished with this versatile medium. From high drama and raw power to delicate nuances, explicit detail and subtle suggestions—pencil can do it all, folks.

You can choose a range of barrel widths, as well as varying lead thickness and hardness. Graphite pencil is one of the most omnipresent of illustration mediums—another staple of every drawing class, basic and advanced. Probably a first choice for the beginner, graphite pencil is a primary tool of practicing professionals everywhere.

# COLORED PENCIL

Like its brother, the graphite pencil, you don't need a lot of materials and supplies to work in this medium. This is another inherently clean process; and just as with graphite, drawing with a colored pencil is simple and convenient.

Continued similarities are obvious. Colored pencils are widely available (and as with anything else, quality can vary). You'll find traditional color/value systems, as well as specific or special ranges (portrait colors, metallics, earth tones, pastel values—to name only a few). Pencils come in numerous sizes and different lengths, plus the standard barrel shapes (faceted, round, oval, and rectangle, and as squared sticks of pure lead). The pencils can be bought in sets (commonly 12 to 120) or individually.

Some illustrators work with one favored brand, others will mix it up, using different types of colored pencil (or mixed media) to get just the right look, response, or killer effect. And colored pencil manufacturers often color coordinate pencils with their markers. This smart continuity gives you significant layout options and creative opportunities.

You will find the scope of both harder and softer leads in a range of lead thicknesses. Sharpening can be handled in different ways. Electric or simple (even specialized) hand sharpeners, knife and razor blades, sandpaper or sanding pads can all shave a pencil to give you a wealth of points.

These fine points, squared tips, tapered or beveled edges (and custom shapes) will give you the cornucopia of marks that makes the extremely popular colored pencil medium a most exciting and diverse technique.

Much like charcoal and graphite pencil, colored pencil has become a popular tool of both professionals and beginners. It is easy to see why: exquisite shading and value work, as well as tremendous variance of line character; buttery smooth blends and gradations; layered,

Figure | 5-7 |

It is easy to see why the colored pencil enjoys such popularity. With one self-contained, multi-purpose drawing tool you can achieve a variety of effects: fine shading, transparencies, and value work; great line character; terrific blends, gradations, and textures. This piece is one of the 12 illustrations I did for a calendar (circa 1993) from Price Stern Sloan, Inc. (© Michael Fleishman)

jewel-like transparencies; the striking contrasts of flat tone with a multitude of both applied and suggested textures.

The versatile colored pencil can give you all this in one set, or one marvelously self-contained, multi-purpose instrument. See Figure 5–7 for an example of a colored pencil illustration.

## Watercolor Pencils

Call them water-soluble color pencils, if you will. This medium offers the same benefits of working with "normal" colored pencils, plus the added bonus of watercolors—all in one!

You enjoy similar advantages. Watercolor pencils are readily available by the pencil or in complete sets, and in the standard barrel shapes. These pencils boast somewhat softer leads, but mindful sharpening can be accomplished in all the typical ways.

Like all art supplies, brands will differ (in quality, build, and feel). Some illustrators prefer one make, others work with a variety, using different pencils for a specific response and/or effect. Regardless of which colored pencils you use (or in what combination), you reap the same artistic returns as when working with regular colored pencil: fine shading and a broad range of values; the ability to capture grand line character; sweet blends and beautiful gradations; rich, radiant transparencies; the same dramatic distinction of flat color against texture and pattern. Water-soluble colored pencil brings all that to the drawing table—without water.

Now throw into this mix the ability to combine line with wash. Do wet on wet techniques, as well as wet on dry (and the reverse). Rub and dab; scrub, dribble, and splatter. Use your finger

## STEP by STEP

## *Colored Pencil and Wash with Benton Mahan*

Obviously, this demo dovetails into our next chapter, Wet Media. Mahan is a seasoned pro and teaches Illustration at the Columbus College of Art and Design. His quick, versatile technique allows you to easily work with a bright palette or a dark, moody concept.

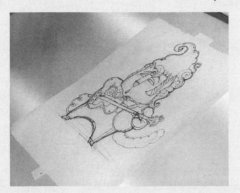

**Step 1:**
Gather reference and refine a sketch with a good solid black line to facilitate subsequent transfer via the light box (as well as for faxing or e-mailing). (Illustrations © Benton Mahan)

**Step 2:**
Next, take a 3-ply Bristol paper and paint it with a very thin mixture of oil paint plus mineral spirits (the mineral spirits make it dry faster). Paint quickly and wipe off to stain and tone the paper with a nicely colored surface. Mahan prefers ultramarine blue, raw sienna, and burnt sienna here.

**Step 3:**
Mahan says you could trace the drawing on the paper *first,* spray fix it, *then* coat with the oil wash and wipe off (one advantage being that you could use a kneaded or art gum eraser to pick out highlights before the wash completely dries). But here—and when the paper is dry (usually about 3 to 4 hours)—you'll transfer a pencil drawing to the paper *after* the staining procedure.

*continued*

# STEP by STEP

*Continued*

**Step 4:**
Before he lays in the color (shown here) Mehan might take a fine line technical pen and outline some of the key areas and erase stray pencil lines.

**Step 5:**
Painting flat color with watercolor dyes or acrylic inks, Mahan uses Dr. Ph. Martin's concentrated watercolors or Hydrus watercolors. His wash technique gives the illustrator a necessary color base.

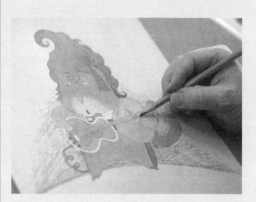

**Step 6:**
This foundation of color is important. Now Mahan renders with soft to medium pastel pencils.

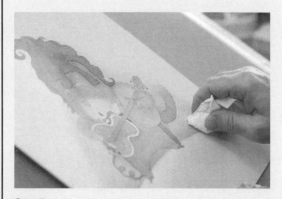

**Step 7:**
He then rubs and moves his color around to establish the crucial value structure.

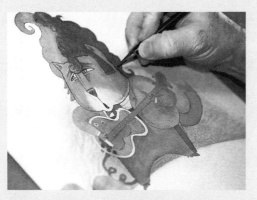

**Step 8:**
Spray with a light dusting of fixative so that the pencil will stick and apply more color. Remember to always spray this fix in a well-ventilated area (and of course, use a fixative that is odor-free and colorless).

**Step 10:**
You can change or enhance colors via a mixture of watercolor (or acrylic) with acrylic matte medium. Glaze with this color mix by layering color on top of color. If you want a darker look, top with oil paint, then wipe out areas with a cloth.

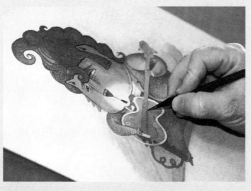

**Step 9:**
Bring out the highlights and dark tones with wax-based pencils such as Spectracolor or Prismacolor. Colored pencil is a marvelous tool to push both lights and darks and really pull that value system together.

**Step 11:**
Coming back in with colored pencil to fine-tune highlights and accentvate lower values. Check out the final of Mahan's rockin cat in the color insert.

Figure | 5-8 |

Wet and dry media mix naturally in my figure study *Red Up* (also see *Red Head Recline*, Figure 6–8). (© Michael Fleishman 2003)

to smudge color, or dip the pencil right into the water and work directly. Brush over a line (or patch) to blend, bleed, or dissolve pigment. Watercolor pencils complement marker, acrylics (indeed any water-soluble media), pen and ink, and graphite pencil. It's really a win/win inventive scenario.

## MIXED MEDIA

Any and all of our dry media can be used together. And consider that pairing dry and wet media can definitely be a tasty recipe (see Figure 5–8).

Sure, there's always some stuff that just won't mix well, and your experience and exploration will certainly demonstrate this point. But the savvy illustrator may be able to utilize the resist or fugitive qualities of certain combinations for a unique look. Saying that, much of the media discussed (in both Chapter 5 and Chapter 6) will work splendidly together, and some groupings are real naturals.

You may want to mix traditional media and methods with digital drawing, as well. The original figure study for Figure 5–9—a sketch from a figure drawing class during my school days—was done in Conté on newsprint. The line character is still fresh, but the thin paper has unfortunately discolored and been damaged in subsequent years. I took a digital shot of the work, brought the image into Photoshop and breathed new life into the old, fragile drawing.

Knock yourself out! There's a smorgasbord of media out there—go for seconds.

Figure | 5-9 |

It's just plain fun to create hybrid illustration, but I was also able to digitally rescue a favorite drawing that had seen better days. (© Michael Fleishman 2003)

# CHINA MARKER

China markers are not ink markers, and they don't originate from the orient. They do come in a variety of standard colors, and are primarily used to write on both porous and non-porous materials (such as *china*, glass, metal, plastics, rubber, etc.) and if anything, they are more akin to a colored pencil or grease pencil.

Like many industrial grade, hardware store, or common household "markers" (the grease pencil just mentioned, carpenter's pencil, Sharpie marker, and the simple ballpoint pen are other instances that come to mind), china markers also double as fine drawing tools that make excellent strokes on papers and canvas.

# ACCESSORIES

Papers and supports are addressed elsewhere in the book, so I'll point you in that direction for a refresher. But let's take a light look at some other drawing accessories. Some stuff will be absolutely necessary. A few items may be highly recommended; still others will be just for fun.

## Stay Sharp

Electric (or battery, as the case may be) pencil sharpeners are a real boon for the pencil artist (colored pencil or graphite). One of my better investments was buying a professional grade heavier-duty electric sharpener. The thing has recouped its slightly higher expense many times over in time and energy savings alone.

Electric sharpeners, of course, won't work with the so-called studio pencils (sketching or carpenter's pencils). Larger round or hexagonal drawing pencils may not fit either. But there is a whole school of thought that says regardless of the pencil, the best—*and only*—way to get right to the point is to fetch your knife and sandpaper to sharpen that sucker *by hand*.

Sharpening manually with the appropriate blade permits you to customize the pencil point. With a knife or piece of sandpaper, you can create a multi-chiseled edge, and facet, square, or round the tip. You also have the control to keep wood loss to a minimum.

This consideration of different leads and casings should not be underestimated. In certain instances, electric pencil sharpeners may eat soft leads alive or chew some woods to nothing, in no time at all.

## Take It Off

We all make mistakes, but don't commit the error of not having a number of good erasers at your drawing desk. Erasers are economical, if not downright *cheap*—get a bunch. Here's what I find to be the most appropriate:

- Kneaded-rubber eraser: gets my vote for the generic eraser to have if you could only afford one. Great for general erasing, as well as "pulling" tone or what's called "subtractive" drawing—*removing* pigment to create negative or lighter marks. You can actually mold the eraser into the point or shape that works best for your drawing situation. I should mention that playing with a finger-softened kneaded eraser can be a fun, harmless, and mindless distraction, as well as one of the great stress relievers for a harried illustrator.

- Pink Pearl and gum erasers (like Artgum): other selections for the MVP of erasers in your studio. A bit more like blunt instruments, these erasers are better for larger areas and good for a thorough cleaning of your illustration surface. They can work to subtract lines, and smudge or blend.

- Vinyl or plastic erasers: hard erasers that can be cut to create a custom tool, these babies can keep a sharp edge, and are great for detail work.

- Mix and match: the slightly more abrasive ink erasers; plain ol' pencil erasers can be anything but typical erasers (some *are* lame, but some are just wonderful); hand-held electric erasers; erasers in a pencil-like paper case or pen-style plastic barrel. Eraser pads contain a granulated erasing substance in a self-contained, self-dispensing little scrubber.

A general caveat would be to use a hard eraser on a harder surface, and a soft eraser on softer supports. But like any good respected rule, a skilled craftsman can break or bend those stipulations and still appreciate the universal guidelines.

| TIP |

One of the ways to create a lighter tone in a charcoal drawing is to *lift* the charcoal *off*. Just rub or press with a kneaded eraser to erase, lighten the value, or soften a texture. You can also replace the kneaded eraser with a piece of soft bread! Pull off a good chunk (try an unsliced loaf for a larger home-baked eraser) and use the same technique as with the kneaded eraser.

## Keep It Clean

They say if it ain't broke, don't fix it. But if you work in most dry media (especially the stuff prone to smearing, like charcoal, chalk and pastel, Conté, and pencil) you'll want to *fix* your work with a spray fixative.

Aerosol fixative is a colorless varnish you spray onto your work which adheres or "fixes" the tincture to the picture surface (alternatively, you could use a mouth diffuser—also called an atomizer—to do the job).

Said simply: I recommend a spray fix. Get the right stuff and nail your technique down. Practice and experiment with any fixative before you apply it to your final. Make sure there's truth in advertising: Is the fix absolutely colorless? Do steady, consistent, slow sweeps; from one direction and back, in complete arm movements. Gauge the proper distance and angle to ensure a light, even mist (with no saturation, splatter, or blobs), as well as complete coverage.

Just a safety warning here: Always—and only—spray in a room with proper ventilation (or out of doors). If available, use a spray booth. Consider wearing a spray mask as well.

## SUMMING IT UP

The dry media discussed in this chapter represent a spectrum of traditional and current drawing tools, which offer exciting visual opportunities and creative challenges for both professional and beginning illustrators.

| TIP |

To prevent smearing a drawing in progress, place a small sheet of paper under your hand and on top of the drawing. Don't slide this sheet, lift and raise it as you work on different areas of the piece.

| TIP |

Safeguard your good work with a cover flap! Two minutes of time and energy can serve to protect hours of creative energy. Accidents can happen, and this will not totally bullet-proof your illustration, but it's a great first line of defense.

# PROFILES

## *Jeanne de la Houssaye*

As Jeanne de la Houssaye says, "Different folks make different strokes, and each kind of stroke needs different materials." The eclectic New Orleans-based illustrator draws in a variety of formats, and runs down her supply list: "Digitally, it's Adobe Illustrator. Traditionally: Winsor & Newton professional grade and Holbein pigments; Arches 140lb or 300lb paper, sable or synthetic brushes—rounds, riggers, flats up to 2 inches. Also: Prisma black on coquille paper.

India ink (rapidograph or crowquill) on Bristol Board. Prismacolor and Conté over marker and watercolor, on watercolor paper. For caricature: Design markers (a friend gives me his old ones, I like 'em kinda dry) on plain ol' card stock from the copy center."

One of Jeanne's specialties is drawing on the scene. "I have a whole trick bag of stuff here, depending on where I'm going. Markers, Prisma, soft pencils, smudges, white and sanguine Conté, watercolor; newsprint, charcoal paper, sketchbook, and a watercolor block."

She feels brand names can be very important. "Good name-brand pigments are saturated; they spread and stay where you want them. Holbein's Opera and Winsor & Newton's New Gamboge (paints) are like nothing else in the world!

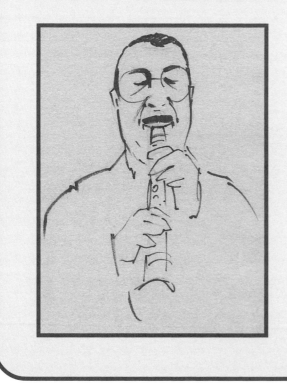

For Jeanne de la Houssaye, drawing on the spot is both a joy and a test. "To carry a sketchbook," she says, "and really *use* it, is a jet-propelled self education." The difficulties—myriad distractions, the noise and wind (as well as the technical challenge of drawing with a pad wedged in the crook of your arm)—are also the glories. All this forces an economy of line and a perception of shape that just may not happen in the studio. The excitement of the moment transfers itself to the page. "Any missing details and lack of polish are nothing compared to the bold, spare strokes drawn in the heat of the moment," de la Houssaye comments. "These lines contain the dynamic essence of the subject. It's in there—you just have to squint and look." (Illustrations © Jeanne de la Houssaye)

"A fine rag paper stands up to use and displays the colors as they were meant to be. Bad brushes don't hold paint, spread unevenly, and leave bristles in washes.

"Only quality drafting pens work consistently, and only the best ink ought to go in them," she continues.

"Venus pencils never have scratchy spots. Prisma makes pencils with lots of pigment in a good, smooth waxy binder." Saying that, de la Houssaye also admits to making nice money with her buddy's dead markers on mediocre-grade card stock.

"One of my favorite techniques way back in life drawing class was a matchstick dipped in any old India ink on newsprint or brown wrapping paper," Jeanne remembers, "and I studied with a watercolorist who used sponges, spatulas, credit cards, plastic rulers, Saran wrap—anything that makes a mark.

"I must come down on the side of the best materials with this caveat: Good supplies are only tools, and they can't replace good skills."

# PROFILES

## *PJ Loughran*

PJ Loughran says materials should never get in the way of *making something*—materials are merely a means to an end. "Using something you're not accustomed to allows for some interesting mistakes, "Struggling through new supplies leads you somewhere you haven't been before," he comments.

Loughran works organically, favoring a variety of brushes that produce very thin lines or chunky, thick lines. "I like what happens when you don't have enough ink on the brush," he points out. "As you're drawing, you run out of ink and get that nice, jagged stroke."

He likes a paper with appreciable tooth, and may paint with acrylics or "whatever colored paint I have lying around." He'll often use pieces of found paintings and incorporate them into a piece, but says, for the most part, "All the color behind a drawing is done in Photoshop—and it's basically collage."

It's all good—cardboard, a crayon scribble, whatever. Loughran looks for any and all elements that will add nuances, textures, and some kind of emotional subtext to the work. No fan of what he labels "digital aesthetics," he is likely to throw in "anything to make it look like it's not done on the computer!"

"It all starts and ends with the drawing for me," he states. The illustration is actually driven by the drawing—I think at the end of the day I'm really a drawer."

© P.J. Loughran

## in review

1. Compare and contrast pastel with oil pastel and chalk. Discuss similarities and differences based on your perception.

2. Discuss working with graphite and its many forms. What is the difference between an H and a B pencil? By the way, who invented the lead pencil, as we know it (and what else is he or she known for)? What's the best way to sharpen a pencil? Why?

3. What's messier—pastel or charcoal? How are these drawing tools made? What are the advantages/disadvantages of working with charcoal?

4. What studio supplies and general peripherals are *essential* for the illustrator working in dry media? What would be good to have? What would be a nice something extra?

## exercises

1. Match game: create a mixed-media illustration using 3–5 different dry media. Suggested illustration problems to solve: Inappropriate animals; the only item rescued from a house fire; who survived the shipwreck; my favorite ten seconds of all time; what's the deal with _____ (name a celebrity)? Work in a larger size, no smaller than 11 × 14 in.

2. Buy a cheap oil pastel box and do a still life (just a suggestion; free choice, if you prefer) with these tools. Now purchase the most expensive oil pastel set (or individual sticks) you can afford. Do the same drawing. One more time: use both sets to recreate the original drawing. Discuss how dissimilar tools affected your process, and any technical differences you discovered. One question to kick off the conversation: Do quality materials make a difference?

3. Crumble up a medium to large-size paper bag. Draw this object in: a) colored pencil; b) graphite pencil; c) pastel; d) Conté; e) crayon. Work bigger.

4. Do a large (18 × 24 in., or bigger) charcoal study of your bed at 8:00 A.M.

5. Pick one object with a pronounced surface texture. Draw this object with your favorite dry media. Draw this object again with your *least* favorite dry media.

© Joe Murray Studio, Inc.

Wet Media

*"Color, style, and paint application can make things look good and finished but they can't cover up bad compositions, boring concepts, or drawing mistakes."*

**Ali Douglass, illustrator**

*"I love the entire creative process of painting. It never feels difficult, because I enjoy it so much. And I relish the moment—somewhere in the middle of the paint process—when I feel the 'life' of that particular painting."*

**Tad Suzuki, artist**

*"When I was in college and some illustrator would come and give a lecture, a student would invariably ask a question like: 'What brand of watercolor paper do you use?' or 'How long do you let the background dry before doing the foreground?' During one such Q and A, a certain visiting artist answered: 'What difference does it make to you? I do what works for me. Figure out what works for you.' I've thought about that a lot and have decided he was absolutely right."*

**Gregory Nemec, illustrator**

## Chapter Objectives:

Explore watercolor and wash

Examine acrylic and oil paints

Discuss tempera, gouache, alkyd, casein and encaustic, oil sticks, and water-soluble oils

Consider combinations and mixed media

## Introduction

Previously, we dealt with dry media, and by extension, drawing. Here we will chat about wet media, and the act of painting. As previously stated (but it bears repeating), painting and drawing are at the ground roots of the illustration process (see Figure 6-1 for a *painterly* illustration that adeptly speaks to both basics), so let's begin the conversation by looking at various wet media and how we use the sundry supplies involved.

WET MEDIA

Figure |6-1|

Brian Shellito's precisely crafted portrait of a younger Katherine Hepburn captures the sophisticated actress as she was during Hollywood's golden age (© Brian Shellito).

# WATERCOLOR AND WASH

The venerable watercolor medium has been challenging and stimulating artists for centuries. Watercolors originated in ancient China, and "modern" watercolor techniques are credited to eighteenth-century artists like Turner and Constable. The paint itself is a mix (a suspension, to be more accurate) of pigment, water, binder, and a wetting agent (this enables a liquid to spread out and soak in, rather than bead up).

## Paint Grades: Student Versus Artist Quality

You'll see watercolor paint assigned to two designations: student quality (also referred to as "second quality" or "budget" paints) and artist quality (or "first quality" or "professional grade").

As a general rule—and even with similarly named colors—paint appearance, quality, and performance (including a color's "recipe," as well as its look, feel, and practical use) vary from brand to brand.

You'll be hard pressed to find set parameters qualifying what's tagged as "artist-quality" and "student-quality" (and, on a relevant side note, the same goes for brush sizing conventions).

So, just who makes those distinctions? As with brushes, it's the manufacturers, of course. But there are some readily apparent differences that dedicated watercolorists point out: Student-quality paints don't perform like the so-called professional grades. Your paint choices and range of pigment may be limited. Second-quality paints are mixed with less pigment and more extender (and fillers); pigment is not as concentrated, nor as pure. Sometimes inferior pigments are used in the paint formulas.

Higher-quality paints definitely warrant their additional expense. But like "bargain" brushes, "budget" paints have their moments and a place in your studio. Reputable manufacturers make good, lightfast paint, regardless of the price point. With paint, bang for the buck is where you find it. Despite classification (or price), if a certain paint works for you, use it.

## Pans and Tubes

Watercolor is typically sold in sets or separates; in tubes (large and small), pans and half pans. Tube watercolors are already wet, of course, whereas you will moisten the pan color to create your liquid media (also available are semi-moist pans).

Explore both tubes and pans. Both delivery systems are common and obtainable. Each offers challenges, conveniences, and advantages. You may prefer one to the other, or mix and match depending on the job or situation.

An interesting alternative to pans and tubes are color-impregnated sheets. You tear off a portion, plop it in water, and you're ready to roll. The size of the chunk—or the longer it sits in the water—determines the color depth. Apply color by dipping your brush into the wash (or work a wet brush directly on the surface of the slip).

| **NOTE** |

Partial to pans? You can squeeze tube color into empty pans, or access hardened paint, by slicing the side (or opening the bottom) of the tube. The result: down and dirty instant "pans!"

## Give 'Em the Brush

In all likelihood, your collection of brushes will be an assorted mix. Some brushes are simply utilitarian, others true bargains—great tools for the price. But many of your best and most treasured brushes will not come cheap.

A good brush will outperform and endure. You must think in the long term: thrifty watercolorists may go through several disappointing and cut-rate alternatives before realizing that they didn't really save money after all! Like bargain brand paints, economically priced—even downright cheap—brushes have their place and moments, but quality tools are a sheer joy to work with, and (if properly taken care of) promise a long and productive studio life.

As with all art supplies, build-quality and pricing really vary, but there are excellent watercolor brushes of every stripe: all-synthetics, blends of natural plus synthetic bristle, and the pure natural hair brushes (such as sable, goat, ox, boar, mongoose, pony, and squirrel).

| **NOTE** |

Mom alert! Take good care of (make that *revere*) your brushes, regardless of price or quality. Clean thoroughly. Store upright and securely. Make a good thing last longer.

Savvy watercolorists revere sable brushes, and for good reasons. While expensive, 100 percent sable brushes are soft yet sturdy, and wonderfully resilient. Yes, you can buy discounted sable brushes, but better sable brushes load water and paint generously, and are very springy. These first-rate brushes make and keep a fine point, and buoyantly bounce back to shape. Look for "red sable" (often labeled "pure sable"), but premium Kolinsky sable is considered the pinnacle here.

Figure **6-2**

Here's Jeanne de la Houssaye's *Feedmill.* One of thirteen paintings commissioned for a calendar, this lovely watercolor combines opaque and transparent pigments. Remember, while quality paint and brushes are certainly something to consider, it's not quite as important as your paint appearance and brush control. (© Federal Land Bank)

## The Range of Watercolor

The full watercolor repertoire of effects can be found in today's illustration: wash (both flat and gradated) and texture; wet-on-wet as well as wet-on-dry; the range of bright lighting and smoky atmospheric work; contrasts of transparency and opaque; a wet, juicy look or mottled drybrush; sponged, splatter, splotch, salted, speckling and grain; use of resists and additives—technically, watercolor gives the creative a mixed-bag approach that sets the stage for some rousing art. See Figure 6-2 for Jeanne de la Houssaye's excellent use of this exciting medium.

# ACRYLICS

Resin (plain ol' plastic to you and me), binder, water, and pigment join together to create an emulsion called acrylic (for *acrylate resin*) or acrylic polymer paint. Once the water in the mix evaporates, the paint dries rapidly, and resin and pigment combine permanently. The results: a long-lasting, hard-wearing, and supple paint—even-drying, water soluble, with easy clean-up. The popular medium attracts beginners and has made converts of many oil-painters. See Figure 6-3 for two examples of this very feasible form.

In development since the early part of the twentieth century, the first commercial acrylics (initially mixed with turpentine and compatible with oils) came out in the late 1940s to mid-1950s.

Permanent Pigments' Liquitex (for Liquid Texture) brand proferred true water-based acrylic paints and mediums (gloss and matte mediums, Gesso, varnish, and modeling paste) in 1955. Heavier-bodied colors in tubes (and gel mediums) subsequently premiered in 1963.

It was obvious something good was cooking. Industry standards, stringent testing, quality controls, and competitive benchmarks followed in due order. Of course, Liquitex was not the only

Figure | 6-3 |

Acrylic paints are widely considered the "best of both worlds." Offering watercolor as well as oil effects, this medium also gives you a broad range of unique results. The first real commercial acrylics only came out in the late 1940s to mid-1950s—a relatively new creative vehicle in the timeline of artistic expression. Jud Guitteau's illustration for *American Lawyer* and Jim Dryden's *One Stormy Night* are both done in this versatile form. (© Jud Guitteau, left, and © Jim Dryden, right)

choice for very long. Steadily, other makers brought out their own acrylic brands (and like Liquitex, continue to introduce and refine their product).

## The Scope of Acrylics

Like watercolor, acrylics offer the illustrator an extensive selection of artistic expression. You can thin acrylics down to a bonafide watercolor (and produce fine flat or gradated washes, as well as wet-on-wet and wet-on-dry).

Like working in oils, the acrylic medium makes it easy to build up a buttery, thick impasto. Other possibilities: layered glazing; gauze-like transparencies. Thick or thin opaques. Eye-catching textural effects, sharp, hard edges, and the complete range of lighting and atmospheric dynamics. Wet and luscious or dappled drybrush. A satiny, matte surface or shiny, jeweled finish are easy to achieve.

You can go from tactile and gritty to flat, slick, and smooth. Scrub and rub, sponge, splatter, and spray; splotch, speckle and grain. Work with resists; introduce additives; mix your media—acrylics are an eclectic instrument of expression for the active illustrator.

Figure **6-4**

Done with acrylics, Douglas Klauba's *Mercury Jack* is simply an exhilarating illustration experience. Klauba promotes brand names and materials of *consistent* quality, but says ultimately, "You must stick to what you know—use what works best for you." (© Douglas Klauba 2000)

## The Paint

Like watercolor, acrylic paint qualities—chemistry, appearance, performance, color range (even names of the colors) will fluctuate between brands. Acrylics are packaged in small and large tubes and jars. And like watercolor, acrylic paint is also assigned the same pesky designations: student quality (or "budget" or "economy" paints) and artist quality ("professional grade").

We can also refer to similar differences: Student-quality acrylic paints won't handle as well as the professional grades. Lower grade acrylics will offer fewer color choices than artists' quality (generally, color choice is a bit more limited than you'll find with oils and watercolors, anyway). The chemistry, ingredients, and the look and feel of the bargain brands may be inferior.

Better acrylics—like better art supplies universally—are worth the money. But, to paraphrase some earlier sentiments, "economy" paints can co-exist productively in your studio. Paint manufacturers are in the business to make money and in the big picture, bad paint doesn't sell. You can find good acrylics at a variety of prices. If a certain paint works for you, use it (see Figure 6-4).

## Paint That Is Definitely Off the Wall

Through the years, paint manufacturers have introduced a wide (and ever-growing) range of acrylics and related products. Makers have pioneered innovative paint formulations that open up new vistas for illustrators. All you need is a sense of exploration, an open mind, and some bucks, of course.

Look for:

- Gloss and matte finishes. 3-D (stiffer, heavy bodied) structural paint.
- Liquid acrylics.

- Light-reactive colors (fluorescents).
- Interference paint (also called opalescent, pearlescent, and iridescent): These light refractive colors seem to shift at different viewing angles.
- Glitter and metallics.
- Textural additives, extenders and retarders, and flow enhancers (in powders, pastes, gels, and liquids) are consistently being improved or introduced, as well.

Cool stuff, creative dynamite, and fun to use; but here's an important consideration—how will that special effect scan and print?

## A Brush with Density

You can use oil and watercolor brushes with acrylics. Both natural-hair (as in hog's hair—white bristle—and sable) and synthetic brushes (or synthetic blends) work well with this medium.

You'll find that the range of standard sizes and configurations (flats, brights, rounds, filberts) pertain, and the same watercolor and oil caveats apply. Construction and prices are all over the place. Some of your brushes will be almost throwaways—cheap beaters or workhorse tools. Others prove to be great utilitarian bargains—practical, cost-effective tools. And of course, many of your most valued brushes will be expensive.

Cheap acrylic brushes can—and do—work, but may *not* stand up to the rigors of your technique; a good, tough acrylic brush will both perform and last. See Figure 6-5 for two illustrations done with watercolor brushes.

## Brush Names

About those classifications: Flats are, well, *flat*. Rounds are indeed softly rolled or rounded. A bright is a shorter version of the flat. A filbert is much like a rounded flat or bright.

You have liner brushes and riggers, too. Both of these brushes are used for making thin and thick lines. The rigger, by the way, is called as such because it was originally used to paint lines of rigging in nautical art.

| **TIP** |

**TRACING PAPER IS YOUR FRIEND** Tracing paper is rather self-defined. We obviously use it to transfer an image; and as an acrylic painter, you can also utilize it to preserve an under drawing when painting opaque acrylic over graphite. Here's how:

1. Put a sheet of tracing paper on the image you want to transfer (or lines you wish to preserve). Trace the outline (and details) of the image with a pencil (perhaps an HB).

2. Flip the tracing paper over (place the back of the paper up), and rub the outlined image with more pencil. Remember, a hard pencil will leave a lighter mark (you may just want subtle lines—it's your call).

3. Flip the tracing paper back to the original side, and place it on the surface to which you want the image transferred.

4. Trace the outline again with a ballpoint pen or hard 2H pencil. Lift the paper and . . . the image is on the new surface!

To preserve an under-drawing when painting with a dark tone, here's a variation. When you reach step 2, rub the flipped image with a gray-colored pencil; then trace back with the ballpoint. The transferred image is now gray on dark.

Figure | 6-5 |

The glory of your brushwork and paint character, combined with the savvy of using the appropriate brush, make the difference. These illustrations are by Milton Knight, and are numbers 3 and 5 of a series of drawings illustrating H.G. Wells' short story, "The Temptation of Harringay." The tale is of a painting that comes to life and attempts to talk its painter into a deal with Satan; the illustrations originally appeared in the third issue of *Graphic Classics,* and were published by Eureka Productions in 2002. Materials: Winsor Newton series 707 watercolor brushes numbers 1,2, 7; FW acrylic artists' ink; Winsor Newton gouache (white). The spattering technique is also done with ink and white gouache. (© Milton Knight 2003)

# OIL PAINT

The bodacious old granddaddy of the painting process, oil paint (along with watercolor) ruled the artistic roost for centuries. A heady medium to work in, oils present a gratifying technical challenge for illustrators looking to exercise their hand skills and test their picture-making acumen (see Figure 6-6).

## Making the Grade

Like watercolor and acrylic paint, brand differences will be apparent when you compare and contrast. The chemistry and appearance, uniformity and permanence, performance and dry times, quality and price, and color range (and even names of the colors) will vary among brands.

Oil paints are offered in small and large tubes. Colors are sometimes grouped in series, based on primary pigment costs.

As for formulation of the paint itself, industry standards are quite stringent. Rigorous testing and tough quality controls are the norm. The competition to make the best oil paint has driven manufacturers to set the bar high. Demanding professionals have expected nothing less, literally for centuries.

Like watercolor and acrylics, oils may be designated as "student quality" and "artist quality." The student-grade paint won't perform as well as professional quality oils. Lower-grade oils offer fewer color choices than artist quality. The chemistry may differ, pigment levels will vary, ingredients might be cheaper and/or inferior (or perhaps diluted with fillers). The look and feel of the bargain brands may be different and inconsistent.

Oil paints as a rule won't be cheap, but good oil paint—like the best art supplies in general—are well worth the added expense. I have said this previously, but it bears repeating: "student colors" can certainly play a fruitful role in your painting routine. Modern paint makers make great paint at many price points. When you find that good paint, buy it, use it, and disregard counter-productive labels. As you grow professionally and artistically, you'll learn and understand what is truly cost and time effective for you (and what's best for your art), and you'll spend accordingly.

Figure **6-6**

Evoking the tradition of virtuoso painters like Pyle and Wyeth, Gregory Manchess gives us a swashbuckling, action-packed illustration, and a technical tour de force of the exciting oil-paint medium. (© Gregory Manchess)

# STEP by STEP

## *Jim Dryden*

Jim Dryden likes the freedom of working independently. In his words, he enjoys that feeling of "making something new, something that didn't exist before I thought of it and made it."

He usually paints with acrylics (either Liquitex or Golden's) on a variety of surfaces. His favorite? "1/4 in. Luan mahogany plywood," the illustrator says. "The grain of the wood comes through the layers of paint and becomes an integral part of the finished work."

Because of problems with color transience and paint flaking (plus the delicacy of his drawing medium), Dryden switched from gouache and charcoal to acrylics. He has been known to paint on scrap sheet metal, watercolor surface scanner board (when drum scanning is required), and on those heavy brown grocery bags. "I love this surface," he adds,. It has a great tooth. It's not an archival material, of course, but so far the grocery bag paper pieces have held up okay."

The illustrator also has an affection for language that has provided him with a smart method to brainstorm concepts for his imagery—he explores words related to the subject matter. So, for example, on a recent project for the American Neurology Society and Foundation, Dryden looked at the root meanings of many Latin neurological terms—words like *astrocyte* and *arborization.*

Another assignment was to do an illustration on death and dying for Blue Cross and Blue Shield. The illustration was to apply "a humanistic approach to a sensitive subject." The client also requested a human face (abstracted in the Dryden style), with "darker hues of blue, purple, orange, green; bright yellows, and a nice mix of mid-tones." Resource information and inspirational reference were forwarded and Dryden was instructed to keep in mind that hospice and comforting care are for everyone—in other words, no age- or gender-specific imagery.

Here's the step by step of Dryden's clearly perceptive visual:

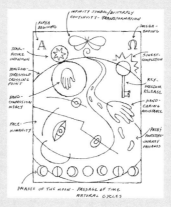

**Step 1:**
The rough sketch with notes.

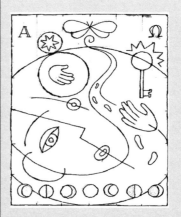

**Step 2:**
The revised sketch.

**Step 3:**
A wooden panel is gessoed.

**Step 4:**
The sketch is transferred to the panel and an under-painting of sepia is applied.

**Step 5:**
Continued underpainting with cadmium red and ultramarine blue is next.

**Step 6:**
Painting in progress.

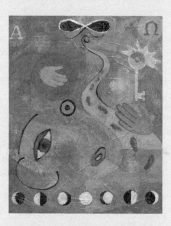

**Step 7:**
Painting in progress.

**Step 8:**
The final.
(Illustrations © Jim Dryden)

## What It Is

Pigment, well ground and very concentrated, is combined with a drying oil (like linseed oil, safflower oil, or poppy oil). This mix is more than likely extended with additives that improve plasticity, uniformity, and permanence.

The combination of certain pigments with specific drying oils will determine the drying rate for a particular paint. Mix colors and that chemistry affects the dry time. Opacity, stain quality, and tint strength will vary from color to color.

Adding mediums (like varnish) and diluents (something that dilutes) like turpentine or mineral spirits will enhance or thin your paint, but we don't want to merely "water down" oils. In the right ratios, these liquids help to explore or exploit different paint treatments, but too much of a good thing (or the inappropriate choice) and you compromise adhesion or drying rates (which can weaken paint quality and stability).

| NOTE |

Even today, you can still mix your own paint and/or media. The process demands some time, but is fairly uncomplicated, may save you money, and (depending on your skill) will almost certainly facilitate better quality control.

## What Oils Can Do

Oil paint manifests vast creative endeavors. It is a medium that is only limited by the artist's hand skills and personal vision, as history aptly points out.

Thin the oil down to a wash; add medium to glaze color. Stroke fine lines or lay down fields of flat, smooth tone. Gradate or blend. Build up a heavy, creamy impasto. Thick or thin, as well as thick to thin opaques, are easy. Layer delicate transparencies to create a jewel-like glow. Simulate a visual texture or aggressively attack your surface for the real thing.

Go from sharp, hard edges to active and raucous. Blur reality, smudge out the facts. Suggest detail or make it all crystal-clear. Scumble and drybrush a parched landscape, or go liquid and juicy. Complex lighting and moody atmospheric effects. It's all there at the business end of your brush.

## Brushes

While you can use oil and watercolor brushes with acrylics, certain acrylic brushes may be incompatible with harsh solvents and the heavy-bodied texture of oil paint (oils may bead and clog the hairs of some synthetic white bristle brushes, for instance). Certainly think twice before using those expensive, precious, and delicate sable watercolor brushes for this medium.

In general, hog bristle brushes are your best choices for painting in oils. But these days, you'll find impressive synthetic bristle brushes (stiff and soft-hair varieties) and bristle blends (natural hair plus synthetic fiber together) that are more than up to the task.

You'll find the standard range of sizes and configurations (flats, brights, rounds, filberts, riggers, and fans). The same watercolor/acrylic caveats apply: Price and construction vary, and you'll use an assorted combination of bargain basement to costly tools.

# ALTERNATIVES

Oils, acrylics, and watercolor are not the only games in town, of course. There are other wonderful (and wet) media out there. Let's take a look at a few other options.

## Gouache

The word may be hard to spell, but this water-based/water-soluble medium is harder yet to resist. Also called "opaque watercolor" or "designers' colors," gouache is highly pigmented, may contain white chalk or paint, flows with ease, and gives you flat, clean, bright color (see Figure 6-7).

Figure | 6-7 |

Robin Zingone's bouncy style and lively composition make this illustration for pharmaceuticals a fun read. It's painted in Japanese Sumi ink and opaque watercolor—also known as designers' colors, or gouache. This paint is similar to watercolor or acrylics, but is a challenging, satisfying alternative. (Robin Zingone 2003. All rights reserved)

Gouache is akin to watercolor and acrylics in process, tools, and supplies. But remember, gouache is neither flexible acrylic, nor fluid watercolor. This presents some technical challenges for the illustrator. Case in point: Beautiful opaque passages or subtle transparencies are possible with this medium. But you would need to mix acrylic medium with your gouache to glaze over that color without breaking down your base coat.

Watch your chemistry, too. If your application is too thick, gouache will crack and flake off.

But the end results are well worth any extra effort. As an endnote, I should mention that there is actually an exciting derivative called acrylic gouache that many illustrators swear by. It's not cheap, but expense is often relative.

## Tempera

Tempera paint has been an artists' favorite for centuries. Classical tempera—or more accurately, *egg tempera*—is formulated from egg yolk and oil. Tempera can also be made with egg yolk plus distilled water. The powder-based grade school art class staple you remember was most likely *not* made with egg yolk (and likewise, some gouache is identified as tempera). No matter what the exact recipe, it's all water soluble.

Store-bought, ready-made egg tempera is available, but many artists doing tempera still prefer to make it themselves, personally exercising a more stringent quality and color control.

As the tempera process can be exacting, impatient illustrators looking for quick, creative gratification need not apply. Painted tempera dries almost instantly, so a picture must be developed slowly, perhaps through layers of glazing; maybe by stippling or dabbing small strokes.

As with gouache, the chemistry is important, too. The wrong ratio of water to paint, and you get an unfortunate eggshell crackle that veins and flakes right off the surface.

But before you write off the process as too high-maintenance, have you seen the results? Like gouache, the technical challenges that go with this territory are well rewarded. Tempera done right can give you detailed pictorial nuances, not to mention vibrant, shimmering color that seems to shine from within.

## Casein

Quick-drying casein is an ancient media that actually derives from milk curd (and yes, thank you, it is indeed used in cheese). The casein base is an ingredient also used in glues. Initially water-soluble, casein turns more insoluble with time. My research here turned up some contradictions. Certain experts state that the paint becomes water-resistant, but not waterproof. Others maintain that, gradually, casein does indeed become impermeable.

Casein paint is somewhat close in look and feel to egg tempera (the more popular historical choice). Not very elastic, casein nonetheless flows easily, covers well, and is a good paint for detail work. You can even polish the finished surface to a soft shine!

## Alkyds

Handling much like oil paint, alkyd paints dry faster than oils but slower than acrylics. Thus, you can take advantage of classical oil painting technique, without the traditional wait times. Alkyds dry uniformly (like acrylics), and to an even sheen. They don't have as much pigment as oil paint, so colors aren't as concentrated; however, the medium can be used with (or instead of) oils and is quite durable and elastic.

## Water-Soluble Oil Paints

It may seem like an oxymoron, but water-soluble oil paints—oil paints that actually mix with water (and clean up with soap and water)—are an interesting breakthrough. Grumbacher's Max and Winsor & Newton's Artisan paints are in this category.

These people-friendly—and environmentally safer—paints (no toxic solvents necessary) don't quite perform like typical oil paints, but the benefits of such a medium should be fairly obvious.

So, after all this, we learn that oil and water *do* mix. Now, does 2 plus 2 actually equal 5?

## Oil Paint Sticks

Check out what might be dubbed solid oil paint—oil paint sticks—at your local art store. We're not talking oil pastel (or pastel pencils). Nor are we referring to crayons or grease pencil.

You can use oil sticks with the media just mentioned (and with all manner of other paint and drawing tools, on all types of supports), and there are some similarities. But there are basic differences: This is real oil paint that dries permanently. The sticks can be thinned and blended, dipped and brushed; they can be manipulated, altered, spread or built up—all with the same tools and additives as tube oil color. The sticks even develop a protective skin between work sessions that must be removed before use.

Well, is it a drawing tool or a painting tool? Frankly, you'll have too much fun to care.

## Encaustics

Painting with encaustics is intriguing. Here, you mix pigments into hot wax (or alternatively, melt crayons) via a double boiler, then fuse this blend onto the surface of your work (I'd recommend "beater" brushes or other tools—palette knives; old metal spoons, spatulas, kitchen knives or similar). You'll need a strong support for the piece as this medium builds up a heavier, raised (but decidedly rich and tactile) surface.

## Mixed Media

For me, just *having* different media available provides one of the bigger imperatives for *using* it all together. Mixing media (and techniques, as well) is nothing new; it's always been a bright idea that makes for some exciting illustration. See Figure 6-8 for one of my mixed-media creations.

Combining similar water-based media is a no-brainer. Watercolor pencils with watercolor is an obvious match. But if you grab your grease pencil, crayon and/or oil pastel, you now introduce stick media *and* resists into the visual vocabulary of that picture.

Figure | 6-8 |

A little of this, a little of that. Combine obvious (even offbeat) media choices to create exciting creative opportunities. I'm just naturally inclined to throw a variety of wet and dry media together, as in *Red Head Recline*. Acrylic plus other water-based media; add some charcoal or colored pencil. Maybe a little grease pencil or crayon with oil pastel? Go ahead—mix it up! (© Michael Fleishman 2003)

Think about those same oil pastels with oil paint sticks when painting with acrylics *or* oils. Permanent marker can mark a surface, or give you an interesting bleed with acrylics. Most drawing media—colored pencil, charcoal, pastels or chalk, and so on—work just great with watercolors. Collaged papers and lighter items, or heavier 3-D elements adhered to a surface, can promote a sculptural aspect of your illustration concept. Bring your photography in as part of the visual mix, too.

What seems like a perfectly natural combination can frequently be a real revelation and significant leap forward. Perhaps this is because the purist in us can sometimes dominate the intrepid explorer. It's always nice to transcend that tightly wrapped part of our psyche.

Regardless of the motivation, you have to go for it. Much of this stuff just screams out at you to shake and bake that illustration to new creative levels.

## SUMMING IT UP

Ripe opportunities for creative challenge and growth are endemic when working with wet media. Painting is one of the core artistic ventures. In its great variety the painting process offers the illustrator an excellent showcase of technical ability and personal expression.

# PROFILES

*Sarajo Frieden*

Sarajo Frieden's art encompasses both digital and traditional formats. "I use the computer and paint mediums for my illustration," she begins. "I work in gouache, acrylic, and sometimes oils. I love gouache," the illustrator says, "because of the incredibly beautiful colors and the way the paint handles—for the control, and how the paint mixes. But I've recently been painting on wood panels and I like acrylic for its layering abilities."

Frieden uses Winsor & Newton or Holbein paints for her gouache work, and experiments freely with different acrylics. She has her eye on oil paint for the future but says, "I don't care for the solvents but, again, I adore the rich colors."

She's on a Mac for digital work, and primarily uses Illustrator and Photoshop. "I'm having a lot of fun exploring Illustrator," she smiles. "Using a computer has probably changed my illustration process. The computer has pushed my work in new directions, but I don't think the two forms—digital and traditional—are so separate, it is more about the intention of the work I am creating.

"In general, I'm trying to continually feed my visual inspiration. There are so many things which go into the mix: travel to wild places; galleries and museums; dance performances, music; handmade signs in my neighborhood—all affect my process.

"I do what I love, and I enjoy the feeling that I am adding something to the world in a positive way. My parents taught me by their example to pursue my dreams with passion. Never, ever give up, if this is what you are meant to do."

Sarajo Frieden's intriguing *Sea Serpent*. The mystical illustration was done in gouache—a down to earth paint that Frieden skillfully exploits with some magical results. (© Sarajo Frieden)

# Accessories and Peripherals

Here's a list of studio items and facilities you may want to consider when working with wet media. This list also applies to dry media and other general studio techniques.

- An easel (or two).

- Drawing table and desk (a real one; above and beyond your drawing board); worktable and additional work surfaces.

- Brushes (of course), but also alternative brushes: toothbrushes, house paint brushes, and rollers. "Hake" or "Sumi" brushes (handy, relatively inexpensive Asian brushes. Heads-up—I dig my "hake" brush, but it sheds a bit). Brush extenders (devise, make, and attach these yourself).

- Alternative paints: good-quality household or industrial-grade paints (like latex, enamels, and aluminum paints). Cel paint (for animation), inks, and dyes would also qualify in this category.

- Storage: shelves, cubbyholes, boxes, containers, etc. File holders or filing cabinets, cabinet or closet, flat files or racks; clothes line and clips (to hang and dry art).

- Color charts, painting how-to books and magazines. Technique and/or professional magazines.

- Access to (and an adequate) water supply; good ventilation; excellent lighting; chair(s), lights, lamps, waste basket(s); bulletin board(s).

- Water, paint, and liquid containers: tubs, jars, cans, bowls, cups; tubs, jars, cans, bowls, cups (to mix and hold paint); containers (in general) to hold utensils and tools; funnels. Be kind to the planet: recycle with/from plastic containers.

- Mixing trays, palettes. Store-bought is fine and dandy, but again, think about Mother Earth: recycle with/from plastic containers when you can.

- Backboard (to stretch paper).

- Scratchers and scrapers; color and paint lifters. Cutting tools (knives, blades, scissors), palette knives, spatulas; burnishers and embossers; utility brushes; foam (or nap) rollers; foam brushes; sticks; rope.

William Ersland, James Bennett, and Peter Kuper have set up comfortable and functional studio environments. Here, they create finely honed and richly detailed illustration. (© William C. Ersland, top; © James Bennett, bottom, and © Peter Kuper, p. 151)

- Rags and sponges; tortillons and rubbing sticks; cotton swabs; rulers and straight edges; templates and stencils.

- Stapler, staple gun; tapes, paper glues, other adhesives; sandpapers and abrasives.

- Toolbox of basic tools; toolbox of any process-specific tools; tack hammer (and tacks).

- Grounds and base coats, varnishes and fixatives; process-specific thinners, solvents, and binders (such as linseed oils, turpentine, poppy or safflower oils, mineral spirits, damar varnish, stand oil); both natural and synthetics, homemade or store bought; both natural and synthetic process-specific mediums (as for watercolor: gum arabic, glycerine, ox gall, gelatin sizing, alcohol, perhaps distilled water).

- A mahlstick (an extended wrist elevation that rests against a canvas, keeping the side of your hand off the surface); a hand/wrist rest.

- Photocopier or fax machine with copy functions (reduction/enlargement capabilities are nice); light table or light box.

- Portfolio or carry-all (more than one, in different sizes).

- Paper cutter; matting and mounting facilities.

- Video cassette recorder and TV; slide projector; music system; overhead and/or opaque projector.

# PROFILES

## *Jud Guitteau*

Jud Guitteau has just a few well-chosen words of wisdom for you: Believe in yourself; find your own visual vocabulary; do work that resonates with some truth to it.

One truth is that as this illustrator sees his work change and grow richer, good materials make a difference. "Don't scrimp here," he says, "especially when it comes to paper and brushes." Guitteau favors Golden or Liquitex acrylics in bottles, which he finds very easy to use.

Guitteau's conceptual process is classically academic and logical. When an assignment comes in, he initially reads the copy (as available), and routinely discusses the theme with the art director. Once he familiarizes himself with the project as completely as possible, he looks for words or phrases that suggest a visual metaphor. He then makes quick sketches in a sketchbook. One to three of these sketches are sized into a roughly 5 × 6 in. format, and a photocopy is then faxed to his art director. To speed all this along, Guitteau sometimes develops the sketches directly in Photoshop and e-mails a color JPEG rough.

These first roughs are his visual cues—the starting point of the actual illustration. Here he is trying to find an overall structure for this assemblage of pictorial symbols. "This structure is important," the illustrator comments. "It could be realistic, cubist, folk, light-hearted,

whatever; the style of which is usually in constant development."

The goal now is to keep the work fresh, and at this point the illustrator will often open up coffee table books of his favorite artists (David Hockney, Milton Avery, Matisse, among others), simply to put his mind into what he calls an "open place."

When an image is chosen, he then scans that sketch into Photoshop, (if he hasn't done so already). Here the artist develops the color scheme, as well as both picture content and size.

Guitteau quickly creates the next version of the image by laying out broad colors and the main elements of the picture *with acrylic paint*. "I find this gives me the best of both worlds, I can use the computer to work out ideas in a loose, free style, and keep the hand-done feel I like—a quality which was missing in my all-digital stuff."

This acrylic painting is then scanned into the computer, and the image is fine-tuned and finished. Working on a Wacom tablet, Guitteau can add any additional, small, or difficult to produce elements digitally. The finish is usually sent as a high resolution JPEG to the art director.

Jud Guitteau says, "The simple fact is that I have a profession that allows me to pour all of myself into my work." And the viewer must do the same: Guitteau's illustration captivates the eye and stimulates the intellect at the same time. (© Jud Guitteau)

# PROFILES

## *Gregory Manchess*

Gregory Manchess paints in oils and uses mostly Old Holland colors. "These have the most amount of pigment in the tube; therefore, they're very strong and cover well," he tells us. The illustrator also uses Gamblin products like Galkyd, an additive that speeds drying and adds elasticity to the paint film. "I usually use hog bristle brights and synthetic flats," Manchess points out, "and Gamsol odorless mineral spirits—turpentine was too toxic."

Manchess feels that his process always begins with observation. "Reading, travel, life in general. Ideas come after you percolate awhile . . . thinking intensely, then letting the mind rest. Looking at other people's work is really exciting, he adds.

Manchess is a painter other painters point out; he's a pro who knows his craft *and* the business. When asked what advice he can give to folks coming up, he begins with this: "Don't take no for an answer—keep going; keep learning; keep observing. The figure is king—*learn it.* There's always work for the one who can do the figure well.

"*Draw;* work to improve your drawing and composition skills constantly. This will help, no matter the medium—especially computer work. Don't let the computer do it for you!

"Use several portfolios in the beginning. One portfolio that caters to clients' needs, then other portfolios that collate different ap-

Greg Manchess says, "Fully explore and be freely influenced, but only in the mad search for yourself. *Your* approach only comes out of *you.*" Greg's exquisite oil paintings make his point abundantly clear. (© Gregory Manchess)

proaches/techniques. For instance, one book focuses on florals, and another carries only figure and portrait work. Don't mix them up. *Know your client.*

"Your 'special' portfolio is the one that showcases your true passion; that particular look or direction that pumps your adrenalin. Work to perfect this portfolio for the rest of your life; this is the portfolio you want them to remember. But show it wisely, and only to those clients that will be interested.

"Stay optimistic. Do *not* get swayed by other struggling artist friends. And don't ever treat your passion as a business!"

# PROFILES

## *Robert Saunders, Steve Dininno, Brian Shellito*

"I like Winsor & Newton watercolors, generic acrylics and brushes, along with D'Arches cold press paper," says Robert Saunders. His favorite art utensil is a "huge, fat sable watercolor brush I bought in Italy 25 years ago—the brand I don't know. You can't replace sable brushes cheaply nowadays; the prices are through the roof. But, a good medium-size sable brush is still my all-time preferred tool."

Brian Shellito tells us that as he gained experience and his paintings improved, he gradually shifted from medium grade Winsor & Newton colors to Old Holland oil paint. Why? "Better texture, and the pigments don't thin out as much," Shellito remarks. "These paints mix fine with my Winsor & Newton oils, so I am basically replacing colors as I run out. With better paints the cost goes up, so I am substituting a tube at a time.

"I am still testing different surfaces a lot. Canvas, linen . . . I am also fond of the look I get from painting on gessoed paper. Different amounts of gesso and thickness of brush strokes will give the painting different looks. And this is inexpensive paper, I might add, but with some strength and weight. Printmaker's paper is my favorite—specifically Rives BFK."

Steve Dininno says, "I work with Liquitex acrylic paint on 4-ply plate finish white Bristol Board (usually a brand called Rising). Before painting, I prepare the surface with Liquitex Gel Medium (over my drawn pencil outline) to make the paper more durable and less absorbent.

"I use Liquitex because it's always easy to find a wide range of colors and, also, because I've just become so familiar with its properties. I recommend trying a range of pigments and deciding what feels right for one's particular sensibilities.

"As for my choice of paper, weight is important because acrylic is a water-based medium, and can cause curling with anything lighter than 3-ply. I choose a plate finish because I don't want to have to fight the tooth of the paper when doing precise, detailed passages. If I want roughness, I can do it myself with the paint. The gel medium enables me to not worry about getting an expensive paper as it will make almost anything that's the right weight and texture suitable."

Dininno today uses a combination of painted and digitally created imagery. He marries the two mediums by painting particular passages of an image and pairing them with other icons and tex-

Nightcap by Brian Shellito. (© Brian Shellito)

tures created in Photoshop. "It's both a time saver and affords me the opportunity to introduce varying textures and elements that I wouldn't use in a straight painting," the illustrator says.

Here, Saunders agrees. "The computer has supplied me a more forgiving platform than just paint on paper," he states. "I can now digitally correct flaws with far less effort than by hand traditionally. I am able to pursue creative routes I didn't before (such as distorting, flopping, montaging, and color substitution), almost at whim."

He has used basically the same "art box" over the years, but now with the addition of a computer, scanner, and Photoshop. Saunders says that new materials and technology have definitely affected his illustration process. He still works on the drawing board, but tweaks in Photoshop. "The original hard-paper version is not viewed as the be-all and end-all anymore,"

Saunders explains. "It is no longer the culmination of the creative process, but one step along the way to a digital result, and one among many possible variations."

It's a slightly different story for Shellito, who says, "I've done a lot of digital work as a staff artist but as a freelancer I'm all traditional." He pauses here and smiles, "I love my Mac, but it just doesn't smell as good as linseed oil.

"For many people the computer made things *too* easy. But I think it's balancing out now. The cream of the digital crop has risen to the top and is pushing the medium in new directions.

"Painting is an ever-evolving process," Shellito sums up. "It can never be 'perfected' or 'mastered' completely. But ask me the same question about materials and methods a few years from now and we'll see if the answer is different."

*Lighthouse* by Steve Dininno. (© Steve Dinnino)

*Pianist* by Robert Saunders. (© Robert Saunders 2003)

## in review

1. What are casein, alkyd, encaustic, tempera, and gouache? What is the difference between tempera and gouache?

2. Research: what do we mean by the term "water-miscible" paints—and what exactly are they? Why/how do these media work?

3. What is the difference between acrylics and watercolors? Acrylics and oils? Alkyds and oils? What are encaustics and oil sticks? In each of these comparisons, what are the similarities?

4. You find a treasure chest on a desert island. With one mighty blow from a handy coconut, you crack the lock and swing open the lid. You're rich! Ten tubes of the finest paint (stolen from a painting cruise of the Caribbean, and hidden by a pirate who painted on Sundays only) are revealed. What are the ten colors?

5. Who are your painting heroes—current or historical? In your estimation, what five painters are vastly underrated? Why? What five painters are greatly overrated? Why?

## exercises

1. Do five self-portraits or (the same) portrait five times. Each version must be done in a different wet medium. Size: 9 × 12 in. minimum.

2. Working larger (18 × 24 in. minimum), do a painting that can be sectioned off into at least 16 squares or rectangles. Each of these subsections will be executed in a different wet medium.

3. Create a painting with your opposite hand. The end result will probably be somewhat expressionistic. Compare and contrast this piece with your "normal" work; what does this piece teach you?

4. Do a mixed media piece involving at least five different wet and/or dry media (including collage and/or embedded elements as one choice). For an added challenge, make it a representational (*not* abstracted) piece, perhaps a portrait or still life.

5. A fun exercise is to do a group or "round-robin" painting. Get a small group of painters together (about five, more if you have the size—certainly a wall mural can accommodate a crowd). Mutually decide the parameters of subject matter and media. Each painter works on the painting in short bursts for a number of pre-determined cycles; or painters contribute for a one-time only, designated time frame before passing it on.

6. Hold a group show with a specific theme.

Pens and Inks

*"The computer is really good for balancing a checkbook. I have Photoshop and Illustrator, but don't really use them much. Part of the pleasure of doing illustration is the work itself—the physical interaction of you and your materials. My friends are always trying to convince me that I could get the same effect with the computer and I could make changes faster. Hey, working on the computer is just fine, but it's not been quite as enjoyable for me."*

**Bill Jaynes, illustrator and educator**

*"Koh-I-Noor made this great yellow and black sketch pen that has been discontinued. This pen featured a fillable cartridge, and the nib was just flexible enough to get a broad variance of line width. Now it takes a myriad of nibs that I must continually dip for ink to obtain the same effects as that one sketch pen! The feel is not as smooth and the flexibility is definitely not the same—these nibs simply don't work as well."*

**Daryll Collins, illustrator**

*"Most of my illustration is first done off the computer with magic markers, brush pens, Chinese bamboo brushes, and various black and white drawing tools. I like the variation of line that a brush gives me. I also use lots of different papers: name brands, off-brands, and no-brands. Using different materials makes it more interesting and fresh each time."*

**Mike Quon, illustrator**

## Chapter Objectives:

Explore pen, brush, and ink

Look at related "specialty" inks, pens, and processes

Discuss markers and related fiber tips, roller balls, felt tips, gel pens, ballpoint

Consider combinations and mixed media

## Introduction

In Chapter 6 we addressed wet media, and looked at painting. This chapter focuses on drawing and painting with pen, brush, and ink.

As we've discussed, the act of painting and drawing is technically challenging, professionally rewarding, and personally, just plain fun. Working with pen, brush, and ink makes for an enjoyable test of hand, eye, tools, and materials. Ink techniques are vital subsets of the

**PENS AND INKS**

illustration practice, while drawing and painting are the very underpinnings of illustration. Let's begin our exploration.

# WHAT DO WE LABEL AS INK?

"Ink" by default is often generically considered to be *black*. Take that a step forward and you might say we routinely call it *Indian* (or *India*) *ink*. This is like calling a photocopy a *Xerox* or asking for a *Kleenex* when we want a tissue.

But inks come in the proverbial rainbow of colors, both water-soluble and waterproof. Traditional black ink is made with pigment. Colored inks are formulated from dyes (and might be thought of as dyes, but there are also *pure* dyes available).

| NOTE |

Lampblack is the superfine, powdery form of carbon left when oils containing that carbon are burned. The densely opaque, liquid black ink we commonly call "India ink" (or "Indian ink") is a solution of that carbon pigment, and a binder. You know India ink—water-soluble when wet, but permanent when dry. You may not realize, however, that India ink can also be found in a range of colors beyond basic black.

Waterproof colored inks are often referred to as "artists' colors" or "artists' drawing inks." A dense shellac is added to this ink to make it waterproof, so this medium might quickly and easily jam a pen or stiffen a brush. With this in mind, you wouldn't normally use waterproof ink in fountain or technical pens that may clog easily.

# WHAT PEN AND INK CAN DO

Pen and ink rather defines versatility. You can do so much with this medium: lines, cross hatching, hatched line, evenly hatched (groups of parallel) lines; gradated vertical lines, gradated horizontals, gradated crosshatch, gradated parallel hatch, broken hatched; thick to thin, thin to thick; toned stipple; dots and dashes; spatter, spray, scribble, line with wash, toned wash; outline (but keep it minimal—too much outline and you get a distinct coloring book effect). Use these line techniques to promote shape, capture details, and push value. See Figure 7-1 and 7-2 for some explorations into the possibilities of pen and ink illustration.

# TYPES OF PENS

There is literally a world of variety out there, and a history of both craftsmanship and penmanship that goes back millenniums. In light of all that, let's take a look at some pen types available for you today.

## Dip Me

The dip pen is an age-old inking device that employs holders and nibs. A nib is the sharp, shaped, detachable metal point—the "pen"—that both carries and transfers the ink. A dip pen

Figure | 7-1 |

The sound, feel, and rhythm of pen tools working a toothy paper. Exploring light and dark (as well as light *to* dark) with fluid ink line and tone. The relationship of values as expressed through the interaction of dot, line, and shape. All just some of the allure of a fascinating medium. *Rat* is by Bill Jaynes, who used a toothbrush to splatter his ink and tracing paper masks to achieve that soft edge. A fine or coarse splatter is controlled by how high above the paper the toothbrush is held. (© Bill Jaynes 2003)

Figure | 7-2 |

Ilene Winn-Lederer's eclectic repertoire features strong ink work. Her thought-provoking concepts, facile pen craft, and interesting line quality make *Hank Greenburg* more than just a routine shot of a ballplayer. Examine the portrait for a subtle clue to this man's character and beliefs. (© Ilene Winn-Lederer)

can come relatively cheap (prices, like all things arty, vary—you can buy specialty nibs that cost a tad more and pricey, exotic holders if that's your thing).

Dip pens are light, nimble drawing instruments; holders are balanced, nibs practically weightless. A word of caution: We're referring to a bit of formed, sharp steel; some nibs may be a little fragile. In contrast, fountain pens can get expensive, but are more chunky and durable. With care, either type will last longer, of course—I have nibs and fountain pens from my college years that I use to this day.

Figure | 7-3 |

Just a plain old stick makes for a potent pen that offers a rewarding and interesting drawing challenge. Marks made by low-tech (but nevertheless responsive) ink tools can give you striking line character. On drawings like *Portrait of Max J. Cooper,* I use thin or thick twigs, old chopsticks, stumps of brushes and broken pencils, straws, and more—anything that can mark or drag a stroke after dipping the utensil into some ink. (© Michael Fleishman 2003)

## Crowquill Pens

Look for crowquill pens—a variant of the mapping pen—as part of the dip pen family. Crowquill and mapping pens require a specific holder, but these pens boast straight points that draw very fine lines, lovely line variation, and are great for getting the details down.

## Organics

In its most basic form, a twig or stick, sharpened or natural, can be considered a pen (and can provide an interesting, challenging drawing exercise). Likewise, the traditional or ancient pens are all organic in origin. Still used in our modern era, these drawing instruments are not just for illustrators "living in the past." A combination of found objects, both natural and man-made, can also yield interesting effects (see Figure 7-3).

While not high-tech or the current rage, all these pen types offer beautiful line character and unique response—naturally.

## Quill Pens

Quills are classical natural pens that are a lot of fun to draw with. These old-fashioned drawing tools are made from the shafts of bird wing feathers, and are among the earliest of the dip pens (as are the bamboo and reed varieties).

## Bamboo

Bamboo pens and brushes are Eastern in origin. Making a bamboo pen is an art itself. Master artisans, continuing centuries-old traditions, carefully select hard bamboo. This wood is then skillfully hand-carved as per long-standing practice.

The classical black ink painting process is called *Sumi-e.* This art process is actually a wonderfully meditative ritual. You wouldn't—or shouldn't—just pick up a bamboo pen or brush and doodle during a phone conversation!

Special *Sumi* ink must be ground from a black Sumi stick, made from the powdered carbon of burnt pine or lampblack (plus a binding agent). Working on a flat grinding stone called a *suzuri* with a water supply, you dip the stick into the water, and rub on the stone in a prescribed rotation. For the artist, this is a time of peace and contemplation while the carbon flakes off and dissolves in the water, making the delicate *Sumi* ink. Calligraphy, painting, sketching, or printmaking is now done on absorbent, white rice (or bamboo pulp) papers.

Careful: *promptly* clean the ink stone (and do a good job)—dry Sumi is tough to get off later and can compromise ink production (and quality).

Now, it should also be said that you can use a bamboo pen or brush for non-meditative creative activity (although it's a lovely idea that you can satisfy your muse and calm your soul simultaneously). These are just greatly expressive illustration tools in general. There are liquid Sumi inks, and certainly other inks and watercolors could be employed as well (exercising good care, adequate consideration, and thought, of course).

Some consider the bamboo pen a blunt instrument that makes crude marks. Others look at those same marks and wax on about audacious, even primal line quality. Try this pen and create your own labels.

### Reed Pens

Invented by the Egyptians, reed pens are cut from garden canes or bamboo stalks. Natural reeds become pens of varying size, length, shape, and color, with flexible tips that can be sharpened like pencils (and adjusted for individual needs). A drawing instrument used by the likes of Van Gogh and Rembrandt, this simple, humble pen gets rave reviews from artists who call it a highly sensitive and remarkably responsive drawing tool.

Thinner and more delicate than bamboo, the reed pen seems to be doing a vanishing act these days. There is still a market out there, however. In particular, my research turned up British specialty vendors and enthusiastic, die-hard users who campaign to keep this tool from becoming a mere anachronism.

# RESERVOIR PENS

Reservoir pens come with a self-contained, internal ink supply. This reservoir—that part of the pen where the ink is stored—is what makes the pen handier and easier to use than dip pens. Let's take a look at some options.

### Fountain Pens

The first truly practical fountain pen was invented by Lewis Waterman in 1884. Classic fountain pens—modern incarnations or the original collectibles—contain the reservoir in the actual barrel of the pen. These pens need to be filled by siphoning ink from a bottle. There were (and are) different means to do this, but most earlier designs favored a lever or button mechanism. Filling a fountain pen this way was standard operating procedure until the introduction of the ink cartridge in 1950.

From the 1950s on, "modern" fountain pens employed this small, handy, see-through plastic (or clear glass) ink chamber. The cartridge attaches to the nib and this assembly fits into the body of the pen.

A few notes are worth mentioning. Fountain pens require non-waterproof inks that prevent clogging. Specialty inks are available (and are more expensive, of course). Pen barrels may be marvels of form and balance. Elegant craftsmanship, quality components, and deluxe materials are usually de rigueur. Nibs can be made from precious metals (like gold and platinum) or with coated tips of exotic alloys (iridium, ruthenium, osmium).

Cheap (even disposable) fountain pens are out there, but won't be the precision drawing instruments their prized, sophisticated counterparts are.

Figure | 7-4 |

I use a Rotring Art pen—it has a light barrel weight and a comfortable shape for my grip. I don't have to dip, and the flexible sketching nibs offer just the right resistance and "scratch." These features combine to give me the line quality I seek for illustrations like this peacock, done for a kid's pop-up book. (© Michael Fleishman 2003)

## Sketching Pens

A reservoir pen that thinks it is a dip pen! The sketching pen hybrid offers fountain pen design and convenience with dip pen feel and line character (see Figure 7-4). Sketching pens (or art pens, if you prefer) use specified drawing nibs and pre-filled, disposable ink cartridges (or converters that let you refill from an ink bottle).

## Technical Pens

Technical pens are also tagged "tech pens" (and generically called rapidographs). This type of pen uses interchangeable nibs and comes with a self-contained ink supply (disposable pre-filled cartridge or refillable. Current variations include low-tech disposable pens, as well as all-in-one pre-filled, disposable nibbed cartridges for specific barrels).

Modern tech pens offer many nib sizes (widths), in a choice of metals. A tech point is a thin, precision tube affair that delivers smooth, precise lines. Ostensibly, at least, this line quality never varies. I temper this statement because on the right papers (and in the right hands), even the fine-tuned rapidograph nib can be manipulated to skip and scratch out a craggy line.

Figure | 7-5 |

I used a rapidograph with a 4 × 0 (0000 or .18 mm) nib to draw *Old Bike*. The pen was loaded with Koh-I-Noor ink, and the illustration was done on 90lb Whatman's watercolor paper to fully push a rough, wispy line quality. (© Michael Fleishman 2003)

Technical drawing nibs are somewhat fragile, particularly the fine points. If you're too aggressive, they will bend or fracture.

Although I was educated to never use India ink with these points, certain India inks are indeed advertised as perfectly safe for technical pens (but I would check chemistry, manufacturer's cautions, and possible dilution ratios).

It's a sound idea to work with inks made specifically for tech pens, but I figure if they can make a water-soluble oil paint (and they did), those magicians in product development may actually have come up with an India ink that won't clog a nib and gum up the works of your rapidograph. See Figure 7-5 for an illustration done with a technical pen.

## Brush and Ink, Brush Pens

Natural hair, synthetic, or blended brushes, brush pens (both resin-based or natural hair), and bamboo brushes are all great painting utensils. Mix and match inks and brushes—the combinations are just terrific (but you'll want to explore and experiment for compatibility, of course). The drawings in Figure 7-6 will give you a glimpse of the possibilities.

I juggle a variety of ink tools, but prefer a brush pen. The double-tipped Sakura Pigma *Sumi Brush* was my clear favorite before it was unfortunately discontinued (also lamented by Ilene Winn-Lederer). My wife returned from a trip to Japan with a number of new brush pens for me to explore. You won't have to go quite as far; you'll certainly find great brush pens at your local art store.

You can work deliberately (layered washes with line) or spontaneously (gesture, contour, or semi-continuous line) with a brush. Brushes are a superb vehicle for a lyrical line quality (or strong drybrush); the full range of value through wash, as well as rich, dense blacks—and vivid positive and negative—are entirely possible with this tool.

(a)

(b)

(c)

(d)

Figure | 7-6 |

My two brush pen illustrations (a and b) were done with a Sakura *Sumi Brush*. Tom Bachtell's drawing style (c and d) is witty with a spontaneous feel. Working primarily in brush and ink, Bachtell pays homage to many of the classic illustrators and cartoonists of the 1920s and 1930s. (a and b © Michael Fleishman; c and d © Tom Bachtell)

## | NOTE |

Rich in consistency, gel inks are water-based, but not transparent (like conventional inks). This is due to the chemistry between additives and pigments.

The vibrant color and sparkle? These gel inks are formulated from metallic pigments and oxides, plus polymer additives and thickeners. The glitter that knocked you out when you first used these pens is actually powdered aluminum.

# MARKERS (AND SO ON)

These pens are everywhere, but may or may not be as artist-friendly as they are consumer oriented. As an illustrator, the first two questions to ask when drawing with these pens will be: "Are the inks lightfast? Are they waterproof?" Archival quality is promoted as a selling point for various pens—it will pay you to know if there's truth in advertising. So, what are you working with here?

## Felt Tips, Fiber Tips, Plastic Tips, Roller Balls, Brush Tips

The generically soft-tipped felt marker, an American innovation of the 1940s, took off in the 1950s. The "Magic Marker" brand name literally became synonymous with this tool. Various refinements (fine-line and medium points, a range of soft to harder tips, etc.) and spin-offs (dry erase, permanent markers, and more) developed throughout the years. For instance, fiber tips were introduced in 1962, highlighters in the 1970s, gel pens in 1984, thin-line dry erase markers in the 1990s, and so on to this day. The classic Sharpie marker (see Figure 7-7) has remained a staple throughout the years.

Fiber tips run somewhat firmer, while plastic tips offer hard points. These pens also come in many sizes and a variety of tip shapes including wedge, bullet, fine, super or ultrafine points. Roller balls boast harder points yet, while brush pens go the other way—these plastic-based tips are flexible and springy; viable alternatives to "real" natural or synthetic-hair brushes.

# BALLPOINT PEN

The ballpoint pen is perhaps the most popular and prolific drawing and writing tool in history. The original concept, invented in 1888, is actually credited to one John Loud. But our "modern" ballpoint was invented (and initially copyrighted) in 1938 by the Biro brothers, two expatriate Hungarians who emigrated to Argentina. The pen was developed further throughout the war years (and beyond).

Some billions of ballpoint pens later, this anything but "common" pen has had its ups and downs. But the *biro*, as most of the world knows this pen, enjoys all the innovation of modern design, chemistry, and industry. Inks are better, ink delivery more sophisticated and much improved; a wide range of brilliant (even specialty) colors are now available. See Figure 7-8 for an example of illustration using a ball point pen.

Fact is, ballpoints are so ubiquitous, we take for granted the exquisitely thin line character the media has historically offered, not to mention the strength and resiliency of this tool's point. Particular mention must be made about the vibrancy and potency of oil-based ballpoint ink. Hey—how loud and long did you curse the last time a ballpoint leaked in your shirt pocket?

## Combinations

Ink plus mixed media provides exciting illustration opportunities—you're in for a surprise (and a treat) if you keep your mind and options open. It's all available to you, why *not* use it in combination?

If we think of pen and ink only from the perspective of drawing; if we never think of combining inks (and inking techniques); or if we seldom use inks with other techniques and media, we severely limit what this exceptional medium can offer.

Use a variety of different inks together. Inked drawing elements can offset the visual mix of a collaged surface. Of course, the addition of other water-based media is a natural direction—watercolor, thinned acrylic, or gouache supplement and complement ink line or wash nicely (see Figure 7-9).

Thinking more opaque, oil pastels and oil-paint sticks, acrylics, or oils can give you an interesting surface for ink marks or splatter.

Line combinations are another obvious direction; markers (both permanent and soluble) pair nicely with ink. In fact, all varieties of drawing

Figure | 7-7 |

*The Window Boy* was one piece of line art for an educational curriculum package. It was drawn with a regular Sharpie marker—a studio stalwart, esteemed by artists of all ages. Much to the chagrin of the competition, the Sharpie brand name is often used as a generic tag for *all* permanent markers. Sometimes nothing else will do when you want a bold and chunky, free-flowing, permanent ink line. (© Michael Fleishman 2003)

| NOTE |

Ballpoints flew high during the war years of the 1940s. The British military was quite interested in the ballpoint pen (for ground and air use). The long lasting ballpoints could work at high altitudes and were quite convenient in a cockpit.

media work in tandem with pen/brush and ink—pencil, colored pencil, charcoal, pastels or chalk; you name it.

Perhaps you want to delicately tone your ink strokes with rubbed charcoal or pencil (or other forms of graphite). Or go the other way: Lay down a hefty ink line and boldly smudge that value or color with grease pencil, crayon, or the aforementioned oil pastel.

Ink is a splendid stand-alone application, but both natural and engineered combinations are entirely possible with this medium—make mixed media part of your ink drawing repertoire.

## SUMMING IT UP

Pens and inks are a creative marriage made in illustrators' heaven. Combining the challenges of both wet and dry media, this is a fun hybrid of great artistic rewards. The pen and ink process is a fitting platform to sharpen your skills, express your vision, and exercise your voice.

Figure **7-8**

*Cow/Boy/Hat* was drawn with the decidedly uncommon "common everyday, garden-variety, run-of-the-mill, standard issue, plain old" ballpoint pen. (© Michael Fleishman 2003)

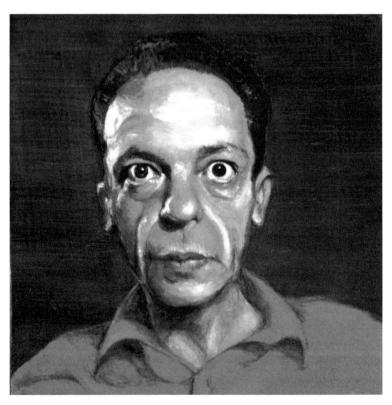

Figure **7-9**

Akiko Stehrenberger combines ballpoint pen, Gesso, and acrylics to create sly, smart illustration and arresting caricature like *Squared Knotts.* (© Akiko Stehrenberger)

# STEP by STEP

## *Paul Melia*

**Step 1:**
This is the basic reference and Melia's core idea of what the painting would be about. He studied this material to pull out V-shapes within the picture elements, highlighting the compositional device with green and orange marks.

**Step 2:**
These small pencil studies of seagulls were also done as reference. Melia then chose certain birds to use in his painting.

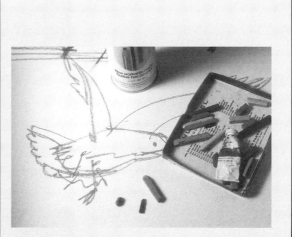

**Step 3:**
A gull drawn in pastels, directly on the piece.

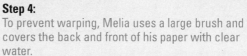

**Step 4:**
To prevent warping, Melia uses a large brush and covers the back and front of his paper with clear water.

*continued*

# STEP by STEP

*Continued*

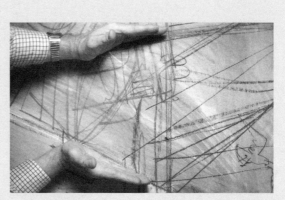

**Step 6:**
Checking composition and the crucial V-shapes.

**Step 5:**
He then flows water and ink together with his brush. Melia lays the paper flat, pours the inks right on the surface, and brushes them out. Inks are diluted to about a 50 percent value. The artist is careful to not go too dark; he doesn't want to cover up the pastel line, thus obliterating the original drawing. Melia comments, "This is a key thing—you're essentially going to paint in between the lines."

**Step 7:**
With a mixture of matt medium and inks, Melia quickly works color into the pastel lines of the drawing. He starts in the logical place to begin—generally the top—putting the background in first, but moving to other sections as he sees fit. "I am conscious of developing the overall painting as a whole," he says.

**Step 8:**
Fine-tuning color and value (and simply having fun with his process).

**Step 9:**
Melia stays close to the basic drawing, but may paint over or patch if something is not working out.

**Step 10:**
The final! (Illustrations © Paul Melia)

# PROFILES

*Akiko Stehrenberger*

Akiko Stehrenberger's delightfully streetwise cast of characters comes to life through "a lot of ballpoint pen, Gesso, and acrylics." She has used Liquitex acrylics since art school, when one of her instructors recommended the paints for a particular class. "I got used to its consistency," she says. "When I use generic acrylic paints, I notice a more gooey quality, which is a hindrance when you're trying to get solid, saturated, and opaque colors."

The plain and simple, generic ballpoint pen previously mentioned is Stehrenberger's all time favorite drawing medium. "This works just fine—as long as they don't smudge or leak," she comments. "Ballpoint gives me a variety of lines; from punchy dark strokes to beautiful gradations and soft value changes. Another advantage of ballpoint is its permanence when painting over it. My paintings feel naked without it, since maintaining an evident drawing in the painting is important to me."

Stehrenberger prefers cold press, double weight illustration board. Here, the roughness of the board gives the artist a desired texture, and the double weight prevents the support from warping.

After an initial reference hunt, Stehrenberger works up "rough and tiny" thumbnails to get an overall idea of composition, and then she says it's "straight to the board. I rarely do a detailed sketch before going to the final, unless a client asks for it." Sketching on board feels more spontaneous for her. "I sketch in pencil until I get the lines I want, then I go over those lines in light ballpoint pen. Unless it's terribly distracting, I keep most of my initial lines because I like them to show through. Most of my favorite paintings are the pieces that show process."

When the drawing is complete, the illustrator then goes through a procedure taught to her by teacher and fellow illustrator Robert Kato. "I take a cadmium red medium or a burnt sienna, and make a thin wash of it over the whole board. This acts as a midtone which makes it tremendously easier to get started—easier than starting from scratch. From this point, I only have to either go lighter or darker.

"I do a lot of back and forth in this process. I begin with the medium to lighter to lightest, and start building the form; then I go medium to darker. In between, I also strengthen lines with the ballpoint pen. This also helps me see how my value is doing."

About midway, Stehrenberger separates foreground from background, working with white Gesso to clean up edges. "The white around the form also helps me judge values. I spend the most time on the face, because likeness is absolutely vital for my assignments. When finished here, I like to emphasize a graphic and simple background, as well as the body. With the value and detail primarily in the face, it's sure to be the main focal point."

© Akiko Stehrenberger

# PROFILES

## *Ilene Winn-Lederer*

Quality drawing is paramount to Ilene Winn-Lederer's craft, and this means brand names only—generic just doesn't cut it. Cheap watercolors don't offer the richness of tone or coverage. Generic colored pencils usually result in waxy build-up when you layer colors. The pigment in off-brand acrylics or gouache tends to separate from the medium and not mix well. "The bottom line is you get what you pay for," says the Pittsburgh illustrator.

Now, saying all that, the artist still prefers her art gear to be direct and simple. Too much attention to the paraphernalia, she feels, "means that the real me stays hidden; the idea is obscured by the flash of it all."

But hold on. Winn-Lederer has actually begun drawing with—are you ready?—ballpoint ink. "Very pedestrian, and very hypocritical to the attitude expressed in my opening statement," she admits. "However, *I love it.*"

The illustrator finds ballpoint pens to be ultimately portable and spontaneous; direct, yet subtle. Not very messy, ballpoint supports watercolor very nicely, as well. "With controlled pressure on good quality paper you can actually create a sort of intaglio, etched line," she points out.

Actually, Winn-Lederer works in several media, sometimes in combination: watercolor, acrylic, gouache, color pencils, graphite, pen and ink, scratchboard, collage, and now, digital drawing. "This is fun and hypnotic," she states, "but does not have the true feel of actual media on real paper or canvas."

This seasoned pro is well aware of a few things, which Winn-Lederer sums up in five words: research, roughs, and "ready-to-wear." Her short list:

1. Research is the most fun. Winn-Lederer looks at everything—anything relevant and irrelevant to the project.

2. Roughs can begin anywhere—on scrap paper, Post-it note, coffee shop napkin, or a handy sketchbook tucked in a purse.

3. Capturing the spontaneity of those roughs in the finish is tough. "Spontaneity," she laments, "can easily become a casualty in the war between inspiration and art direction."

Ilene Winn-Lederer's *Ballpaper* showcases her strong line quality and vivid brush work. For more of the same, look for Lederer's *Owl and the Pussycat*, Figure 18 in the color insert. (© Ilene Winn-Lederer 2003)

4. You must draw as though your lines could speak; make a definite statement or no statement at all.

5. Don't be timid; but don't "noodle" or over-work the drawing. "Often, a concept that is implied is more effective than one you send home with a sledgehammer," says the artist.

# PROFILES

*Rob Rogers*

Rob Rogers creates his editorial cartoons using brush and/or pen and ink on Grafix 32-L Uni-Shade bristol board. The board comes with invisible even lines printed on it that only show up when a liquid developer is applied.

"It works a little like photo paper," the nationally known cartoonist says. "The lines are so uniform, they give the impression of a solid gray tone. But instead of having to shoot it as a halftone, you can still shoot it as black and white."

But watch out for a slight speed bump. The Grafix Uni-Shade board is not archival. It turns yellow and the chemicals break down after a couple of decades (or sooner if left in a humid place or exposed to light). "It reproduces great, but there's a trade-off," Rogers tells us. "I often threaten to switch to a plain archival bristol, but I haven't made the leap yet."

Rogers likes Higgins Black Magic ink for solid blacks and line work (since it dries quickly), and his favorite brush is the Grumbacher Series 197 Kolinsky Sable watercolor brush—he uses a No. 1 for the ink and a No. 3 for the developer. "I've used other brushes, but none have worked as well with my style," he comments.

For lettering, it's either a Pigma Graphic No. 1 or a Staedtler Pigment Liner No. 03 or No. 05 (depending on how fine the lettering). For cross-hatching, Rogers leans towards a Staedtler Pigment Liner No. 03 or "My favorite pen in the world, the one I never leave home without—the Sanford Uni-Ball Vision Micro Black. It is great for sketching (I do all my roughs with this pen) and it is waterproof and fade-proof. If I don't have one with me at all times I get separation anxiety."

So just how is a Rogers editorial cartoon produced?

After reading the newspaper, Rogers writes down potential topics in a sketchbook. This serves as both inspiration and reference. "If I hit a dry day I can always look back at the previous list of topics to see if something is still worthy."

Next he does a rough sketch in the sketchbook (with his favorite Uni-Ball Vision Micro pen). It might take a few tries to get a keeper. He takes this rough, reduces or enlarges it on a photocopier (and keeps the original intact in the sketchbook).

The photocopy is placed on a light table, and penciled on the Grafix Uni-Shade drawing board. "Before inking I do the lettering; any lettering that goes outside of the pencil lines can then be adjusted during the inking stage. I next use brush and ink to ink in the pencil rough."

Once the ink dries, Rogers erases the pencil and brushes on the Uni-Shade developer. With a pen, he cross-hatches where needed, and uses process white gouache to correct any mistakes.

"When everything dries I make a photocopy of the original cartoon and reduce it down to an 8.5 × 11 sheet of paper. I scan the photocopy of the cartoon, save it on my computer, and send it by e-mail to my newspaper and my syndicate."

## in review

1. What is a dip pen? A reservoir pen? Compare and contrast these pen types.

2. From your own experience, and in your own words, what are the differences and similarities between felt-tip, fiber-tip, roller-ball, plastic-tip, and brush-tip markers?

3. Describe the various "organic" pens. Have you tried any of these pens? If so, relate your experience. If not, choose an organic pen and explore your technique with this particular tool.

4. What is *Sumi-e?* Can illustration be meditative? Spiritual or zen-like? How about medicinal or healing?

5. Are ballpoint and gel pens valid illustration tools? Why or why not?

## exercises

1. One hundred marks (or more): Choose any pen; any ink. Do a style sheet of 100 marks (minimum). Each mark must be different from the last. Consider all the basic elements of design: line and line quality; value and color; pattern and texture; shape and form; spatial and sequential relationships such as size, position, repetition, and rhythm spacing; movement and progression; harmony, unity, emphasis and variety; balance.

2. Draw with your favorite inking tools, but with your opposite hand. The final may be rather expressionistic, but compare and contrast this piece with your "good" hand— what do we learn from such an exercise?

3. Create a mixed media piece. This illustration should involve your pen and ink process with at least four different wet and/or dry media (including collage as one possible choice). The piece can be representational or abstracted. For an added challenge, make it a portrait, self-portrait, or still life.

4. Do an ink drawing with the most basic or crudest (or perhaps the most contrived) tool you can find. For example: a plastic coffee stirrer or straw becomes your "dip pen." Fray a thin branch to act as a brush. For more of a challenge, do a larger drawing (8.5 × 14 to 12 × 18 in., or bigger).

5. Choose a fine nib, thin-line marker, or ultra-fine tech point to do a *big* drawing (12 × 18 to 18 × 24 in., or larger). Next, pick a broad point marker, larger nib, or tech point to do a *tiny* illustration. Go with challenging dimensions that will still give you the opportunity to produce a complete picture of multiple lines.

© Lori Osiecki

Scratch, Spray, Dimensional, Extended, and Peripheral

8

*"Once I discovered that Photoshop would give me a non-digital look, I sent my airbrush (and all its small, impossible to clean and reassemble parts) flying across the room and into the trash, without hesitation."*

**Lori Osiecki, illustrator**

*"Woodcut is a challenge of human against grain—which keeps me more creative and my lines and tones more alive and less controlled."*

**Carla Bauer, illustrator**

*"If it's a medical malpractice story, draw a stethoscope and see if that reminds you of anything. 'Oh, the stethoscope looks a little like a snake, snakes represent duplicity and danger, so I can turn the stethoscope into a snake!' It's usually a lot of trial and error. Once the concept is down, and the sketch is refined, simplified, and improved, I run through a short mental checklist, and ask what would make this even more interesting—an unusual point of view, some strange angle, should I change the relative scale of things?"*

**Gregory Nemec, illustrator**

## Chapter Objectives:

Provide an overview of illustration techniques beyond "traditional" painting and drawing

Explore airbrush, stencil, and scratchboard

Review dimensional techniques

Discuss calligraphy and graffiti

Consider the relationship of these forms to general illustration

## Introduction

Painting and drawing may justifiably provide the framework for general illustration, but what about those processes that complete and complement the structure? Let's examine some extended and worthy techniques that branch off from "classical" illustration.

# SCRATCHBOARD

I don't mean to short change or discount the venerable woodcut, and its sister, the linoleum cut. These are certainly viable, time-honored, and stimulating illustration media. Each produces wonderful pictures.

| NOTE |

If you opt to work in woodcut, you'll find that woodcut *illustration* is one thing. But because you'll also make editions of prints that people buy, your materials *must* be archival.

But for our purposes, there is a related process that does not require specialized inks, specific cutting tools, or a printing press. Let's immediately segue into what is perhaps a more user-friendly and time-efficient process for the illustrator: scratchboard. Yes, you can make a good argument that scratchboard is not terribly time-efficient, but I'm not talking man-hours—you don't want to rush through *any* of these demanding techniques, especially the labor-intensive scratchboard process.

## Beginning

When just starting out in the scratchboard technique, a "student-grade" board will work just fine. Scratchboard (sometimes called scraper art) manufacturers like Esdee offer several different grades of board—professional, student, as well as a "gosh my kids want to play on something" category. Claybord is a widely available brand found in most art stores and catalogs. Scratchboard can be an unforgiving medium at any budget, but I think the learning process can certainly be worked through on a less expensive surface.

In general, the words "student grade" don't necessarily *always* equate to "cheap" or "lousy" art supplies, but in terms of components, ingredients, and/or build quality, there are reasons you're getting that price break.

When you determine the need to move up and on, you'll want to work on a quality surface like the commercial-grade Esdee, a British scraperboard many illustrators regard as the absolute best (as well as the most expensive) scratchboard available. Buy it mail-order and buy in bulk to meet your needs (it'll be somewhat cheaper).

Why does a good or better board make a definite difference? The grade of the clay coating on a scratchboard determines the smoothness of the line being scratched (see Figure 8-1). The thicker the coating (and the stronger the cardboard underneath), the more chances you will have to re-ink and fix mistakes.

Figure | 8-1 |

This illustration is by Robert Zimmerman who, like most scratchboard artists, emphasizes that a quality board is essential to the scratchboard process. (© Robert Zimmerman. Comedy Central logo © Comedy Central)

## Inking

When using white scratchboard that needs to be inked before scratching, a good quality India ink will cover the surface in two or three coats, even if you are watering down the ink with a little distilled water.

That's right; this scratchboard surface is *sans* ink—you paint the surface of the board with black ink. But you can buy pre-inked board, if you like.

## Stay Sharp

A sharp blade is an absolute scratchboard essential. X-acto blades are hardly exotic art tools. Your tool set will probably combine both classical scratchboard tools *and* improvised utensils.

You'll find triangular and sharp points for making fine lines, shovel-shaped and rounded points for scratching away large areas. Gregory Nemec buys metal scratching points made to fit crowquill pens. But he also uses X-acto points with the very tip broken off to make fine lines, and a rounded linoleum cutting tool to scrape larger segments (see Figure 8-2).

These semi-accidental discoveries should tell you that the type or quality of your scratching tools is not crucial. Every sharp implement has its own personality, and different tools will suit different illustrators. Some scratchboard artists use medical scalpels or penknives or dental

Figure | 8-2 |

Gregory Nemec uses both manufactured and improvised scratching utensils to do his thought-provoking, eye-catching scratchboard illustrations. (© Gregory Nemec)

Figure **8-3**

Mark Summers' engravings in scratchboard have netted numerous awards, many exhibits, and a growing list of clients. You've seen his work for the *New York Times* Book Review, and on Barnes & Noble shopping bags, banners, and trucks. (© Mark Summers)

paraphernalia—it's whatever works for you (and come to think of it, we probably all have an X-acto with a broken tip lying around somewhere). It's pretty simple, actually—make your choice, then just start scratching! See Figure 8-3 for another example of scratchboard illustration.

## Transfer

There are a number of ways to get your drawing onto the scratchboard. Some illustrators may use the sketch as a pure reference and work directly on the scraperboard. Others may use a projector to transfer the sketch to the scratchboard. If it's a silhouetted image or one with large white areas, transfer the sketch to white scratchboard and ink in the areas that will be scratched out. A predominantly dark image or one with predominant texture should be transferred to pre-inked scratchboard.

Robert Zimmerman works his roughs out on economy-grade tracing paper, which makes revising and tweaking the sketch much easier. It's all very simple—put one drawing on top of the other and refine the visual. Using drafting tape to secure the tracing paper sketch to the scratchboard, transfer the image with transfer paper (placed between the tracing paper and the scratchboard, the transfer sheet acts just like carbon paper). The Saral Paper Corporation makes transfer paper in five colors; Zimmerman uses a yellow sheet, by the way.

## In the Beginning—Value

You will be scratching lines—perhaps a flurry of lines—or you will be scratching out shapes—creating the object and giving it value. This may be true of any drawing, but in scratchboard the illustrator is doing it in one gesture, *simultaneously.* To facilitate this tricky course of action, you may want to photocopy a tight sketch and add tone to this image via ink washes or hatching.

This can give you a roadmap of values when doing the scratchboard, but there might be no set system—no real rhyme or reason—to this part of the process.

And you may find that once everything is all scratched off, the sum effect is rather gray and even. To create more contrast and variety, you'll want to refine the values.

Scratchboard (woodcut and engraving, too) is all about black and white lines creating the illusion of tone. Spend time to selectively make areas lighter (by scratching the white lines to make them wider) or darker (re-inking the black lines to make them wider). This adds depth and promotes a three-dimensional quality. It can even change the overall values in the entire piece.

## Scratchboard and Digital

For many illustrators working in scratchboard, the computer has re-vamped their routine (see Figure 8-4). Jumping ahead to the end of the process, one benefit of a digital final is delivery time and conven-ience. These days it's quite common for illustrators to attach and e-mail small work or burn and send a CD-rom for larger illustrations. You may never have to send the actual artwork anymore.

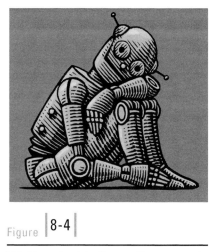

Figure |8-4|

This illustration is by Gregory Nemec, one of many illustrators who feel that working digitally complements and enhances the scratchboard process. (© Gregory Nemec)

But there are substantial returns during the work-in-progress stage, too. You can scan your art and clean it up in Photoshop, a step you'll find much to your ad-vantage. "If you've botched an area, or a client wants you to change an element, it's difficult to make corrections in the unforgiving medium of scratchboard," as Nemec relates.

To remedy an unhappy accident, simply redo the section in question on a separate piece of scratchboard. Scan the new section, then cut and paste it digitally into the original—the patch will be absolutely invisible. "Once an image is manipulated digitally," Nemec goes on to say, "it's always cleaner and better for reproduction than the original physical piece on the scratchboard!"

The computer advantage gives you the versatility to creatively stretch without destroying the original artwork. Also consider that there are always myriad tasks with any assignment. Now, throw in the everyday demands of an illustrator's work schedule. Working on the computer is very clean in a number of ways. Save your work, walk out of the room, come back and con-tinue. Nothing to tidy up at the end of the day.

The computer will make your process a lot more forgiving. You'll now have the ability to *go backwards*. You can play, explore and experiment, painlessly dig deeper to find what's not work-ing exactly—and not have to go back to square one.

# SPRAY

## Stencil

As you experiment with different techniques, you may initially start out drawing with pen and ink. You will no doubt paint a bit. Perhaps you'll do scratchboard, wood or linoleum cuts, and possibly dabble in collage as your learning moves forward. But there's a marvelous and very basic technique you just may overlook—stencil. Give the technique a shot; you may find the unique and appealing stencil style invigorating and revitalizing.

The stencil technique moved illustrator Peter Kuper away from what he labels as "certain bad drawing habits." Drawing with straight pen and ink, Kuper's line work fell somewhere between a kind of fine art, realism, and cartooning—ultimately a type of drawing that didn't energize the artist.

He sought to separate from those influences and noticed that many of his pure pen and ink drawings seemed more pedestrian than when he *mixed and matched* different techniques. Stencils gave a distinct "oomph" to Kuper's work, exactly what the illustrator was looking for. When he landed on it, it stuck (see Figure 8-5).

Figure **8-5**

An exciting shift from his illustration routine brought Peter Kuper to stencil. The technique invigorated Kuper and compelled him to dump some old, restrictive drawing habits that just weren't working for him. (© Peter Kuper)

### A Hole in One

When we think "stencil" we may dwell on the obvious: cut stencils with spray paint, but a) paint need not be sprayed to take advantage of the stencil effect; and b) paint is not the only medium that can be stenciled—oil pastels, for instance, can be rubbed to create a fine, soft focus stencil; c) cutting is not the only way to create a stencil; and d) you don't have to be too particular about brands here.

Your illustration may involve stencil/spray paint with added watercolor and/or collage elements. Archival materials are recommended, such as glue sticks (never rubber cement), fine-quality watercolor paper (hot press for a smoother finish or cold press for more tooth), high-grade watercolors and colored pencils, good pens with archival-quality ink, and sharp knives.

Because of the nature of the technique and components, there will always be something surprising with stencil. "It never gets boring," says Kuper. "And that's probably the biggest issue for me—there must always be that element of surprise in the work."

# AIRBRUSH

An old can of spray paint is a self-contained painting system, but hardly offers the fine-tuned control of its more sophisticated sister, the airbrush. Let's take a basic look at the hardware involved when working with this tool. Simply put, it all breaks down to the following items: a vehicle—in this case an airbrush or airgun—and a propellant to disperse your medium (which could be paint, inks, dyes, pigments, etc.).

### The Set-Up

But that's obviously the bare bones of a far more complex and hardware-intensive operation. What type of propellant do you use? Compressed air in cans—handy, but very low-volume, thus expensive? Electric air compressors that need a power source (widely available and economical; certain models may get a bit bulky)? Compressed $CO_2$ tanks which are clean, quiet; cost and time efficient—no power necessary, but will need to be refilled (can get a bit heavy, but offer a longer "shelf-life")? How about a regulator to control air flow and pressure?

How about the tool itself? Airgun or airbrush? An internal mix airbrush (where air and paint are combined inside the unit) or external mix airbrush (where air and paint are integrated outside the unit)? Single action (one trigger movement down is all it takes; the beginner's favorite) or dual action (two distinct movements—down and back—to get your spray)? Gravity-feed, side-feed, bottom-feed, or siphon-feed?

These decisions will really depend on what you intend to do; much in the same way that you pick a paintbrush—or any tool—to match the job at hand. Size, style and quality all must be duly considered for a particular application. See Figure 8-6 for one artist's airbrush choices and methods.

Figure | 8-6 |

Douglas Klauba's *All You Ever Need* is airbrushed acrylic. He works on a Crescent #110 illustration board (gessoed or ungessoed), bringing his drawing in with graphite pencils plus Prismacolor and Derwent colored pencils. He next blocks in darks with Liquitex tube acrylics, using both brush and airbrush. "I cut friskets (masks) and apply acrylics in a glaze method, mostly with an Iwata HP-C airbrush," Klauba says, "but drybrush acrylics over these areas to model the form." (© Douglas Klauba 2000)

## The Paint

Airbrush paint, like all paints, may be transparent or opaque. Opaques may be a mixed blessing. Rich, lustrous, and creamy paint usually means a heavier viscosity, so opaques may readily clog. Color blends (or color coverage with certain hues) may present some technical challenges, as well.

The thinner transparents are the flip side to that coin. They offer superior flow, provide better blending and translucent color overlays, *but may not cover as well.*

Inks, dyes, and watercolors fall into the transparents category, and are all good airbrush options. Gouache, also called opaque watercolor, is a viable choice for airbrush, with due care and clean-up. You can thin oil paint and sign paints to work in an airbrush, as well.

Many illustrators use both opaque and transparent acrylic paints. All the traditional benefits of acrylics can be recognized when used with an airbrush. Boasting great color and tone, water-soluble acrylics are versatile—both thick and thin are very easy to attain. They dry fast and are long-lasting. Tough and durable, acrylics are resistant to the wear and tear of the frisket process. But like gouache, due care and thorough, immediate clean-up must be practiced.

You will probably find it best to stick with name brands like Dr. Ph. Martin's, Liquitex, Createx, or Winsor & Newton (amongst others) to insure a consistency in pigment color, as well as the amount of color pigment to filler. The Internet has sparked a global buyer's market for art supplies; you can find good off brands out there, but remember, there will be no substitute for high-grade ingredients and quality control.

## On the Surface

You see airbrush on all kinds of stuff, including body art, arts and crafts, tee shirts and other wearables, even cars and trucks. But for our discussion of the airbrush as an illustration tool, let's focus on papers or boards.

Canvas, cardboard, and other appropriate-weight and appropriately-textured art papers can handle the technique. Scratchboard is airbrush compatible. In fact, Claybord, a clay-coated hardboard (and considered by some to be the best scratchboard out there) is a first-rate surface for airbrush.

With a variety of surfaces to choose from, many airbrush artists have a preference for illustration board. John Jinks tends to use an extremely smooth, hot-pressed board especially made for inking and airbrushing. Besides providing a wonderful picture plane, it's a forgiving surface as well. For instance, you may need to scrape your surface to touch up paint that has seeped under a mask. Hot-pressed boards manufactured by names like Letramax and Bainbridge are very hard and facilitate this clean-up process.

## The Mask

You can, of course, do a freehand airbrush technique—graffiti, or graffiti-style art taps into this freeform approach—but most likely you'll be buying, cutting, or forming masks and shields.

Such stencils are a real mixed bag. Frisket film is probably a first choice—it's transparent, low-tack, and easy to cut with precision. Mylar drafting film is tough, also easy to cut, but is not adhesive backed. Acetate or hand-cut papers of appropriate weight can work. Natural materials (like lace, for instance) make for interesting masks. There is masking tape, masking paper, and sheet plastic for rougher or larger stencils. You can buy or create custom shields, as well.

## Cut!

Get some strong, well-made, sharp scissors (and buy a backup, too). As when we covered scratchboard and discussed the importance of a good, sharp blade, the same goes for cutting masks in the airbrush process. There are other blades out there, but the common household name in art knives is the X-acto brand (and a #11 size blade is pretty much the standard).

While a knife *cuts* with a nice, neat edge, you can also use an electric stencil burner that *melts* the frisket film (and leaves a softer edge).

It sounds like a no-brainer, but *only* use a clean, keen blade (and scissors). Buy in bulk, keep an adequate supply, and maintain all your cutting tools.

## STEP by STEP

*Airbrush with John Jinks*

Airbrush virtuoso John Jinks considers many factors when doing an airbrush illustration. "Your visual approach is very important," he says. "I tend to look for inspiration from many sources and reference. To generate truly inspiring stuff means that sometimes it has to germinate and form in your mind before you can produce it.

"I think knowing when to stop is just as important as exploring more ideas. This can take time and a client that knows this will get the best you have to give."

Jinks' personal best thrills his appreciative audience. He indeed knows how to start and when to stop, as he demonstrates here in this step by step.

**Step 1:**
Sketch ideas sort out the composition. These roughs allow for type and get the image right for the book cover (the book is called *Trombone*—in the story, a trombone player has a fatal attraction for a woman who is an arsonist). Jinks picks the best sketch to show to the client.

**Step 2:**
A color study for the final is done in colored pencil and presented to the client with a traced overlay of the type treatment.

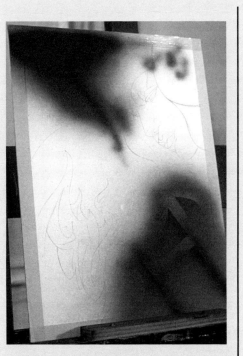

**Step 3:**
Starting the painting. The sketch is projected up to final painting size. Using the sketch as his guide, Jinks traces the outlines of all painted shapes that will complete the entire painting.

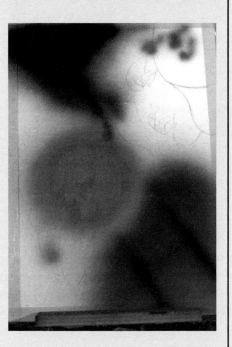

**Step 4:**
Jinks covers the entire surface with a low tack frisket, cuts out an area, and begins. He starts with a green base, to which he will add browns and blacks (before covering and moving on to another section).

*continued*

# STEP by STEP

*Continued*

### Step 5:
Several areas are done at this point. All previous masks were done using frisket. The frisket is cut; an area is painted, and the frisket is then *very carefully* repositioned *exactly* in place. This particular section requires an acetate mask taped down with low-tack drafting tape.

### Step 6:
In the upper right are several acetate masks used to create the shapes in the flame. Jinks started with a red/orange base and built up color layers with the same masks. Next, yellow is applied to the flame. This will be followed by a brown to make it "pop" a bit.

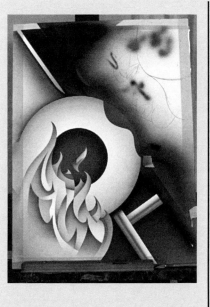

**Step 7:**
The frisket masks have been pulled off several areas to show the modeling of color used, and how the sections look together. The purpose of the initial color study—and the tough thing about this process—is that you have to cover an entire area after completion to work on another. This is a bit like doing a puzzle one piece at a time. When you've pulled off all the frisket masks to reveal the full painting, you usually have to go in and adjust the contrast and make the painting look even throughout.

**Step 8:**
Here, Jinks is using the same basic layering techniques, but this time with blues. The tan colored paper on the left is newsprint. This scrap paper is where Jinks sprays the airbrush first. He makes sure the paint is flowing properly and smoothly before hitting the painting.

*continued*

# STEP by STEP

*Continued*

The final. (All illustrations © John Jinks)

"I use acrylic paints on illustration board," says John Jinks, "I stick with better brand names as there is a consistency in pigment color, and the amount of pigment to filler is usually good.

"Good brands are Liquitex and Winsor & Newton. There are many surfaces to choose from; I prefer a hot pressed illustration board—quite hard and good for scraping. I tend to use a very smooth board made for inking and airbrushing—sometimes you need to scrape the surface to touch up paint that has seeped under a mask. Brands by Letramax and Bainbridge will get the job done.

"I also use a No. 11 X-acto knife for all cutting and scraping on the surface. My airbrush is an Iwata HPBC-2—I like the response of this brush the best. This is a bottom-fed brush with removable color cups to allow quick changing of colors.

"I also use a high-tack frisket film for masking. This allows precise cutting, plus effortless removal and reapplying of the frisket onto already painted surfaces. I also use a .003 clear acetate—this makes for clean scoring and breaks (which leaves precise edges). These masks are then taped to the board with drafting tape. Drafting tape is a low-tack easily removable tape that can be reapplied without pulling up existing paint.

"Unfortunately, there are some materials you can't get anymore…for instance, Frisk brand illustration board—the highest quality board made specifically for airbrushing. Their frisket film was also excellent, but sadly is no longer available. Badger film is good, though, and I try to use that when I can. You must go with what's available and adapt."

# DIMENSIONAL TECHNIQUES

Illustration does not have to be *flat*. There are (and have been) many artists who illustrate in three dimensions. Carving, bas-relief, sculpture, assemblage, and construction (in clay or resin, metal or stone, papier maché, wood, engineered and cut paper, felt, etc.) are every bit an element of the illustration vocabulary.

Some illustrators work dimensionally when the job demands it. Others formally embrace 3-D as their main method, working flat when the assignment dictates. Look for the illustrations of Walter Einsel, Raymond Ameijide, and David Wisniewski to get a taste for yourself. See Figure 8-7 for Bob Selby's 3-D illustration.

Illustrating in 3-D usually means that your work will have to be shot photographically. I say *usually*, because there are computer artists who build or shape digitally. Incredibly powerful and sophisticated software and hardware now translate objects in minute textural detail and majestic beauty. The forms do not physically exist, but are nonetheless breathtakingly dimensional in print or on the screen. There may not be a tangible object to shift in your hands, turn, or walk around, but this is still dimensional illustration that takes the word *render* to new heights.

Figure | 8-7 |

*The Aloof Jim Rice* is a 3-D illustration done for the *Providence Journal*. The sculpture is polychrome plasticene. Here, Bob Selby literally adds dimension to a striking statement about attitude and personality. (© Providence Journal 1986)

# GORGEOUS SCRIBBLES

A classical definition of *calligraphy* is "the art or skill of producing beautiful or artistic handwriting." We spent some time earlier defining *line*, and you may also have heard certain lines labeled as *calligraphic*. I won't quibble with those who don't lump calligraphy into the illustration category per se, but the two endeavors are closely related—cousins, certainly, if not brothers.

I had a friend in art school who studied Japanese calligraphy and practiced making the traditional letterforms incessantly. This was not for any class, mind you, he just did it to improve his

brush skills. His brush ultimately danced with an amazing grace, skill, and speed. To this day, I remember those pages and pages of good-looking strokes—a seemingly boring exercise turned into handsome results and visible dexterity.

When I look at the creative directories, I always check out the calligrapher's section. I love seeing what sharp and skilled artists can do with a finite set of components—after all, there are only 26 letters and 10 numerals.

To me, if illustration is about the message, then calligraphy is certainly illustration (see Figure 8-8).

## The Style of Graffiti

For some, it will be a bit blasphemous to mention graffiti or the graffiti style as legitimate illustration. But it's not so far-fetched, at least in terms of visual influence and cultural impact.

Folk art (also called naïve art) is done by comparatively untrained amateurs, with social, ethnic, or traditional overtones (you may want to research the work of Grandma Moses as one prime example).

Outsider art, as defined by art historians Paul Zelanski and Mary Pat Fisher, is created by "sheer individualists . . . self-taught and . . . working totally outside of both community traditions and establishment ideas about what constitutes good art. This nonconformist work is highly personal, spontaneously expressive, and often spiritual."

Both folk art and outsider art have achieved prominence, influence, and collectibility. Graffiti stylization has similarly affected conventional imagery and inspired many contemporary illustrators (not to mention current design and advertising—plus the visual arts in general).

Graffiti can certainly fit definitions of folk and outsider art. Graffiti—for better or worse—is perhaps the ultimate outsider art; our generation's ubiquitous folk art. Call it street or performance art, if you will; think of it as modern day hieroglyphics. Regardless of the moniker, it's a round peg that jams quite visibly in the square hole of mainstream creative accomplishments.

By no means do I sanction, nor wish to glorify, the vandals that foul public works or desecrate places of worship. I *am* trying to say that graffiti is all about self-expression (again, for better or worse).

## SUMMING IT UP

This chapter provides an overview of illustration techniques that go beyond the traditional borders of painting and drawing. Stencil and airbrush, scratch and cut techniques (scratchboard, lino, and woodcut), 3-D processes, calligraphy, and graffiti, as well, can help us grow and stretch—to push our technical skills and creative thinking in fresh directions, to new benchmarks.

## | NOTE |

The most influential and successful graffiti artist was, and remains, Keith Haring (1958–1990). Remember that "success" is a relative term. Perhaps it would be better to say that Haring was the guy who truly fused the guerilla art of graffiti with recognized mainstream arts. Haring's graffiti became quite legitimate, to say the least. His art was critically and popularly acclaimed, socially and culturally iconic, and a very lucrative enterprise. That's success on many levels, in almost anybody's book.

# PROFILES

*Scratchboard Artists Lori Osiecki, Robert Zimmerman, and Gregory Nemec*

© Lori Osiecki

Illustrator Lori Osiecki put in 8 years at Hallmark, where she really was a Jack (or Jill, as it were) of all trades. She dabbled in different styles, many techniques, and a variety of approaches, which all changed with every different assignment.

When Osiecki left the greeting card giant, she understood that to make it in a freelance market, she needed a specific direction. "When people call for your work," the illustrator explains, "they must know what they are going to get; no guessing games. Clients are really buying a look."

With the advice of good friend (and noted children's book illustrator), G. Brian Karas, Osiecki opted for scratchboard as her signature look. She has done well with it. Using a jagged edge to the line, Osiecki's work is not your traditional scratchboard illustration. The illustrator's visuals jump with great energy. You'll notice that the Arizona artist does not attempt to maintain pristine whites on her board either, she doesn't try to make it clean—Osiecki leaves a lot of the little pieces in, so there is purposeful movement to the line.

Robert Zimmerman says that the job of an illustrator is to "Pull the most from an assignment and take it as far as you can." Indeed, the illustrator once traveled 200 miles to visit an old minor league ballpark for an assignment about baseball.

For Zimmerman, inspiration comes from within. "If I'm motivated by anything, it's thinking of the person who will end up seeing what I have done. I keep the end audience in mind, not the art director. I extend an invitation to be entertained out to the *audience* and hope that they'll accept and participate."

Zimmerman started out in the business working frequently for the *New York Times,* which in those days almost meant living at the newspaper. "One of the lost benefits of those old days," Zimmerman recalls, "was the chance to meet and hang out with a lot of great artists."

Two marvels of technology changed just about everything. The fax machine enabled Zimmerman to actually do a sketch at his studio and fax it to the *Times.* He could get approval by phone, do his final at home, and deliver it when done.

Then the Macintosh came out. Zimmerman recalls those pioneer days of working in Photoshop and sending files directly via modem. "Transferring 5 meg files often took all night," he smiles. "I no longer need to live in New York to work for the *Times*. I now live in the mountains of North Carolina, and my illustrations arrive at the *Times* building less than a minute after I'm finished."

What motivates illustrator Gregory Nemec the most is a very tangible excitement of making something new while doing a good job. "You can renew yourself every time you make an image," he tells us. "The excitement I had as a kid *making* art is still there. And the excitement I had as a kid *looking* at art informs what I do now."

And Nemec's genuinely exciting scratchboard illustration begins with extensive sketches. The artist says he'll even sketch *bad* ideas, just to get them on paper and out of the way of better concepts he has in his head. Research is important; not just for reference, but to gather different points of view, as Nemec feels it's better to have more than one source. "Ten artists who represent 'alienation' spark more

original ideas than looking at one, limited resource," he says.

Art and photographs inspire, of course, but ideas often generate via books (perhaps with *no* pictures in them) and movies. Often mundane objects or settings spark an idea. "A good Scrabble player moves his tiles around and around until a word appears; the elements of a drawing can be manipulated in the same way," the illustrator comments.

And when stuck for an idea, it's those sketches that invariably do the trick—not concepts, but pictorial elements that might be in the final image.

Once a concept sketch is refined, simplified, and improved, Nemec asks himself what would make the illustration even more interesting: "An unusual point of view; some strange angle; should I change the relative scale of things?" None of these changes would alter the *basic concept,* but they do help Nemec create a stronger, tighter second sketch.

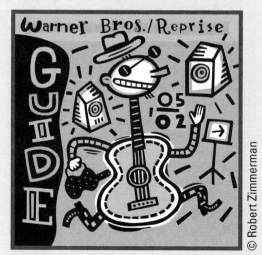

© Robert Zimmerman

© Gregory Nemec

# PROFILES

## *Peter Kuper*

You could certainly label Peter Kuper's work as narrative—which the illustrator nicely equates to visually "picking a moment." Kuper simply enjoys telling a story, and revels in the opportunity. "Putting together writing and drawing like this is ideally suited for all the areas I want to cover," he says.

When Kuper does an illustration, he thinks about the flow of the piece—how your eye will enter the picture and move through it. Not coincidentally, this is just the way you *read* the story; he is conscious of the fact that you are usually going to enter the illustration from the left. "It's the same way I think when I draw a comic page, where I direct your eye to go from panel to panel," he compares.

The comics he refers to are dictated by either a personal experience or an issue that concerns

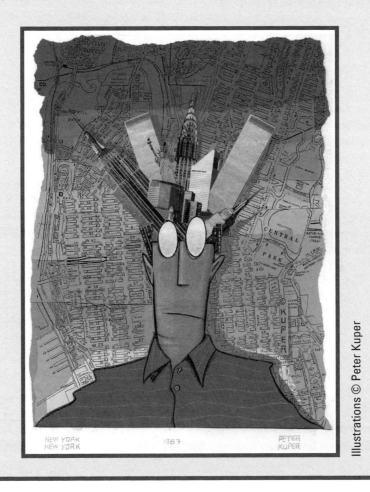

NEW YORK NEW YORK    1987    PETER KUPER

Illustrations © Peter Kuper

the illustrator. Kuper says he also keeps up with the news. His travels have been a great source of material for him, as well. Mostly driven by cultural, social, and political subject matter, the artist is often called to do assignments with which he is already familiar.

To get the ideas rolling, Kuper may simply think about what his subject would say, and the associated images with such a dialogue. There may be one line from the text that strikes and inspires the artist. He may doodle, or just write the words down. Kuper will look at the word forms and often incorporate those word forms into illustration; perhaps because the subject is rather hard to describe with an image alone.

An actual illustration starts with a pencil sketch that, when fine-tuned, is then photocopied. A stencil is cut from that copy. Areas that are to be black (or color) are actually cut-out holes in the stencil paper.

In the spray booth, a loose spray is applied. If it's a color piece, Kuper usually sprays red first, and without moving the stencil, sprays black on top of that. This gives the element just an underspray of red with what the illustrator calls a "hard-holding black."

Back at the lightbox, another photocopy of the original image is used to tighten up the drawing. "Because of the nature of the stencil," Kuper instructs, "you have to have connecting places. Here I will put those connections back in."

A background may be a separate stencil, but this varies. The illustrator may just use watercolor. Or, he will go back to doing colored pencil and watercolor, and then add one or two collage elements. "I like to do this because the stencil itself makes a very iconic, reasonably flat image; using a little bit of photo collage gives a quality of reality I want a piece to have. Social topics need that sort of reality."

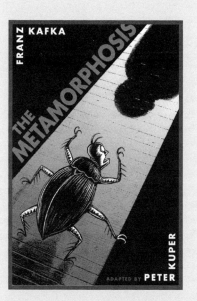

# PROFILES

*John Jinks*

That good, sharp knife we mentioned in the text is one of John Jinks' first priorities. Jinks uses a #11 X-acto blade for all cutting and scraping on his work surface. His airbrush of choice is an Iwata HPBC-2, a responsive, bottom-fed brush with removable color cups to allow quick changing of colors.

The illustrator also prefers a high tack frisket film for masking (and here, Jinks recommends going with a high-quality brand like Badger). Better frisket allows the precise cutting Jinks demands, as well as the easy removal and

reapplication of that frisket on already painted surfaces.

Complementing this, Jinks also employs .003 mm clear acetate. "It makes for easy scoring, breaks very clean, and leaves clear-cut edges," Jinks says. These masks are then taped to the board with a low tack drafting tape. Drafting tape is made to be easily removed and reapplied without pulling up existing paint.

When considering process, the artist says that every job involves many factors. One big concern is the client relationship. "Sometimes the art director or creative director can influence a job to the point of brilliance or mediocracy," Jinks comments.

He feels that getting *mutual* needs in line can make or break the gig. "I really like the interaction," he says. "Most of the time it's more like fun than work. A great client, a mutual respect, can be very satisfying."

Once those needs are determined, Jinks can form his visual approach. This is important be-

All illustrations © John Jinks

cause it saves time, provides the motivation, and makes it easier to get satisfactory results for both parties.

The illustrator looks for inspiration from many sources. "Sometimes it comes easy; other times, you have to dig," he says. "I don't think I have a set way of going about this, and it's most often dictated by the job and the client." He may look at art, explore nature, study the lyrics to a song; it might even be a commercial or news broadcast on TV.

Jinks usually starts a job by sketching a lot on tracing paper, forming rough ideas and refining them to the point of presentation. While he may need figure or object reference, he invariably tends to draw his subject matter from scratch. "This lends my particular style to the piece," he points out.

The sketch is then scanned into the computer for refinement, usually in the form of scaling or distorting. There are often several versions of this rough, and after working on the visual, Jinks may just walk away from it to look later with fresh eyes. When the sketch is satisfactory, the illustrator sends it via e-mail to the client. "My sketches are rather tight and a good representation of the final artwork," Jinks adds.

Once the client likes the sketch, a color pencil study is done (time and budget permitting) before moving on to the final piece. Also pretty tight, this version gives both illustrator and client a true guide to the end result. "I then project the sketch up to final size on illustration board and begin the painting."

## in review

1. Why does a good or better scratchboard make a big difference? In general, what are the plusses and minuses of working with premium-quality materials? Would this be important in the airbrush process in particular?

2. Name at least one advantage to working a scratchboard illustration digitally.

3. Exactly how could a process like stencil move you away from bad drawing habits? What are *your* "bad" drawing habits? What steps could you take to remedy these problems?

4. To your way of thinking, has the computer replaced the airbrush?

5. What are your thoughts on 3-D illustration, calligraphy, and graffiti? In your estimation, are any of these *not* bonafide illustration forms—and why?

## exercises

1. Airbrush involves equipment. If you (or your school) do not have the hardware, find a secondary tech or trade school that does. Volunteer your art/design teaching time in exchange for a class or studio access to explore this process.

2. Try scratchboard. Here's the assignment: Isolate a 1-inch square (or perhaps a 1 by 1.5 in. rectangle) *of anything* and blow it up to *full* board size.

3. Ask a friend to name an adjective, ask another to supply a noun, find a third person to give you a verb, and one more to come up with an adverb. Visually express this phrase in a multi-color stencil illustration. No smaller than full-page size, and no words!

4. Pick a passage from a Shakespearean play. Do a multi-color, modern graffiti-style visual interpretation (words are optional). But there's a kicker: Do it *wall-sized* (extra credit if you *legally* do it on an actual wall).

5. Do a calligraphy portrait (or self-portrait) using only descriptive and visually interpretive words and letterforms. Variation: do a group calligraphy portrait using only descriptive and visually interpretive words and letterforms (and different words and letterforms for each individual).

**notes**

© Mary Thielen

Collage, Cut Paper, Fabric

*"I try not to use too many digital effects, and basically for the most part I work on the computer much the way that I collage by hand. It was a gradual transition; very gradual. But one day it hit me—I can do all this on the computer—and I went the opposite way."*

**Tom Nick Cocotos, illustrator**

*"When I first started creating collages I was using any handmade paper I could find, starting with Arches cold press watercolor stock, metallic gift papers, and Pantone gradient papers. I went through hundreds of X-acto #11 blades a month (and band-aids for that matter)."*

**David Bishop, illustrator**

*"I work quite hard, but a person trying to replicate what I do on the computer would probably work almost as hard to simulate that effect. When I show my portfolio, people often try to feel the texture of the piece. They really want to experience the effect of the actual texture—the very nostalgia of fabric: a favorite corduroy; a certain plaid you wore on that first day of school; a sweater of your Mother's. Color, texture, and fabric really say something about you."*

**Margaret Cusack, illustrator**

## Chapter Objectives:

Provide a continued overview of illustration techniques beyond "traditional" painting and drawing

Look at both traditional and digital collage

Talk about cut paper (and related) illustration

Examine techniques done on fabric: both stitched and batik illustration

## Introduction

As stated in Chapter 8, painting and drawing may justifiably provide the framework for general illustration, but what about those processes that complete and complement the structure? Let's take a look at some popular techniques that veer somewhat left or right off the cornerstones.

Figure **9-1**

Collage can incorporate almost anything—if it can be digitally applied or traditionally adhered to the picture plane, go for it. Tom Garrett created *Walk* by layering paint, glazes, and a variety of paper elements into place. (© Tom Garrett)

# COLLAGE

The beauty of collage—in either digital or traditional manifestations—is that the process allows you to grab, cut, and paste just about anything (see Figure 9-1). What goes into a collage? You name it—photographs, papers, foils, and cardboards; clay and cloth; wire, strings, and stitching; recyclables or throwaways; visual treasures or aesthetic junk—if you can adhere it some way, you can collage it. Add paint, mark or stain the surface (if so desired). Fashion it by hand, create the thing digitally, or play with a best-of-both-worlds hybrid. But do it.

## Stick to It

How to adhere the design elements to your piece? Serious collage artists will find that one's glue of choice is as important as anything else. There are a variety of bonding agents out there. The wealth of available liquids, sheets, roll-ons, tapes, aerosols, pastes, and sticks have individual advantages and disadvantages. Most glues are usually cheap enough, so that's probably not going to be your main consideration. Hold, durability, wrinkling and bleed, archival concerns, plus very real health and environmental impacts are more the issue.

We must mention immediately that those handy and super-strong spray adhesives are also environmentally unfriendly and rather toxic health hazards. They present a questionable option, so take good care. Use these sprays with caution and adequate ventilation, if and when you must use them at all.

Based on the recommendation of another collage artist, Tom Garrett began working with glue sticks. "It changed my life," he states, and Uhu sticks are this illustrator's favorite glue. "The purple glue stick is a must," Garrett insists. "You can see where you are putting the glue before the sucker dries."

## A Photo Finish

When selecting photography, avoid imagery that is already powerful and artful. Instead, seek out pictures of ordinary things that you can creatively empower—images that will be secondary players to your concept.

Be sensitive to copyright, and pay usage fees when applicable. There is also the quality control issue—the final illustration must look like it was created *by you*, rather than cut and pasted bits of other photographers' imagery.

## The Advantages of Digital Collage

For many collage artists, an actual finish will start with "real" papers, paints, and boards (an so on), but it's next scanned into Photoshop for color correction and revisions. Art that was formerly shot as an $8'' \times 10''$ transparency can now be e-mailed to the client. The give and take of corrections, revisions, and shipping could literally take days and days. Working digitally, the entire process is not only easier, but much quicker (see Figure 9-2).

Figure **9-2**

This is digital collage. The artist is Tom Nick Cocotos, who tells us, "I don't want to create something digitally that looks unnatural. I don't want it perfect—I just do it quickly and roughly. As in my traditional collage, I don't try to get too exact with my cutting, I like to keep that sort of choppy look." (© Tom Nick Cocotos 2003)

# CUT PAPER

I want to briefly mention two related processes to begin our discussion. *Papier-maché* involves cut or torn paper (see Figure 9-3), and has been used to create furniture, jewelry, and objects d'art for centuries. It is a base material for the quintessential elementary art school experience, but also the heart of some slick and stylish (and truly adult) art.

Figure **9-3**

*Norm and Dot* is acrylic and oil pastel liberally laid on top of a *very* heavy base of paper. I built up successive layers of scrap to create a rough surface relief and texture. It was this collage technique that gave the illustration a particularly rich and tactile face. (© Michael Fleishman 2003)

I mention it here because paper *scrap* is also the core ingredient in the production of paper *pulp*—in and of itself a viable art medium. Check out the work of author/illustrator Denise Fleming (and no less an art world luminary than David Hockney) to qualify that point. You'll be amazed at what gooey gobs of blended, liquefied, and strained paper can do.

## A Snippet of History

Scherenschnitte—the traditional art and craft of paper cutting—dates back centuries, and flourishes yet today. Silhouettes and lace cutwork have been popular since early times. The 1980s saw an updated wave (for that day) of what I would call a faux Scherenschnitte/paper-cut-style illustration. And while that particular drawing approach is no longer hot, you will find that the many variations of the cut-paper look are still pretty cool.

## Basic Stuff

Paper cutting supplies are, at the essence, quite basic: good scissors and a sharp knife (with the emphasis on quality), a pencil or pen, a decent glue, and—of course—paper. Serious paper cutters learn quickly that higher-grade utensils are a definite plus, and that a variety of papers is the spice of life, but at its heart, the medium is highly portable and very cost efficient.

## I Got a Paper Cut

Cut (or torn) paper illustration is a visual treat because of that mix of papers and the resulting range of shape, hue, values, and textures achieved (see Figure 9-4). There is a big world of papers out there. Many artists also create their own surfaces, producing an eclectic fusion of patterns, grains, tone, and color. It's a stale old chestnut, but the only real limit is you—your imagination and creativity, and how you put all these components together.

Cutting and pasting is not an Olympic event, and that's the meat of it. But artists like Romare Beardon, Mary Thelen, Eric Carle, and Christopher Myers are all world-class creatives working with cut paper.

# FABRIC: STITCH

Let's clarify that you may be using two different techniques when working with fabric. Machine appliqué is one method. Here, you are actually applying many pieces of fabric onto a backing cloth using a sewing machine zigzag stitch (FYI: There is the hand appliqué method, as well). The other process, hand embroidery, is stitching by hand onto one piece of fabric (see Figure 9-5).

Simply put, your supplies will be a bit different from most illustrators' needed materials. In many cases, you will employ standard and traditional sewing techniques and materials, as well as the more specialized tools of the trade.

Figure |9-5|

Yes, this is stitched illustration, made the old-fashioned way with needle and thread! Margaret Cusack creates samplers, quilted illustration, soft sculpture, and so on for clients like *Time* magazine, the *Wall Street Journal,* the U. S. Postal Service, and more. (© Margaret Cusack)

## A Classical Process

This is a process where digital technology plays a secondary role to traditional thinking and hand skills. Like illustrator Margaret Cusack, you may use your Mac to create and manipulate typography, but not actually go to the computer for design work. Traditional pencil and tracing paper, a projector to re-size sketches and trace images onto fabric, and a photocopier (to repeat or flip an image), plus "normal sewing supplies" will round out the supply list.

Depending on the size of your final, a yard of fabric may last a long time, and having a variety of fabrics on hand is important. As with drawing or painting, you will develop a visual vocabulary of color and texture. But remember, the language of this palette will be the variety of fabric you collect.

A piece featuring complicated, minute lettering means scaling the original up so the lettering will be easier to work with. A note here: in some cases, lettering can be painted on and then stitched over. In other cases, you may actually cut out the individual letter forms—a rather intense proposition, to be sure (Cusack works with existing typefaces, but also designs the lettering from scratch). Stitched typography presents an interesting and challenging alternative to the traditional mindset and manipulation of print letterforms.

### Roughing It Out

With any illustration assignment, doing a rough is a smart idea. A fabric paste-up based on an initial sketch is helpful for both art director and artist to better understand the image and resolve important decisions *before* working on the final. Simply discussing cloth and fabric colors or textures doesn't quite, well, *cut it* (especially because most art directors are novices when it comes to this unusual medium).

### Next Steps

Prepare your final fabric choices. With glue or fusible webbing, secure the fabric pieces in place (this will facilitate the sewing process). All edges are overlapped slightly, and with everything held in position, the pieces are sewn with the aforementioned zigzag stitch to hold it all together.

Quilted edges, zigzag, and other decorative stitches can also telegraph the idea that you are creating a stitched piece. Stitches like the blanket stitch (which looks like a straight line with small, perpendicular stitches) do nothing for the piece physically, but simply enhance the sewn look of the art.

### Final

In terms of presentation, the finished artwork is stapled to canvas stretchers or foamcore board for a trip to the photographer. You read right; getting the job to the client means that your finished piece will then be photographed.

It's important that the photography enhance the dimension of the stitching and that the lighting be even. We should mention that this step is a client expense and completely up front in the job contract.

# FABRIC: BATIK

Batik is not tie-dye, although the two processes share similar materials and basic procedures. Batik is a demanding, technical, and overtly physical process. There is chemistry involved as well as organization, and you must keep things moving—you're not just sitting and doing the same daily routine.

What's so exciting about this process is that the distinctive crackle effect Batik is known for is just a pure, natural occurrence that comes from swishing the fabric around in the dye. The wax cracks, and the dye gets in those cracks, creating a visual testament to the whole kinetic process. The look is exhilarating and rich, whether it's reproduced for publication, on clothing, hanging on walls, or hanging in front of windows (pretty cool—light coming from behind a Batik produces a sparkling stained glass effect. See the profile on Robin Zimmerman for more on this).

Yes, dye is messy and *very* permanent. Batik can be frustrating, but as you get better at it, you'll master the dyes and control the wax. You can make brilliant images with the process.

As an illustrator, the style can be a unique signature—very distinct and definitely not mass-produced.

## The General Process

Please note that in this particular Batik technique you will not dye in boiling water, as doing so would melt the wax. You'll be using specialized dyes that are fiber reactive, and specifically suited to the Batik process.

Dyes are set with ordinary table salt (this you can buy in bulk from a feed and grain store). Setting the dyes also requires soda ash, purchased from a swimming pool supply company and bought in bulk (large quantities of this stuff saves money).

Paint the wax on with ordinary, good-quality brushes or perhaps bamboo Japanese watercolor brushes.

## Step One

Wash unbleached muslin cotton in extremely hot water with a degreasing agent. This takes any of the oils out of the cotton that may impede the dying process. When the cloth is dry, a design is then drawn with a Sharpie marker. Use a lightbox so you can see the sketch through the cloth. As assignments can be ganged in batches, you may find that you do all this line work on one day.

## Step Two

Mix up small jars of dye. The dyes are only good for about six *hours,* after which they exhaust themselves and lose permanency. Mix up tiny amounts of the dye powder plus a fixative right into the little containers. Add a thickening agent so the solution does not just spread out immediately when it hits the natural cloth fiber. Thus, you can maintain a clear crisp line of color. Master Batik artist Robin Zimmerman recommends that you apply darker colors first.

In classical Batik, you dye your cloth a light color, wax, dye another (perhaps darker) color, then wax *that* area. You end up with more of an earth tone (or at worst, a muddy) background color because you are *over-dying.*

Like working on paper, your themes may dictate that you paint directly onto white. So remember, you are painting directly onto the cloth here—you layer the image via a variety of colors, much like traditional illustration.

Thus, you can establish a range of value—lighten value by diluting with water; darken value by adding more powder and dye setters to the mix (which makes the dyes more permanent to the cloth). It's similar to working with watercolors, actually.

Colors are dried very slowly, and longer. This means the rich colors set deeper, and last longer.

## Step Three

Heat up a mixture of beeswax and paraffin in an electric skillet. Paint the wax onto the fiber. As it cools, the wax hardens and will act as a resist when you take the cloth to a tub of dye.

Next mix up the same powder dyes used in the paint process, but now in much larger quantities. About one cup of powdered dye to 10 cups of salt will give you intense, vibrant color. The salt wets the fabric out and drives the dye into the fiber. Hot water (not so hot that it melts the wax, though) makes a difference.

Add the cloth to the water. Keeping the fabric agitated allows the dye to get in every crease. Go for the most solid, uniform background color you can get, with no hint of it being left folded in the tub.

## Step Four

When this solid background color is achieved, the dye fixative (soda ash) is added. Once this color is thoroughly saturated, the dye has set. Put the cloth in the washing machine, spin and rinse out the excess dye, then fill the washing machine up again with the hottest water you can get. Wash the fiber, agitate it all out slowly and air dry the cloth on the clothesline.

| TIP |

Newsprint ink can sometimes dirty the cloth. It may be better to use plain newsprint paper (no ink) as opposed to the good ol' Sunday news to sop up the wax in your ironing process.

When the cloth is dry on the line, iron the wax out. Use a "newsprint paper sandwich" to absorb the wax. Change the newsprint repeatedly to catch the residue, but you'll find that this does not get all the wax out. So head over to the dry cleaners. Dry cleaning fluid dissolves and removes the remaining wax, bringing the cloth back to its original softness. See Figure 9-6 for a lovely sample of Batik.

Figure | 9-6 |

Robin Zimmerman's shimmering Batik is a fine example of this captivating technique.
(© Robin Zimmerman)

## SUMMING IT UP

While these techniques may be considered left of the traditional center of illustration (drawing and painting), they are hardly secondary to an inventive illustrator's repertoire. All offer creative challenges and rewards and are well worth your exploration.

# PROFILES

## *Tom Garrett*

*Love Hurts*

One of Tom Garrett's buzzwords is *perseverance.* "Have faith and original ideas will be eventually rewarded," he offers. The road to that reward starts by free association; jotting down words that first come to him with crude thumbnail sketches. For example, a "Walk" illustration, done for a local AIGA began by writing down visual clichés dealing with taking a walk: shoes, landscapes, birds, and so on.

This first list prompts him to rethink the obvious and to keep asking: *how can it be done differently?* Complex visual metaphors can often throw the viewer off, but simple symbols combined *just so* might actually say something *brand new.*

Garrett deals with all that, right up front. Thumbnails, then enlarged images, come next and keep the freshness of his ideas alive. Once roughs are at the working size, Garrett redraws the sketches into "something legible and hopefully interesting."

Then the illustrator tweaks the composition. Here, Garrett says he simply "draws and draws. I go through quite a bit of tracing paper to refine my ideas into something that works. This might take anywhere from 10–20 sketches."

Garrett notes that he now uses the computer in many stages of his collage process. He can create roughs manually, scan them, then modify and rearrange these drawings in Photoshop.

"This might be a minor compositional change or flipping an image to rework and improve the sketch," he says.

Once the sketches are up to par and approved, a larger version of the sketch is transferred to tracing paper. Used as an overlay on the board for the final, this helps to position and size the elements in the illustration as per the original sketch.

With this done, the illustrator starts painting the background on bristol board, employing everything from wet-on-wet to drybrush technique. He builds layers by further painting, glazing, and collaging different papers into place.

Simplifying complex information into readable visual metaphors, and empowering a more human quality into a dry topic are welcome challenges. Making a "better picture" sounds simplistic, but that is the goal, and Garrett is truly excited about these opportunities. The final collage may represent a most satisfying completion and closure, but the beginning of the process is rich with all the *possibilities.*

# PROFILES

## *Margaret Cusack*

You might describe Margaret Cusack's illustration as realism, but the fact that it is done with stitchery and fabric throws a bit of a curve at that label. Based on the graphic design skills she learned at Pratt Institute, the artist has created her own special niche of stitched illustration. "I like to think that in the back of every art director's mind is a 'home-sweet-home'

stitched image that they can use to warm up their client's picture," she says.

When Cusack is asked to approach a conceptual problem, the artist does a series of what she calls "postcard-size" thumbnail sketches that tap into her own thinking process. For reference, she goes to an extensive resource bank that she keeps in her studio.

This is followed by a dialogue between art director and artist, via many rough sketches. "Drawing and thinking things through is one stage of an assignment I really love," the illustrator states. A *Time* magazine cover for an article on small towns is a good case in point. The article discussed the idea of people moving to small towns to avoid big city problems.

All illustrations © Margaret Cusack

Cusack's cover concept targeted the basic idea of moving (physically and metaphysically) to a small town "The image that we agreed on was a hill with a small town at the top of it," she tells us, "and then a lot of road curving up and little cars and moving vans heading towards the top of the hill. A small banner reading 'Why More Americans Are Fleeing to' and the words: 'Small Towns' are stitched.

"That particular idea was one of about ten sketches that I sent them. Some were icon-like images, others dealt with moving vans or with city streets; street scenes—there were many different things I went through before we settled on this particular concept. There was definitely a give and take exchange with the art director and *a lot* of faxes back and forth."

When the state of the sketch is resolved, Cusack refines the drawing and presents a rough fabric paste-up to her client. This preview of the color palette and textures helps the art director get a better understanding of the image. This stage also lets Cusack make certain color and value decisions *before* cutting out the final shapes.

Once selections are made, Cusack next prepares, places, and sews down her final fabric

choices. In this day and age of computers and instant digital shortcuts, the viewer may look at this illustrator's delightful art and quickly say, "This must be done in Photoshop—it looks *just like fabric*." No, no, no. Margaret Cusack will tell you it is actually done the old-fashioned way, it really *is* stitchery and fabric.

# PROFILES

## *Robin Zimmerman*

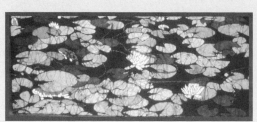

Everybody owns a few Sharpie markers, right? Robin Zimmerman uses the pen for a different reason than most illustrators, however. Robin does Batik illustration, and uses this workhorse drawing tool because it will last through the rigorous physical process of dying—"Right to the very end," she says.

Zimmerman's conceptual process is all about her surroundings. She's an extreme lover of nature, and all of her work is realistic. Lately the illustrator is moving towards landscapes, but her work will almost always contain imagery of animals and birds, trees, or flowers.

This comes from living on an 8-acre farm in the country (and another place in the north woods of Michigan's upper peninsula) plus extensive travel. A recent journey to England, Scotland, and Wales provided the inspiration and reference for a study of shaggy redhead cattle. "I am painting the animals, the cliffs, and the highlands of that region with dyes," Zimmerman tells us. "The colors I saw are a challenge."

But adroitly meeting such creative tests by way of a truly demanding medium is what Zimmerman has been doing for years. It's quite evident in her print work and book covers. And it's exactly why the Audubon Society recently commissioned Zimmerman to design a series of 4-foot long, 2-foot wide banners for their bird, reptile, and amphibian educational room.

"The Society wanted the panels done in fiber to help absorb sounds in what is a really loud room. Fiber will help soak up the noise, quiet it all down. Batik, when hung in the windows, will interact with incoming light almost like stained glass—it has that glow to it. This client felt that this would be the perfect solution to the problem—colorful and educational, with a look like glass, but weighing only half a pound!"

The influence of technology for this artist and process? Not much. Zimmerman has bought a color copy machine—an HP all-in-one color copier scanner and printer. "However, the only button that I push is the one that says reduce and enlarge," the artist laughs, "I did utilize an overhead projector for the Audubon banners. But, that's it; I don't use a computer."

Hey, that's the point. With Batik, you never know *quite* how it's going to turn out—it's not an exact science. There are happy accidents, the final result is not going to be "perfect." The work-intensive, overtly hand-done technique offers that one-of-a-kind vibe that people see and say, "Yeah, I can tell this is something that is not mass produced—it just doesn't look like everything else."

# PROFILES

*David Bishop*

In his textbook cover illustration, David Bishop used foamcore, ping pong balls, and Christmas ornaments, as well as gradient paper, gold foil, acetate gels, glass marbles, and Japanese art paper!

Plate glass was suspended vertically, allowing the disk and some objects to be suspended in air. A second set, laying flat, holds the other elements. Film is exposed first on one set, then the other, shifting components until the registration is correct.

The technique was modified later by exposing the transparencies separately, then combining both to make a duplicate, single transparency.

For a poster announcing a state-of-the-art heart monitoring system, Bishop's eclectic materials remain a staple of his collage technique. However, digital compositing has changed his method.

Bishop's components were a blue glass heart, satin fabric, Japanese paper, gold braided paper wire, and metallic gold paper. Bishop originally shot the heart suspended and backlit to reveal its depth. Later he added highlights to reveal the surface contours, but simply registered the two layers in Photoshop.

The fabric was one of three different materials photographed, and only one of several different folds. The gold paper was on a separate set with the Japanese tissue paper, and the gold wires were shot later against black. The composition is one of several layers, each with a selective mask that hides or reveals important details of that object.

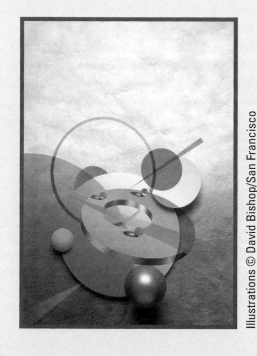

Illustrations © David Bishop/San Francisco

## in review

1. In your interpretation, what exactly is a collage? Is there such a thing as a collage of ideas? If so, how could you apply this in a visual context? What are the advantages of digital collage? Indeed, what are the advantages of using the computer in any or all of the extended or peripheral techniques discussed?

2. How does the Batik process described in this chapter differ from "typical" Batik technique?

3. How should we compare digital "stitchery" and collage with the "real thing"—hand-stitched art and traditionally cut and pasted collage? What are the differences?

4. When putting a collage together, why avoid photo images that are already powerful and artful? What's the problem here?

5. What are your thoughts on 3-D illustration, calligraphy and graffiti?

6. In your estimation, are any of the above not bona fide illustration forms? If so, why?

7. What is transfer paper?

## exercises

1. Create a traditional collage *self-portrait* incorporating a variety of found and devised elements. The collage can include photography. However, no photographs of *you* are permitted! Work larger—no smaller than 11 × 17 in.

2. Variation: Create a *digital* collage *portrait* without photographs, please.

3. Do a diary quilt: one week or a day in your life expressed as a stitched illustration.

4. Variation: Do a *digital* diary quilt: one week or a day in your life expressed as a stitched illustration.

5. Do a representational Batik about the love of your life.

6. Variation: Create a non-objective Batik of your most pressing problem.

**notes**

Digital Illustration

© Brian Zick 2000

*"Use new tools and technology if you can—don't reject them out of hand. I'm sorry that one-of-a-kind original illustrations disappear as more and more illustrators turn to the computer, but I think it's a small price to pay when I see creative artists pushing the digital envelope. Technology doesn't kill creativity, a closed mind does."*

**Elwood H. Smith, illustrator**

*"Modern illustrators, whether traditional or digital, face an ever-growing myriad of creative and tactical challenges. Successful veterans and emerging talents alike must work hard to fill niches that their competitors don't successfully occupy. Today's artists must remain true to their inner creative desires and succeed by being original, brilliant, and memorable, as well as savvy and resourceful."*

**David Julian, illustrator**

*"New technology does not mean a change in the creative process, new technology provides a different means by which you spit out your ideas—the delivery. The means of getting there are a little faster and more convenient, a little more controllable. It all happens in your head, anyway."*

**PJ Loughran, illustrator**

## Chapter Objectives:

Discuss the relevance of digital illustration, and provide a perspective on the role of digital illustration

Compare and contrast traditional and digital illustration

Review digital image-making and look at some important illustration applications

Explore a digital project

## Introduction

History points out that as computer speed and storage go up, up, up, price goes down, down, down. Hardware and software will have certainly changed between the time of this writing and the time you read these words. What you will get for your money will be bigger, faster, cheaper, and more powerful for sure. Use this chapter as a point of information—only as a guide—*not* as the definitive last word.

# UPGRADING TRADITION

Computer illustration is our era's breakthrough innovation, to say the least. Going digital has radically changed the illustrator's world. For the present generation of burgeoning professionals, it may seem that the computer has always been *the* illustration tool, now and forever. These folks may very well believe that we chronicle time by addending the suffixes B.C. (Before Computers) and A. D. (After Digital).

But even with the advance of the computer, you can still work as a traditional illustrator, with all those timeless tools of the trade. If that is your direction, please keep going, and don't stop.

This book is all about choices, and trust me, not *everybody* works on the computer. I myself work in both traditional and digital arenas and, like many of my colleagues, often marry the two processes in the same operation (see Figure 10-1).

There are die-hards who refuse to accept the computer on any artistic level, and some folks are just afraid to jump. No judgments from this corner, but I will say that you must embrace the computer if it will *advance your art,* not because "everybody works on the computer now," or because you think you have no choice. Work digitally if the computer is the right tool to get your job done with flair, precision, and efficiency.

# DIGITAL ILLUSTRATION DEMYSTIFIED

What would we do without computers? In terms of the *end result,* I would think exactly the same great illustration we were doing *before* the digital revolution.

Figure | 10-1 |

An illustration by Michael Wertz. Illustrators often combine digital and traditional techniques; this nicely syncopated portrait of musician Caetano Veloso was done in just that way. Wertz may begin with collage or screen print. Or he might use pastel or acrylic, pencil or photography. The artist then scans his preliminaries into his Mac to make the finish. The client was the Los Angeles Times Book Review; Carol Kaufman was the art director. (© Michael Wertz 2003)

My first Macintosh was grossly underpowered in every respect but potential. Exciting new tools (even humble tools in retrospect) are always terrific springboards. After all, it wasn't the crayons that produced the wonderful drawings of your elementary school days—it was the kid!

Bottom line, the computer is really just another art utensil. Okay, okay, that's a bit too pat. So, tools are just tools, huh? And technology is all relative? You *could* make that argument. Einstein used a humble piece of chalk to develop his theory of relativity; imagine Albert paraphrasing my opening sentiment every day: "What would we do without chalk?"

The computer immediately fit right in with my drawing supplies. It comfortably co-existed with the bulk of my art materials; just as my paints sat next to the inks, 90lb watercolor paper rubbed up against tracing pads, and the pencils worked with my markers (true, if you're smart, you don't use your airbrush in the same room, of course). In no time, my Mac became just as indispensable as any of those valued tools.

Fast, powerful, and versatile, the computer streamlined both my craft and the business end of my organization. And I still get a definite thrill when I see a new box of crayons. See Figure 10-2 for another artist's view of computer illustration.

Figure | **10-2** |

A computer can be central to both art and business. For many illustrators, the interaction is so extensive, the indispensable tool takes on real persona. C'mon, tell the truth—*you talk to your computer all the time*, don't you? This bright illustration is by Jeanne de la Houssaye. She works on a Mac; her software of choice is Adobe Illustrator. "I'm keeping this computer until he's truly obsolete," she smiles. "His name is G Whiz. When he has something to tell or ask me, he politely says 'A thousand pardons, gracious lady.'" (© Dynamic Graphics, Inc.)

Figure | 10-3 |

*Sit Straight* was done for this book, and is a combination of traditional and digital painting techniques. The hybrid figure study retains the brush, color, and paint qualities I push in my painted work, but is decidedly different than my cartooning or humorous illustration (either traditional or digital). (© Michael Fleishman 2003)

## No Paper? (Part One)

I keep hearing that paper and print will disappear; that all production and product will be totally digital. I hope this doesn't happen. It's a big world, with room for everyone, and all sorts of methodology.

My traditionalist side revels in the very act of drawing or painting on a real surface, with actual tools and physical materials. The computer can't *replace* the little rush you get from the silky flow of watercolors or the scratch of a great pen on good paper (and in a related issue, I wouldn't want screen time to supplant the fun and mystery of turning pages). Also, there is something quite intimate and primary about holding (and looking at) a final illustration in both hands.

It must be noted right here that no matter how you proceed—traditionally or on the cutting edge of technology—skills make all the difference. No software filter or preset will truly disguise meager drawing ability; just as thick paint can't hide poor color savvy.

## VARIETY

I paint, so I'm a *painter,* but this generic label merely places me in that big, metaphorical ballpark where all the "painters" play. Digital style and technique are not fixed classifications. You may work digitally, but that doesn't have to typecast you.

The ways and means to do digital illustration are as varied as traditional painting styles and techniques (or *any* medium, for that matter). Chris Spollen's illustration is decidedly different than David Julian's work. For that matter, Spollen's new digital style looks nothing like his old approach. But we *can* safely say that you will be illustrating with vectors or pixels. See Figure 10-3 for an example of illustration using both traditional and digital techniques.

## A CHOICE

Illustrators work on the computer in two main image-making categories: bitmap (also called raster) and object-oriented (or vector). A bitmap image is made up of pixels (the "bits") arranged on a grid (or a checkerboard, if you will). The pixels are square dots of color or tone that, in combination, carry all the information about that picture you see on your monitor.

A big difference between vector and raster images is the imagery itself. Conventional wisdom points out that vector graphics boast a solid line with predominantly flat color, or perhaps a gradient-heavy look. Bitmapped images, on the other hand, usually offer photographic realism, a smooth blend of tone, and a subtle (or painterly) variation of color and texture. But these days, programs like Adobe Illustrator and Photoshop are evolving in some similar directions, as we will discuss.

## Bitmaps

Graphics software programs that use bitmaps are often labeled as *paint* programs. Analogous to the actual physical act of painting, these applications offer brush, pen, pencil, eraser, and other tools that push the metaphor and work much like their authentic counterparts. Like applying real paint, a line or stroke adds to, deletes, or replaces pictorial elements.

In a bitmap program you can work with individual pixels, whole shapes, or the entire image. Bitmap images are at a fixed resolution (each dot is one set size), so resizing the picture means that picture quality will change. If you enlarge a bitmap illustration, edges get jaggy and stair-stepped; the pixels become very obvious (the image becomes pixellated); you lose detail and clarity. The larger the image, the more pronounced the effect; therefore, we say that raster illustration is resolution dependent.

## Vectors

Software applications that employ object-oriented graphics are also known as *draw* (or *drawing*) or *illustration* programs. This type of format creates an image composed of objects (or groups of objects) built of lines, curves, and geometric shapes.

So, vector shapes are actually *mathematical* in origin, and thus can be manipulated and scaled without any loss of quality. You can enlarge a tiny vector object (or the entire illustration) to gargantuan proportions and your lines will still be crisp and clean on the page or on your monitor. Thus, we say that object-oriented drawings are resolution independent.

No matter how big the image, vector files are relatively small in size, especially in relation to bitmapped graphics. Why? A larger bitmapped illustration contains more pixels and the size of a raster file is determined by the number of pixels involved (and that's why full-color images or big photos are such monsters to display, store, and print). It's relatively easy to rasterize a vector image, but not quite as simple to go the other way (turning a bitmap image into a vector graphic entails conversion software like Adobe Streamline).

# Formats

Currently, the most common graphics file formats are:

- AI (Adobe Illustrator document.)

- BMP (.bmp—the basic DOS or Windows bitmapped file format.)

- GIF (Graphics Interchange Format—.gif. With an interchangeable hard or soft *g;* I've heard both. A basic format for images on the Web where limited colors and lower picture quality may be all you need.)

- EPS (.eps—Encapsulated Postscript. Can handle both vectors and bitmaps, but you'll need a Postscript printer to maximize scaling and resolution. Works great with object-oriented graphics.)

- JPEG (.jpg—abbreviated from Joint Photographic Experts Group. High-quality and fidelity with a range of image compression.)

- PDF (Portable Document File. This file will look exactly the same on any computer, any system.)

- PICT (.pct—the stock Macintosh designation; you can store both bitmap and vector information simultaneously.)

- PSD (.psd—Adobe Photoshop image format.)

- TIFF (.tif—Tagged Image File Format. These bitmap files can contain black and white, grayscale, color and photography. Great format for scanning images. High quality and fidelity can mean whoppin' big files.)

Other formats to mention: CDR (CorelDraw), CMX (Corel Exchange); CGM (Computer Graphics Metafile); DRW (Micrografx Draw); SWF (Shockwave Flash); DXF (AutoCAD and CAD software); WMF Windows Metafile.

© Phillip Mowery

Phillip 's Photoshop TIFF file could be saved in a number of formats: as an EPS, JPEG, or PSD (even as a GIF for the Web). Evaluating file formats means determining final usage, dimensions, and image quality.

Mowery works in Quark, so he'll likely be using TIFFs for CMYK images created in Photoshop (and ultimately placed in a page layout document).

And generally, an EPS format would be fine and have all the quality and versatility of a TIFF file (or more). For this particular image, Mowery may use the JPEG format for the Web rather than a GIF. "I think that a JPEG would represent subtle color variations better and be clearer overall," he points out.

Mowery's 350dpi TIFF file is 47MB. Saving the illustration as a PSD reduces the file size (but print output and quality may be an issue).

Likewise, creating a JPEG at a higher level of picture quality (lower compression) drops the file size, but brings up the same issues (saying that, many illustrators send jobs out electronically in the form of high-quality JPEGs).

A JPEG setting of low quality (which means higher compression) is quite small (Mowery's file shrinks to 852K), but there's no real print quality to speak of.

# THE PROGRAMS

Let's look at some applications you will use. There are other choices out there beyond Photoshop, Illustrator, Freehand, and Painter, but I'm going to limit this synopsis to the preceding titles.

Without slighting any fine products or makers, the following software established the industry standards, and, with every version, these programs continue to raise the bar for power, speed, features, versatility, and relative ease of use.

It's risky to speculate in regards to this volatile market; but it is also a pretty safe bet that these programs will endure for all the aforementioned reasons.

## Photoshop

Calling Adobe Photoshop a "simple" bitmap paint program is, well, a *bit* of an understatement. You can *illustrate*—"draw and paint"—in Photoshop with panache, but it is more. Yep, it's the premier photo-editing tool on the market, but saying it is "only" for photo-editing won't do this remarkable program justice either.

Photoshop is, and has been since it's debut, the hot rod application of the graphics world. It is the yardstick by which other image-manipulation programs measure their worth, and is the standard benchmark for users everywhere. In short, if you work in our industry, you know about Photoshop—or know how to use it.

All this for good reason. Photoshop's feature set is comprehensive. Each version expands and improves on an already broad array of smart, efficient tools and powerful capabilities. Plug-in architecture gives you the opportunity to adapt and customize through third-party add-ons.

There is a learning curve that comes with such grace, brain, and brawn, but it's well worth it— the program's potential feels only limited by your imagination and expertise!

As Photoshop evolves, new vistas have opened up for the program and made it even bigger and better. Of note: the raster-based program has acquired features found in its vector-oriented sister (Adobe Illustrator). Working with text is much improved, and Adobe has expanded Photoshop's ability to create images for the Web, as well. Photoshop's plug-in architecture allows the user to adapt and customize toolsets with third party add-ons (called, appropriately enough, plug-ins).

Something else to mention is the elegant interaction between Photoshop and Illustrator. You can easily put together an illustration that taps into the best aspects of both programs, resulting in a hybrid visual you couldn't achieve working in one application alone.

In fact, Adobe gives the user a well-designed, consistent interface shared by all its software. This integrated work environment is a master stroke of ingenuity—learn Photoshop and you'll feel right at home working in Illustrator (or the other Adobe titles).

## Adventures in Photoshop

*Hey, Look* began life as one of my "kitchen sink" mixed-media pieces—acrylic, marker and ink, pencil, crayon, and grease pencil on masonite board. I regarded the final illustration as only semi-successful, and always wanted to rework the composition.

On the plus side, I loved the surface texture and was quite happy with my rendering of the face itself. I particularly felt that I really nailed this gentleman's "dead" gaze. So I brought the illustration into Photoshop via my digital camera. I painlessly cropped a new composition out of the old (the original still exists intact).

I then futzed a bit with the Unsharp Mask filter. Next, I applied the halftone pattern option (filter > sketch > halftone pattern—if you must use filters, that's a decidedly cool choice; you can get a hip, faux "cheap reproduction" look when you fool with this effect).

Then I began to paint and play with color and value. One note: I abandoned the standard brush and pencil, and only used the dodge and burn tools (to lighten or darken), a large airbrush (set to dissolve, and at lower pressures) plus the clone stamp tool (a nifty retouching device and a fun and interesting "paint brush," as well).

A word about using filters: Filter "magic" is not necessarily personal creative power. Filters are fun. Filters are sweet. Filters produce all kinds of nice effects. But you actually expend precious little creative energy if all you do is hit that button. Filters *will not* and *do not* make you an artist; *you* are the artist. A filter can be a fine tool or a cheap gimmick. A filter effect should be used by choice (and with skill) and not by default.

I seldom use any filters on actual commissioned work or self-promotion. I prefer to explore these tools on experimental or personal pieces where serendipity won't confuse the issues.

© Michael Fleishman 2003

## Illustrator

Like Photoshop, Adobe Illustrator has set a standard for drawing programs since its launch. And for the same reasons: Illustrator is feature-laden and incredibly powerful. It's sophisticated and effective; a real workhorse that keeps improving with each upgrade.

Illustrator is simply a neatly engineered creative tool and a wonderful production environment. It works, and works well. Nicely integrated with Photoshop, the program is loaded with artistic rewards. But remember, we're not pushing pixels around here. Doping out points and segments, manipulating handles to maneuver paths, and understanding the intricacies of

Figure | 10-4 |

Adobe Illustrator is my "go-to" graphics software. This line art was used as the cover for a middle school curriculum package. I added the color for this book. (© Michael Fleishman 2003)

Illustrator's gear and options is downright tricky at first. Is it more difficult than mastering Photoshop? No, just different. And there's the same great payoff. See Figure 10-4 for an example of an image created in Adobe Illustrator.

And, we should say, as goes Photoshop, so goes Illustrator. The vector-based Illustrator has acquired features found in its bitmap-oriented complement. The application includes fine text-handling chops. Adobe has also stepped up the program's capability to generate Web graphics. More of that smart Adobe "one-stop shop" mindset has only made a great program sweeter yet.

This illustration for an education curriculum package was done in Macromedia Freehand, a great vector-based drawing application—and Adobe Illustrator's stalwart competition. (© Michael Fleishman)

As good as it is, Illustrator has a worthy "adversary"—Macromedia Freehand. And this presents a wonderful "dilemma" for the illustrator—the availability of two first-rate vector-based applications.

## Macromedia Freehand

The other nifty object-oriented illustration program and Illustrator's main competition is Macromedia Freehand. The two applications seem to run neck and neck in terms of features (bang for your buck), upgrades (this is truly a veritable horse race between these two programs), and advocates.

There's a lot of debate as to which interface is cleaner (Illustrator will win this one), but it's generally said that Freehand offers better text and page editing (especially when creating multiple-page documents).

Freehand is every bit as capable as Illustrator, and it's a tough call as to which program is *better*. Each has its *advantages*—I think the choice comes down to personal preference and the requirements of the assignment at hand (case in point: Freehand—like Illustrator—boasts ever-improving tools to create Web graphics, but Freehand offers a direct path to Macromedia Flash, a bulwark for Web animation). See Figure 10-5 for an example of an image created in Macromedia Freehand.

If you're thinking that the programs sound similar, you're absolutely right. These days I'm working far more in Illustrator; but when I work in Freehand I'm soon reminded what the good buzz is all about. Like its competitor, Freehand is just nicely done. It's an efficient and extremely capable vehicle for illustration. It also works and works well (if it didn't, there'd be no contest—Illustrator is that strong).

Figure | 10-6 |

The *digital* pastel work of David Milgrim. This buttery, amusing illustration was done with Painter software. (© David Milgrim)

## Corel Painter

For the illustrator, Corel Painter is a must-try application. Yes, this application offers both raster and vector capabilities, as well as typographic and Web facilities. So in that sense, it too adopts the "keep up with the Joneses" approach of most current software. All well and good, but if you're looking for one piece of software that truly and successfully emulates the variety of natural media, this is it. You'll swear it's as if you're using the actual stuff in this program—Painter uncannily and accurately mimics real-world techniques and materials (see Figure 10-6 and Figure 10-7).

The options and controls are vast and deep, and it's a complex program of tremendous creative power. If anything, Painter takes the rap for being too complicated and dense, offering *so much* that the interface tends to be confusing and cluttered.

I've worked with the program over the years and each upgrade offers even greater power and tools. Yes, Painter can be quite daunting (but to be honest and fair, no high-energy application escapes this ding), and every new version continues to clean up and streamline Painter's very busy act.

You'll just have to try it for yourself. I think you'll find that the only thing missing will be the pastel dust in the air, ink under your fingernails, and paint stains on those new jeans.

| NOTE |

I can't recommend one program over the other. Each shines in its own right; all have strengths and weaknesses. Before a trial run, I *would* highly recommend you read magazine and Web reviews, as well as talk to friends and pros for insight and input. When you compare Illustrator and Freehand, it really comes down to your need and the job requirements. Photoshop and Illustrator could be used together to maximize each program's potential. Ditto with Painter and Photoshop.

Figure | 10-7 |

*Prince Paul.* Overton Loyd scanned line art (done with his trusty Bic) and rendered color with a simple watercolor brush in Painter. The film strip in the background represents the performer's "cinematic" form of rapping. (© Overton Loyd)

## A DECISION

Let's talk some shop. What *is* the better professional choice—PC or Mac? I have used and owned Macintosh computers since 1986. Most "arty types" I talk to prefer the Mac, hands down. It is our industry's standard for good reasons: you work on a Macintosh for high resolution graphics, an intuitive (and consistent) interface, plus the availability of powerful illustration (and design) software. Mac hardware boasts speed, strength, and capacity, as well as a slick and sleek design—big power in a cool package, and for decent money.

But the lines are blurring. A die-hard PC enthusiast will contest any Mac advantage. The argument over which system is the "best" will not end soon. Truth is, over time, the Mac and the PC move ever closer. Great software is available for both formats. On either format, new systems and software developments emphasize ease-of-use, icon-based interfaces, sleek graphics (and of course, the capabilities to create slick art). Hardware evolves constantly and consistently. Maybe someday you won't have to make a decision. But currently you do, and the primary choice of your peers and your client base is Macintosh.

# HOW THE COMPUTER FITS IN

Many people simply fixate on the *economic* advantages of new media. These advantages can be substantial, and are obviously important, but surely that's not all.

New media means new technology, and this means innovative shortcuts and inventive techniques. While generally regarded as an appreciable boon, there are still those artists who remain steadfast traditionalists—sticking to "classical" methodology, if we can label it as such.

You can tap into the computer in many different ways—as a fast sketch tool, or for down and dirty color and/or compositional roughs. There are illustrators who use the computer as just *part* of their process. For instance, line work is done by hand and scanned into the computer for clean up. The line at this stage may be refined as necessary; color, texture and pattern are then added digitally to create the complete package. Many illustrators, myself included, work just this way.

Other illustrators scan picture elements into the computer, then incorporate or collage this material to produce the art. The artist processes these design components, and literally pieces together the digital final.

Some illustrators sketch on paper and transfer the rough to the computer. This drawing is then used as a template in their software of choice, with final art executed digitally.

And, of course, many illustrators work directly—*digita prima,* so to speak—no paper sketch, no scans, no template. It's all done completely on the computer.

Your approach will be a highly individual thing. See Figure 10-8 for one artist's unique digital method.

On a peripheral matter, the artist can also efficiently convey an image electronically. Many illustrators use the computer to deliver roughs (or finals) as attachments to e-mail, or burn visuals onto disk.

Art can also be picked up at a website (through a link and/or password the illustrator supplies). This is a good way to get big or complex art—which usually means a large or unwieldy file—to the client).

# PAPER IS DEAD . . . LONG LIVE PAPER?

As I mentioned before, some forecast that it will be a *paper-free* market in the near future; but currently, the traditional avenues for illustration are all still there (and will hopefully be there for the duration).

There are options for illustration apart from the standard advertising and editorial opportunities. Some of these openings are coming into play as a direct offshoot of the digital revolution.

Figure | 10-8 |

Your approach is an individual thing. Some illustrators really emphasize digital quality, others keep computer technique somewhat anonymous. David Bishop's intriguing combo of 2-D and 3-D elements blends paper assemblage, photography, and digital process into his own brand of mixed media.
(© David Bishop/San Francisco)

Some classical venues are picking up more steam as the computer's role in the design and illustration process grows. Let's take a look at digital illustration "off paper."

## The Net

The Internet thrives for many reasons, but let's narrow that book-length discussion down for our purposes. A big part of the appeal of the Internet is that the forum is so compellingly *visual.*

For illustrators, the Net offers a terrific showcase of creativity, an easily accessible, readily available portfolio review, and is an excellent marketing tool—websites have revolutionized the whole concept of marketing and promotion. All this at all hours, any day of the week, and global to boot.

Savvy illustrators can take full advantage of the interactive nature of the Web experience to promote, sell, and entertain, with just one sentence—"Hey, check out my website and my latest work."

The Web is a vehicle for illustration to go to work for a client (as in: sell a product, tell your story, drive home the concept, etc.). Illustration on the Net even advertises and enhances the Web experience itself—it's fun to "surf the Net," and cool, and diverting graphics are a big reason why.

## Video (Games and Otherwise)

The video game market has exploded and illustration is a considerable part of the mix. Play any video game and you will find illustration—in fact, video games are almost all illustration! A video game without illustration is unthinkable, but funny enough, this market is fairly tied into traditional illustration packaging.

There is, of course, character and environmental design and development. Labels on the cartridges and media; graphics on packages, holders, and sleeves; instructions, manuals and strategy guides; posters and game cards; advertising and promotion. With any video game, illustration is all over the place.

Video on DVD, CD, and VHS also employs illustration—primarily in packaging and in support, advertising, and promotional material. You may also find illustration as part of opening and end credits, as well as for menus and navigation.

## Animation

We are in a new golden age of animation (and its sister act, cartoons and comics). Just surf the Web, flip TV channels, head over to the Cineplex, or check out your video store to see for yourself.

As mentioned previously, the adult and juvenile market for animated product is absolutely *huge*. Traditional cel and sequential animation is struggling somewhat, as digital animation is no longer the "next big thing"—it is *the* big thing (see Figure 10-9).

Digital animation is booming on the Web, and on screens big and small, everywhere. This genre is a stomping ground for talented and visionary (and tech-smart) artists. Highbrow or lowbrow content doesn't seem to be a factor, computer animators are doing landmark work for a substantial, hungry market.

## Media

This entire chapter focuses on digital media (computers). Clearly, illustration has impacted print media: printing and publishing, journalism, advertising and editorial, comics and cartoons. Illustration plays a certain part for electrical media (telegraphy, telephony, music and recording): in packaging, or as part of promotional, informational and instructional materials or graphics.

Illustration also factors into the mix for mass media. Radio uses illustration for printed self-promotion. Besides animation, film taps into illustration for marketing and promotional purposes, as well as for (or during) end and opening credits.

While not to the same degree that animation has impacted the medium, "static" (non-animated) illustration has always played some part in the appeal of television. Whether it be as part of an-

Figure | 10-9 |

imated credits or graphics behind credits and titles; commercials (in whole or part); a station's ubiquitous logos; courtroom drawings; spots behind the news reports; or weather charts, illustration can be found on TV.

## MY STORY, AND I'M STICKING TO IT

For many years I could honestly say that my output (and not coincidentally, my marketing) ran about 50/50—half digital, half traditional. But gradually the tide turned, and I found myself doing more and more assignments on the computer.

My computer technique had already taken a nice little left turn from my traditional style. On paper my materials of choice were pen, brush, and ink; with watercolors or gouache, and colored pencil (see Figure 10-10).

When I began working digitally, I made a deliberate decision to do something different (see Figure 10-11). My characterization and line style remained, but I consciously skipped the colored pencil gradations. I opted for flat, brighter, bouncier, *pure* color and kept the gradated approach on the back burner.

Technically, this felt both revolutionary and evolutionary—I wanted to shake things up a bit, but maintain a certain comfort level and link to my existing process. To get this, I started out in Photoshop, and used a wonderful little paint program called Colorize.

Frankly, I resisted any object-oriented applications. Manhandling paths and points seemed foreign to my method—it just wasn't *me.* That's true enough, but I was also being somewhat complacent. Those dreaded vectors seemed a bit *too* radical, and I had a comfy "if it ain't broke, don't fix it" routine that was working.

But as both a freelancer and a teacher of illustration, I was smart enough to know I had to at least *try* to keep current, so I occasionally dabbled with Illustrator (actually, in retrospect, I tried Freehand first). And eventually some jobs came around that challenged and changed my cozy bitmapped attitude.

Figure | **10-10**

An example of my work B. C. (Before Computer). (© Michael Fleishman 2003)

The jury was in, if I wanted certain gigs, I had to make a jump and do a bit of a juggle—and I did. The more I got into Illustrator and Freehand, I saw that I actually *liked* the vector environment. I kept wondering why I hadn't realized how sweet this all was. I was challenged by the learning curve, and stimulated by the experience.

Figure | **10-11**

One example of my work A. D. (After Digital). (© Michael Fleishman 2003)

As I progressed, I gravitated more towards Adobe Illustrator. I could scan line art into Photoshop and then bring the drawing into Illustrator as is, or convert the bitmapped lines into vector shapes via Adobe Streamline.

Or I could do it all right in Illustrator. You can draw wonderfully calligraphic and nuanced strokes within the program itself, and these lines look *good*. In fact, I even created a library of my own lines (hand drawn, scanned, and brought into Illustrator through Photoshop). Well, this was just *too* cool.

And when all is said and done, the element of pure *fun* was a major factor in my move to vector-based illustration—and definitely a good reason to work digitally, in general.

## ABOUT WORKING DIGITALLY

A very short note about equipment. My set-up continues to evolve over the years, but there are constants that make the digital illustration process a whole lot easier.

A digitizing tablet has been on my drawing table from the very beginning. I prefer the Wacom $12 \times 12$-inch size, but this invaluable tool comes in many configurations, both small and large (including a tablet that doubles as your screen, and enables you to draw directly on the monitor). Get the hang of working with a stylus and you'll never draw with a mouse again.

A large monitor is a must. In fact, consider using *two* monitors that are coordinated to act as one (much bigger) display. Size the screens to fit your economic, space, and pictorial needs (for instance, these days I link a 19-inch with a 17-inch CRT). After working with this expanded real estate you'll wonder how you ever got along with just one screen.

And if you create large files, heed David Julian's good advice: "The most important thing aside from processor speed," he says, "is to have very, very fast drives, and to get the most amount of RAM you can."

### Let's Begin

Get a concept together. My illustration (digital or traditional) always begins with a *drawing*—the line. For my demo here, I was actually inspired by a certain section of the roughs snapshot I put together for an earlier chapter.

So begin here, as well—dope out your concept, then create your line work (see Figure 10-12a). For the sake of this sample project, we're going to mix and match our approach—let's draw the line art traditionally. Thinking about color is important, but comes just a bit later.

## The Scan

Scanned pencils can give you some interesting line quality—it all depends on what you're after with your concept; but let's scan an ink (or inked) drawing for this demonstration.

You have other decisions at this point. Your drawing may be very polished or rather loose. While I usually choose to refine my pre-liminaries—my roughs are seldom very *rough*—I want to draw directly in Illustrator for this demo. And as I said, we must first scan that sketch right into Photoshop.

## Where to Next?

Now you can go a number of ways.

1. The scanned art is cleaned up and finessed, then finished in Photoshop. Here, your grayscale or bitmapped line art should be somewhere in the neighborhood of 300–400 dpi and saved as a TIFF.

2. You could take the bitmap file into Adobe Streamline and convert it into a vector-based illustration. Streamline permits you to ad-just the conversion setup, but "streamlining" often adds its own flavor to your line quality. Explore and learn the settings that achieve the tightest fidelity to your work. Once streamlined, the art is now editable in Illustrator or Freehand.

3. Or think of your drawing as a template. Here, you scan the line art into Photoshop, then create the actual illustration in Pho-toshop or Illustrator on top of this visual—sort of like virtual tracing paper (hint: if you use the art as a template in Illustra-tor, you may want to save the scan as a smaller-sized PICT). Again, this is the method we will use for this demonstration (see Figure 10-12b).

## What a Character

There are many ways to create great line quality. You may opt for the tried and true, time-honored method—you do it by hand.

In Photoshop, you might select the *brush tool,* open up the brushes palette, and choose a brush. Use as is, or tap into the program's exten-sive control set to customize that brush.

Figure | 10-12a |

The initial doodles and notes for the concept for *Buds*. This sketch was scanned (as is) into Photoshop as line art. (© Michael Fleishman 2003)

Figure | 10-12b |

I've cropped the rough in Photoshop, then placed it into Illustrator as a template. (© Michael Fleishman 2003)

Illustrator offers some slick brush options. Brushes come in different categories that present a tremendous range of line opportunities. I should clarify: You're not actually drawing a line; you're creating a *stroke,* of course. You're still making a path composed of segments with anchors that have direction lines and points. But you get a stroke that looks remarkably natural and is surprisingly responsive.

You can manipulate that stroke with a wide variety of tools and commands, and *redrawing*—reshaping—is a dream. Literally, it's a snap; you can redraw a stroke by simply dragging another line adjacent to an existing stroke—the initial line magically snaps to the new stroke. You can reshape with the pencil, brush, smooth, and erase tools, as well as the classic pen tools.

Make a mistake? Change your mind? No problem—do a Command Z (undo) until you're back to square one. Want more choices? Go to the brush libraries for other alternatives, or customize existing brushes. And as said before, you can even create personal brush libraries using your own actual lines.

## Ready, Set . . .

When asked to comment about his use of third-party special effects to interact with his Adobe software, David Julian smiles and says, "I'm not a filter hound."

I see exactly where Julian is coming from. It's educational to dabble with all the many bells and whistles a good graphics application has in its repertoire. It is fun to try out all the on-board gizmos. There are various filter, preset, and style packages you can add on, as well.

But like many digital illustrators, I like to keep things clean and simple. To my eyes, there is an obvious (and often overblown, in the wrong hands) "computer look" I never cared for, and still scrupulously avoid.

So, let's continue our little clean and simple demo that taps into some basic Illustrator tools.

## Go!

Open up a new Illustrator document and place your drawing as a template (make sure the template and link boxes are checked in the dialogue box). Once we're back to our document, the Layers window should indicate that the rough came in with a *template* designation. On your screen it will be grayed around 50 percent (you can lighten the value even further).

Your rough should be the second layer down on the list (under *Layer 1*). Unlock the layer, so you can size the template up or down. Size it and lock the template layer again (so you don't move it inadvertently).

Rename *Layer 1,* if you wish. *Make sure you're working in this layer* (*not the template*). Under Window in the Menu Bar choose *Show Brushes* (if the Brush palette isn't up already), and/or choose a brush library from *Brush Libraries*. Grab a brush. Select the Brush tool from the toolbox. Make sure you are working with the Stroke and that Fill is set to none (you could also draw with the pencil tool and apply the brush to these strokes, but I usually just draw with the brush tool directly). See Figure 10-12c.

Now—trace over your template. It's that simple.

## Keep Going

That's the beauty of it—it's easy to do, but your control over these lines is quite powerful and extensive. Reshape, resize, and reposition your lines at will; the toolbox offers so many options to get your drawing exactly the way you want it. When you have your line work just right, it's time to lay in the color (see Figure 10-12d and Figure 10-12e).

## Color

I created and closed my color fields with the pencil tool, but you could select the pen tool for a more geometric look. While I chose the more freeform shapes for this demo, the angled look is just as lively. Here's how to exercise this option.

Figure 10-12c

My rough is now the template for my illustration; renamed and in the right layer—below the actual illustration. Once I have the grayed-out image to size and position, I'll relock this template layer and start the drawing. (Illustration © Michael Fleishman 2003)

Select (from the swatch libraries), create (with the CMYK sliders), or load (from another Illustrator file) a color palette. Choose a color. Make sure you are working with the Fill and that your stroke is set to none. You're going to create colored shapes through a series of clicks and drags.

As you almost "skate around" with the pen tool, you'll see the color field taking shape with each anchor point you put down. Close the shape by bringing the pen point over your starting point (see that small circle right next to the pen symbol? Look for the same tiny icon when closing a shape with the pencil tool, as well).

Send the color field to the back—or bring the line work to the front—of the layer (one way to accomplish this is to go to Menu Bar > Object > Arrange). You could also work in multiple layers, but I didn't need to for this basic demo.

Create, size, position, shape, and color all your fields. You could apply blends, gradients, and textures to your color shapes, if you wish.

When you have tweaked your color and line components to taste, put a fork in it, you're done (see Figure 10-12f and Figure 10-12g)!

Figure | 10-12d |

The drawing for *Buds*. I went with a clean, thin, but wiggly line character. This stroke works well with the color shapes I will knock in and out of my line. I developed my cast of characters as I went along; tweaking characterization many times for each of the crew. (© Michael Fleishman 2003)

Figure | 10-12e |

The color layer for *Buds*. (© Michael Fleishman 2003)

## Color Models

Common digital color models are: HSB (hue, saturation, and brightness); RGB (red, green, blue); and CMYK (cyan, magenta, yellow, and black).

HSB is based on *our perception* of color—the "name," purity, plus lightness and darkness, of the color.

RGB deals with the spectrum of colored *light*. RGB colors combine to create white (as all light is reflected back to the eye), and are called *additive* colors.

The CMYK model is based on the light *absorption* of ink printed on paper (color *not* absorbed is reflected back to the eye). Mix cyan, magenta, yellow (and black) to create *subtractive* colors. Combining CMYK inks gives us four-color process printing (the CMYK inks being called process colors).

## FAIRLY SAFE PREDICTIONS

I'm not a fortuneteller, but I'll make an educated guess on some things. Our industry is largely geared towards the Macintosh, and I'll say that won't change. I also foresee much faster and cleaner connections to the Internet. FTP sites and PDF files will continue to trim delivery times (however, there will always be clients complaining it just takes too long to download your file).

Figure | 10-12f |

Line and color combined. Notice both line/color shading effects. The final shows the important relationship between the black line, color fields, and white space in this illustration. (© Michael Fleishman 2003).

Figure | 10-12g |

The original line plus color created with the pen tool. The geometric color is a dynamic alternative to the organic shapes produced by the pencil tool. (© Michael Fleishman 2003)

## Image Resolution

Image resolution is a pretty complex issue. But said simply: more pixels = higher resolution. More pixels means sharper detail, better color, smoother blends, and gradations of tone. So, illustrations at a low resolution (less pixels) may look *pixellated* (those dreaded jaggies or stairsteps).

The size of your illustration—the actual *dimensions* of your image—impacts resolution. Increase size and you make the pixels bigger—you decrease the resolution. Decrease the size, and you increase resolution.

Monitor resolution is characteristically 72 dpi (dots per inch). We know that monitors just *display* the image; thus a displayed illustration is a much different animal than an illustration in print.

So, let's follow a logical thread. Those Web images on your monitor look just fine *displayed on your monitor,* but when printed out, they look awful . . . *why?* Because images off the Web are not usually vector images (thus resolution independent) but are typically bitmapped JPEGs or GIFs, and are generally produced at low resolution— 72 dpi—your standard monitor resolution, as you'll remember.

*Output resolution* from an *output device* (your printer) can range from 300 dpi inkjets to 2400 dpi (and higher) imagesetters. And as they say, your mileage may vary: What you get from your trusty desktop printer might not compare to the output of that high-end imagesetter.

The ability to efficiently network hardware will get easier yet. Software will be phenomenal—and yes, you'll still spend way too much time online or fooling around in Photoshop 17, instead of going to bed at a reasonable hour.

The digital revolution/evolution will mean continued "creativity on demand and at the speed of light," to paraphrase Ilene Winn-Lederer. Unnecessary plus instantaneous changes and corrections will be required simply because clients will think the new technology makes it effortless. It's happening now as we speak. The value of "think time" may ultimately become obsolete.

But, of course, "New technologies are creating a lot of opportunities that simply didn't exist," reminds Robert Zimmerman. "There are programs which require some technical skills, but are fun and challenging in ways that illustration never was before."

## SUMMING IT UP

The relevance and impact of the computer has pointed the way for both the illustrator and the illustration business. You can compare and contrast digital media and methods with traditional resources and technique, but the relationship does not have to be rocky, by any means.

Digital image-making abides by the core precepts of traditional illustration, while offering another exciting creative environment to pursue the dream.

# PROFILES

## *Chris Spollen*

© Chris Spollen

Chris Spollen started working on the computer in 1990, some twenty years down his freelance road. Spollen maintains that working digitally completely eclipsed his hand skills to that point in time. He had spent years developing an inking style based on drafting templates, working with a stat camera, and mechanically producing four-color art in his studio.

But the computer literally knocked Spollen's extremely labor-intensive process right out his shop door. His first ten years in the digital arena were spent almost entirely in Adobe Illustrator.

Currently, the Staten Island-based illustrator is once again in the process of reinventing himself, and has gravitated towards Photoshop. Spollen takes sketches of a particular concept or specific pose, and using a digital camera, sets up models to photographically match his thumbnails. "After shooting several digital photos," he says, "I knock out the color and digitally paint on top of the image to create the desired angel or fairy I have in my mind's eye."

As this process continues to evolve, Spollen finds he is working extensively in layers, digitally tinting and glazing with each additional step. "I distort, flip, plop, color burn, color dodge, and reduce opacity, until the work becomes more and more *art*," he states. Check out Spollen's evocative imagery and see how a visually arresting illustration can evolve from perfunctory photo reference.

# PROFILES

*David Julian*

David Julian has used Apple computers since 1985. Julian believes that the Mac interface is well-engineered for artists, and he primarily uses Adobe Photoshop and Illustrator software for the same reason. Julian will use third-party software to interact with his Adobe programs to get specific techniques and effects, but doesn't like to call attention to the obviousness of his digital artwork.

A Julian illustration starts with brainstorming on paper, *away from* the computer. The artist feels that this is a very important part of the conceptual process. He points out that idea-making does not happen in the computer any more than it does inside a camera. "The pixels won't come together until you get a concept," he advises, "no software will advance your creative process *until you have an idea.* You must have concepts as well as skill (and equipment).

"I must also add," Julian continues, "that to be on the cutting edge of concept, you must think about the *less obvious solution* mentally, and *then* create that idea graphically."

Most of Julian's work has strong photographic content, and he is a firm believer in originality. He does not rely on clip art, stock, or royalty-free images. To capture the unique visual he seeks, the artist simply shoots, scans, *or creates it* himself. He may assemble all the needed elements from his extensive personal photo library, or head out into the field to photograph his target.

By and large, Julian has cross-trained between photography, illustration, and a very real, ever-present mental game. "There are all sorts of conceptual things that are thrown your way that you just have to figure out. You must be inventive and resourceful; you have to get to *the answer.*"

© David Julian www.davidjulian.com

# PROFILES

## *Michael Wertz and John Coulter*

"Years ago," Michael Wertz tells us, "a friend sat me down in front of his tiny little proto-Apple with one of those teeny little black and white screens. He turned MacPaint on and let me play. My world changed forever.

"There was a short period of time when I was using pastel to make my illustrations," he continues. "They invariably came back damaged, smeared, and smudged beyond repair, so now I use a Mac and Photoshop, and I send all my illustrations via e-mail."

To start these illustrations that end up as high quality JPEGs, Wertz taps into a veritable arsenal of media: collage, prints, pastel, acrylics, pencil, and photography. "I scan the rough stuff in to make the finish.

"And I love flat color," he comments. "I'm starting to discover (and use) screen prints. I've been

*Iris D'Origio* was done for the Los Angeles Times Book Review; Carol Kaufman was the art director. Wertz melds low-tech and high-tech with fine flair. (Illustrations on pages 249–250 © Michael S. Wertz 2003)

*(continued)*

doing Gocco prints at home. This is a system that produces nifty 4.25 × 6.25-inch prints. These I'll scan in or let stand as the final product."

And oh, yes—Wertz blogs. What *is* a blog? "I've been doing this blog thing—Web logging—every chance I get," he says. "For one thing, it's an excuse to make a quick drawing and post it on the Web. (To see the blogs Wertz has done so far, log in to www.wertzateria.com.) Each one has an illustration attached. Sometimes the pictures are finished, sometimes they're just sketches.

"The point is to stay motivated and interested in doing artwork. The 'blogging' process also keeps my friends, family, and clients up-to-date with my work and life. But most of all, it's fun."

John Coulter uses "plain old 8.5 × 11 white paper (the kind you find in printers and copiers). I like Papermate Sharpwriter No. 2 mechanical pencils," he says, "They're plastic, disposable, and you don't have to sharpen them. Pilot V ball pens (fine point, black ink, disposable) have a good ink flow, and never clog. Pentel Clic Erasers are great: This is a white eraser in a retractable barrel. Sanford's Magic Rub eraser, another white eraser, has a bigger block."

It's with these tools that Coulter's process begins. A pencil drawing is inked, scanned in at a higher resolution (about 300 dpi), and enlarged (around 150 percent). This is preparation for step 2.

Coulter now saves the drawing as a TIFF file, and opens it in Adobe Streamline. Streamline basically traces the black line art and makes it vector compatible. "The higher resolution and enlargement of the scan gives more information for Adobe Streamline to work," Coulter fills in.

After streamlining, he does a "Select all," then copies and pastes the selection into a new Adobe Illustrator file. From there—and while it's all still selected—the artist chooses the Pathfinder tool. "I now hit the divide icon. This separates the black line art from the interior white areas.

"Then I click on one of the interior white areas (with the hollow arrow—the direct selection tool). I next choose the *Edit > Select > Same Fill Color* option, which will select all the white areas. I then hit 'delete' which leaves a black line illustration with a clear background."

From here, Coulter creates another layer, and draws shapes with the pen tool underneath the black lines, coloring as he goes.

"It's funny," Coulter says, "if I didn't have the scanner and computer, I would have a much harder time creating my work—which actually ends up looking kind of traditional and not computer generated."

## in review

1. What does it mean to be a "digital illustrator"?

2. Why is the computer—and digital illustration—considered our era's breakthrough innovation? Do you agree or disagree with this assertion, and why?

3. Do *you* believe that skills make all the difference? Do you have to know how to draw in this day and age? Defend your point of view. Now defend the opposing viewpoint.

4. What is a bitmap? What is a vector? What are the differences between Adobe Illustrator and Photoshop? What are the similarities?

5. Name at least five of the most common graphics file formats.

## exercises

1. Based on your level of expertise, create a digital project and assign it to a classmate. Make it as tough and encompassing as you'd like. Establish deadlines and specifications. Do a demo, schedule critiques and grade the piece when it's handed in (but justify the score with a comprehensive written or oral evaluation).

2. Read today's newspaper or the current issue of *Time* or *Newsweek;* perhaps watch the news on TV, or listen to National Public Radio. Choose an event, subject, or theme that stirs or concerns you. Do a completely traditional illustration (any media, any style, any technique) that expresses your take on this topic. Next, create that *same* illustration, but start it traditionally and finish it on the computer (using an application—or combining applications—of your choice). Finally do this *same* piece one last time. However, this one must be *totally* digital.

3. Do a practical A/B comparison of Photoshop and Illustrator by trying several different tasks (for instance: create basic shapes with fills of solid color, blends or gradations, set a headline or block of text, do a line drawing, build a grid, blend and gradate colors, etc.). Do the same A/B comparison with Freehand and Illustrator, Photoshop and Painter, and so on.

4. Filter Lab: Shoot a photo of yourself and bring it into Photoshop (scan it or take the photo digitally). You could do a different shot each day as an option. You're going to do a *daily* digital self-portrait and explore *at least one* filter per day. Apply only one filter to your photo at a time (don't combine filters with this exercise either), but play with *all* the parameters available. Keep a filter journal for future reference. Give

yourself a deadline and establish a regimen. At the end of the assignment, print out each self-portrait and "publish" in book form (perhaps with your notes for each).

5. If you are on a Mac, find out if your school has PCs loaded with the Windows versions of your favorite graphics software. No good? You may have to head to a computer store, or locate a friend working on a PC. Explore the PC side of your preferred applications; compare and contrast both hardware and software.

© Lori Osiecki

index

# *index*